Postmodern Philosophy and Law

Postmodern Philosophy and Law

Douglas E. Litowitz

 University Press of Kansas

© 1997 by the University Press of Kansas

Published by the University Press of Kansas (Lawrence, Kansas 66049),
which was organized by the Kansas Board of Regents and is operated
and funded by Emporia State University, Fort Hays State University,
Kansas State University, Pittsburg State University, the University of
Kansas, and Wichita State University

Library of Congress Cataloging-in-Publication Data

Litowitz, Douglas E.
    Postmodern philosophy and law / Douglas E. Litowitz.
        p.   cm.
    Includes index.
    ISBN 0-7006-0857-5 (alk. paper)
    1. Law—Philosophy. 2. Law and politics.   3. Postmodernism.
    I. Title.
    K230.L4482P67   1997
    340′.1—dc21   97-14922

British Library Cataloguing in Publication Data is available.

Printed in the United States of America

10 9 8 7 6 5 4 3 2 1

The paper used in this publication meets the minimum requirements of the American
National Standard for Permanence of Paper for Printed Library Materials Z39.48-1984.

Since Copernicus Man has been rolling from the center toward X.
—Friedrich Nietzsche

To realize the relative validity of one's convictions, and yet to stand for them unflinchingly, is what distinguishes a civilized man from a barbarian.
—Joseph Schumpeter

Contents

Acknowledgments

This project would not have been possible without the love and support of many people, all of whom have made my world a much better place. First I want to thank my parents, Norman and Bonnie Litowitz, and my brothers, Malcolm and Alec, for their love and encouragement, as well as for their support during my exodus from law to academics. I also want to thank my girlfriend, Helena, for her continuing love and support.

This book grew out of a dissertation in philosophy at Loyola University of Chicago, where I was fortunate to have David Ingram as my teacher and adviser. In a very real sense, this book would never have been written were it not for his encouragement and careful reading of prior drafts; David's support and friendship have been a real blessing. I also benefited from countless interesting and often heated discussions with faculty members at Loyola, especially Vince Samar, Olufemi Taiwo, Heidi Malm, and Howard Klepper.

I would also like to thank Gary Minda and Peter Schanck, the two readers who carefully reviewed my manuscript for the University Press of Kansas. Their incisive comments have led to a much improved book. Nancy Scott and others at the press have been unusually helpful and responsive, which has made this project a pleasure.

An earlier version of this book was reviewed by Jack Balkin, who offered important advice on how it could be improved. Three chapters reflect changes suggested by readers at Loyola University of Chicago. The chapter on Nietzsche was reviewed by Hans Seigfried, the one on Foucault by J. D. Trout, and the one on Derrida by Andrew Cutrofello. My thanks to all three for their comments.

Finally, I received financial assistance during the writing of this book from my late grandmother, Alice Ellenbogen, who unfortunately did not live to see the completion of this project. I never had the opportunity to properly thank her and wish to do so here.

Introduction: The Emergence of Postmodernism in Legal Studies

In academic circles, the most influential trend of the last quarter century is without doubt the rise of postmodernism.[1] The core group of philosophers subsumed under this rubric generally includes Jacques Derrida, Michel Foucault, Friedrich Nietzsche, Jean-François Lyotard, Jacques Lacan, Fredric Jameson, and Richard Rorty.[2] Over the last decade or so, the basic themes of postmodernism have worked their way into jurisprudence and the philosophy of law, with the result that law professors are now writing about postmodern legal movements,[3] postmodern jurisprudence,[4] and postmodern legal feminism.[5] In addition to conferences on postmodernism and law,[6] symposia have been organized to consider the work of such postmodern thinkers as Derrida,[7] Foucault,[8] Rorty,[9] and Lacan.[10] There can be no question that legal scholars are joining with the rest of academia in expressing a growing interest in postmodern theory. As one legal scholar recently commented: "Postmodernism is all the rage. Discussions concerning the culture of postmodernity and the significance of postmodern thought fill an increasing number of pages in leading law reviews, and postmodernism dominates contemporary legal theory."[11] Twenty years ago there was no such thing as postmodern legal theory, whereas we can now identify a coherent and growing body of literature which falls under this heading.[12] In short, postmodern legal thought has arrived.

Contemporary legal theorists writing in the postmodern tradition include Stanley Fish, Pierre Schlag, Peter Goodrich, J. M. Balkin, Richard Delgado, Drucilla Cornell, Duncan Kennedy, and Allan Hutchinson. All of these thinkers are pursuing valuable and interesting work which has its roots in the insights of the founding postmodern figures discussed in this book. While it would be worthwhile to devote an entire study solely to this new wave of legal scholars, my focus here will be on those thinkers who might be called "classic" or "old guard" postmodernists, namely, Nietzsche, Foucault, Derrida, Lyotard, and Rorty. I will, however, be making repeated references to many of the cutting-edge theorists.

In my opinion, the growing interest in postmodernism among legal scholars is something of a mixed blessing. On the one hand, there is always something to be gained when the parameters of existing scholarship are widened to include new approaches, especially when a new approach purports to be radical and challenging. Yet one has the nagging suspicion that there is something missing at the core of the work presently being done in the area of postmodern legal theory. There appears to be an overabundance of unsubstantiated verbiage with a decidedly postmodern flavor. Radical lawyers are now speaking the language of postmodernism, writing about the law in terms of "floating signifiers," "logocentrism," "difference," and "marginality."[13] Unfortunately, this verbiage (or verbal drift, if you will) is often unsupported by hard scholarship devoted to the philosophical positions which undergird the colorful terminology. Strangely, there has been a paucity of detailed scholarship devoted to finding out exactly what the most influential postmodern thinkers had to say about law. Even as postmodern thinkers such as Derrida, Lyotard, and Foucault are becoming increasingly influential in legal studies (indeed, they are cited at an almost alarming rate in recent law review articles),[14] there are very few sustained efforts being made to wade through the complicated texts of these authors to find out what they thought about basic concepts such as justice, law, and right. This has become *my* task: to provide a close textual reading of selected works by these thinkers in order to discern the implications of their work for legal theory.

To be sure, this might seem like an obvious task that should have been attempted long ago. Surely someone should have taken the time to work through the writings on law by Nietzsche, Foucault, Derrida, Lyotard, and Rorty. Yet very few scholars have undertaken this project in a systematic way, instead choosing to focus on a single thinker or borrowing selectively from a range of postmodern thinkers. Despite the occasional well-written book on postmodern *politics*,[15] there has been very little written in a clear, analytic style on postmodernism and *law*. Furthermore, there has been no book devoted to explaining the arguments of postmodern thinkers as a *collective* movement in legal philosophy. Finally, much of what has been written in support of postmodern legal theory is shrouded in a jargon and style of argument which is accessible only to those who are already sympathetic to the postmodern approach.[16] To analytic philosophers, texts written in this style can be daunting or even incomprehensible. Not surprisingly, there has been little or no genuine dialogue between Anglo-American legal thinkers and the adherents of postmodernism.

This last point is especially troubling. It sometimes seems that the gulf which separates mainstream legal scholars and postmodernists is so wide that they are speaking different languages, working on different problems, and largely ignoring each other's work.[17] Those who are working within the postmodern approach (e.g., those who focus on Derrida, Lyotard, and Foucault) tend to be derisive of those who are working in the tradition of mainstream thinkers such as H. L. A. Hart and Ronald Dworkin on the view that mainstream legal thought is hopelessly outdated in the postmodern age. On the other side of the dividing line, the leading Anglo-American theorists (such as Rawls, Dworkin, and Ackerman) do not purport to respond to the major postmodernists, not even to point out errors in their work.[18] In any event, there has been no rapprochement between the postmodernists and those who are within the more mainstream schools in Anglo-American jurisprudence. This book is intended to bridge this gap between Anglo-American and postmodern theory by examining postmodernism from the perspective of analytic jurisprudence (and vice versa) and by explaining the differences between the two approaches. My study represents a melange of Continental and analytic theory. Since postmodern theory is largely derived from French and German thinkers, any investigation of this subject will require an excursion into a philosophical landscape largely staked out by continental figures. Yet my methodology—specifically, my focus on argument and critique—remains decidedly within the tradition of analytic philosophy. Ideally this book will prove accessible to legal thinkers from both schools.

This book operates as a two-tiered analysis of postmodern legal thought: on one level it is concerned with postmodern legal theory as a *collective* approach in legal studies; on another level it is about the views of the *individual* thinkers who are central to the postmodern movement. My aim is to provide a simultaneous introduction and critique of major figures from Continental philosophy (and Rorty as well) who have become increasingly important in the philosophy of law. If nothing else, this investigation should have the effect of loosening the parameters of legal scholarship to make room for new thinkers who have not been central figures thus far but whose work is of growing interest to legal scholars.

At the outset, it is crucial to realize that postmodern legal theory does not revolve around a particular work functioning as a kind of manifesto, nor is there a key postmodern thinker. Indeed, there are some quite significant differences among the postmodern thinkers discussed in this book. A basic question, then, is whether postmodernism can or should be seen as a coherent brand of legal philosophy in its own right. In other words, one must ask whether there is such a thing as "postmodern legal theory" as a coherent whole, or, alternatively, if one is dealing merely with individual viewpoints that do not share a set of core attributes. Obviously, I will be arguing that there is something akin to a postmodern orientation (or approach) in legal philosophy which unites the various thinkers I discuss.

Certainly, if the postmodern thinkers shared nothing in common in their writings on the law, then the best approach to their work would be to simply discuss their various positions in serial fashion (passing from one thinker to the next) because there would be nothing to say about them collectively. Yet I feel that these thinkers *do* have quite a bit in common in two key senses. First of all, they share a set of basic *philosophical* assumptions about such central issues in philosophy as selfhood, truth, justice, language, interpretation, and history. Second, they share some basic assumptions about the proper methodology and goals of *legal theory*. I will demonstrate that the first set of beliefs (the more general philosophical notions) has a profound effect upon the second set of notions (about legal theory in particular). Because the postmodern thinkers share these collective assumptions about philosophy and legal theory, I will be taking the position that they can be viewed collectively as presenting a unique approach to law, which I will refer to variously as "postmodern legal philosophy" or "postmodern legal theory," even though there is no distinct intellectual movement which has adopted either of these designations.

Since I will be dealing in great detail with some very complicated themes put forth by some very oblique thinkers, I would like to provide the reader with a road map, an overview of the forest, if you will, so that the reader does not get lost among the trees.

Chapter 1 is intended as a general guide to postmodernism for those readers who do not possess a background in postmodern thought or who seek a broader context within which to place the individual thinkers discussed later in this book. Here I establish that the postmodernists share certain basic assumptions about selfhood, justice, truth, and interpretation. Although these basic assumptions are not about law per se, they form the framework for the postmodern perspective on legal issues. These views are set out here in order to provide the necessary context for my discussion of postmodern theory and individual postmodern thinkers.

In chapter 2 I examine postmodern legal theory as a collective intellectual movement. I present two fundamental beliefs which postmodernists seem to hold about the way in which legal theory should operate. The first is that legal theory should be conducted from an external perspective which need not privilege the first-person accounts of the officials (judges and lawyers) of the legal system. This external perspective is common to Marxist and sociological accounts of the law, yet it stands in stark contrast to the perspective of Anglo-American legal theory, which tends to adopt an internal approach to the legal system, viewing the law from the perspective of judges and lawyers. Throughout the book I will be referring to the perspective taken by the postmodernists (and Marxists) as "the external perspective."

A second approach shared by the postmodernists is a deep distrust and skepticism of the metaphysical and/or epistemic foundations which have historically been offered by lawyers and philosophers in support of particular arrangements of the legal system. Some of these foundational concepts include natural law, dialectical materialism, maximization of utility, inherent human dignity, autonomy, God, and self-evident rights. The postmodern distrust of foundations extends beyond these metaphysical foundations and applies with equal force to such nonmetaphysical foundations as John Rawls' "overlapping consensus," and Jürgen Habermas' "ideal speech situation," to the point where the postmodernists seem almost dubious of foundations per se. This radical skepticism toward foundations shall be referred to as "extreme antifoundationalism."

At the conclusion of chapter 2 I pose the overriding question which runs through the remaining chapters of this book: Can the postmodernists' external perspective and extreme antifoundationalism give rise to what I call a "positive jurisprudence," that is, a normative theory of right and justice which can be used as a framework for deciding cases and enacting statutes? Without a positive jurisprudence, postmodern legal theory will be relegated to what I call a "negative jurisprudence," a purely critical approach which has limited use for those who desire a plan of action for creating an improved legal system. All of these preliminary questions are raised—but not resolved—in this chapter.

Chapters 3 through 7 look closely at the legal philosophies offered by various postmodernists. A separate chapter is devoted to the work of Nietzsche (3), Foucault (4), Derrida (5), Lyotard (6), and Rorty (7). For each thinker I first attempt to formulate a general conception of law and justice and then subject this theory to a searching critique. I also try to determine whether the postmodern thinker can provide a positive jurisprudence. Each chapter ends with a balanced assessment of the strengths and weaknesses of the particular thinker's approach to law.

In chapter 8 I argue that although the postmodern treatment of law is useful as a critique or "check" against the existing terms and concepts within both the practice of law and the enterprise of mainstream legal scholarship, it nevertheless fails to offer a positive jurisprudence. Although various postmodern thinkers have met with varying degrees of success, none have set forth a workable, normative vision for the reform of the legal system. I argue that postmodern legal theory correctly points out that we can no longer naively rely on the foundations once offered in support of our legal system, and that we must perform a genealogy and deconstruction of our existing legal concepts. But this interesting *critical* effort is accompanied by a less successful effort to *build* a new vision for the law. When postmodern antifoundationalism is wedded to an external perspective on the legal system, the result is a line of thought which is of limited value to the players within the legal system, who must decide cases and enact statutes from an internal perspective. While I am generally critical of postmodern legal theory, I nevertheless attempt to explain four significant contributions postmodernism can make to legal theory.

Having anticipated my conclusion, let me now offer a gentle reminder about methodology before I begin my analysis in earnest. Earlier I spoke of the attitude of distrust and derision which surfaces between philosophers working in the different traditions of Anglo-American and Continental theory. My goal in this book is to present a fair and honest assessment of postmodern legal theory. In order to accomplish this, I must make every effort to outline that theory in its best light. This much is required of the so-called principle of charity, which requires that an interpreter make the object of his or her interpretation the best that it can be before portraying it in a negative light.[19] Ultimately one can only view the postmodern movement in its best light by approaching it sympathetically, on its own terms, before subjecting it to a critique.[20]

1 &❧ Understanding
Postmodernism Generally

Understanding Modernism and Postmodernism

The best way to understand postmodernism is by contrasting it with modernism. This comparison can take place on both a *historical* and a *theoretical* level. The historical level looks at the sequence of events surrounding the emergence of postmodernism as an intellectual movement in the late twentieth century. The theoretical level looks at the doctrinal and philosophical views which distinguish postmodern thinkers from thinkers of the so-called modern period. I will begin with the historical analysis and then turn to the theoretical plane.

THE HISTORICAL EMERGENCE OF POSTMODERNISM

In historical terms, the modern period spanned the mid-Enlightenment to the 1960s and early 1970s. It was characterized by a belief in the power of reason and the inherent dignity and uniqueness of individuals as ends in themselves. A basic tenet of modernism held that the faculty of reason could operate as a neutral court of appeal to weed out beliefs and practices based on superstition and blind tradition (e.g., the belief in the divine right of kings). Among the purveyors of modernism one would include Descartes, Locke, Kant, Jefferson, and Rousseau. In political and legal theory, the modern approach strove to justify a participatory democracy which guaranteed civil liberties and due process of law, justified on the basis of God's plan, natural law, reason, inherent dignity, or the social contract. One can safely say that most Americans (and perhaps even most legal theorists) remain within the modern mind-set in terms of their attitude toward politics and law. As Roscoe Pound said earlier in this century, "The American lawyer, as a rule, still believes that the principles of law are absolute, eternal, and of universal validity."[1] In legal theory, the modern approach generally took the form of an attempt to justify a legal arrangement by reference to ahistorical and acontextual truisms about human nature, God, reason, and natural law. Indeed, each of these concepts is mentioned in the

Declaration of Independence and found its way into Supreme Court decisions handed down from the founding of the Republic until the early part of this century. As a matter of American history, one can safely say that the modern epoch extended from the colonial period until shortly after World War II.

Historically speaking, the postmodern period began as a movement within the arts, originating just after World War II but gaining momentum as the sixties approached. In a sense, the postmodern movement was a spin-off from certain trends within modern art and literature, especially the experimentation with new narrative techniques in the work of such writers as James Joyce and William Faulkner, as well as movements in the visual arts such as cubism and expressionism, which challenged the notion that paintings should be created from the perspective of a single, ideal vantage point. Taking its cues from radical strains in the visual arts of the early part of this century, the postmodern movement was led by representative figures such as painters Andy Warhol and Robert Rauschenberg, composers John Cage and Philip Glass, and filmmakers Jean-Luc Godard and François Truffaut. All of these artists stressed the breakdown of linear narrative, the rise of pastiche and "blank parody," as well as discontinuity, diffusion, and schizophrenia.[2]

As the sixties gave way to the seventies and eighties, postmodernism became less tied to artistic movements and allied itself to philosophical speculation and abstract theorizing, especially in the work of Jacques Derrida, Jean-François Lyotard, Jean Baudrillard, and Fredric Jameson. By the mid-eighties, with the English-language publication of Lyotard's seminal book *The Postmodern Condition,* postmodernism had become an identifiable theoretical approach in philosophy.[3] By the nineties postmodernism had become a force to be reckoned with among political theorists and legal scholars.[4] Historically speaking, postmodernism began as a movement in the arts and has become increasingly theoretical, to the point where it can now be identified as an *intellectual* movement separate from its namesake in the arts. Nevertheless, the artistic origins of postmodernism remain highly visible, which explains why each of the postmodern thinkers discussed in this book has written extensively on the arts. For example, Derrida has written on painting,[5] Foucault has lectured on Magritte,[6] Lyotard has written about painting and about Kafka,[7] and Rorty has written about Nabokov and Orwell.[8] At present, however, one need not be concerned with the arts to qualify as a postmodernist.

THE THEORETICAL EMERGENCE OF POSTMODERNISM

One can now turn from the historical perspective to the theoretical perspective.[9] As a matter of philosophical theory, modernists such as Locke, Kant, and Jefferson were wedded to foundational metaphysical notions of a stable human subject or self, a belief in objectivity and undistorted rational dialogue, a commitment to freedom from superstition and tyranny, and a general optimism that science was moving steadily toward the Truth. Some thinkers have taken to referring to this set of beliefs as the "Enlightenment Project,"[10] understood broadly as the project of bringing reason and science to bear on social and political beliefs, thereby freeing humanity from superstition and slavish tradition. This approach can be seen in Kant's seminal essay "What Is Enlightenment?," where he says that Enlightenment represents man's emergence from self-imposed immaturity through the use of reason and public debate.[11] A distinguishing feature of modernism, then, is the reliance on sweeping metaphysical and/or epistemic claims to undergird positions in political and legal philosophy. A concise summary of this attitude is provided by Robert Hollinger:

> Modern philosophy, whose archetypal figures are Descartes and Kant, seeks to provide necessary and universal criteria for discovering truth and universal moral principles. This gives rise to the Enlightenment ideal of the moral and epistemological unity of humankind which was to provide us with the tools for "relieving man's estate" (Bacon) without theoretical limit. This led to the notion of a scientific culture, in which everything was grounded in scientific doctrine or method, or committed to the flames as sophistry and illusion, as Hume put it.[12]

Two examples of this project come to mind: Kant's claim that the faculty of reason generates laws which can be used to justify legal rights; and Marx's claim that history is unfolding according to a series of necessary laws.[13] Kant appealed to reason and Marx to science as ways of grounding a political vision.

In *The Postmodern Condition* Lyotard refers to the foundations espoused by modern thinkers (such as Descartes, Kant, and Marx) as "grand narratives" or "metanarratives": "I will use the term *modern* to designate any science that legitimates itself with reference to a metadiscourse . . . making an explicit appeal to some grand narrative, such as the dialectic of Spirit, the hermeneutics of meaning, the emancipation of the rational or working subject, or the creation of wealth. . . . I define *postmodernism* as incredulity toward metanarratives."[14] For Lyotard and other postmodernists, the grand narratives of the Enlightenment are no longer tenable; hence Lyotard's claim that postmodernism is "incredulous" toward metanarratives. This incredulity can be seen in Nietzsche's rejection of the Lockean (and Jeffersonian) reliance on God and natural law; Foucault and Lyotard's rejection of the claim that history has a telos or end point; Rorty's rejection of the Kantian notion of human beings as ends in themselves; and Derrida's rejection of the notion that the just state can be founded upon first principles. These thinkers (together with the postmodern-influenced Critical Legal Studies movement) deny the existence of a neutral and objective faculty of reason which can be used to generate first principles of morality and law.

All of this talk about rejecting foundations may sound vaguely nihilistic; as we shall see, there is a certain sense in which postmodern theory is doomed to fail at finding a foundation (even a tentative one) for a political vision of the just state. Part of the postmodern malaise derives from the impression that two hundred years of an "Enlightened" quest for reason, truth, and rationality has led to the present state of gross inequality, class warfare, the death of any hope for socialism, two world wars (in this century alone), the threat of nuclear annihilation, sexism, racism, neurosis, and other ills of the modern era. While most people would argue that inequality, racism, and violence are due to the failure to use reason in public affairs, postmodernists like Foucault argue that it is precisely what we call "reason" which has brought us to the state we are in: "The relationship between rationalization and excess political power is evident. And we should not need wait for the concentration camps to recognize the existence of such relations."[15] Given this situation, one way to understand postmodernism is to say that it is a movement which is skeptical about the modernist claims for the use of reason as a way of solving problems, as well as about modernist conceptions of truth, justice, and selfhood. There is a sense among postmodernists (and perhaps this is borrowed from certain critical theorists in the Frankfurt School) that the Enlightenment has been something of a failure.[16]

The Death of Grand Narratives
(Reason, Truth, Self, God, Meaning)

In order to realize the full extent to which postmodernism has rejected the basic approach of modern philosophy, it is necessary to compare modern and postmodern positions on such key metaphysical and epistemic issues as reason, justice, selfhood, truth, natural law, history, texts, and God.

REASON

The Enlightenment modernism of Descartes and Kant saw reason as a universal faculty held by all humans which could be used to articulate a set of rational, true beliefs. The goal was to separate reason from such contingent and distorting features as tradition and emotion.

Kant: Reason proceeds by "eternal" and "unalterable" laws.[17]

Descartes: I observe that there is in me a certain faculty of judgment that I undoubtedly received from God, as is the case with all the other things that are in me. Since he has not wished to deceive me, he certainly has not given me a faculty such that, when I use it properly, I could ever make a mistake.[18]

Locke: Reason teaches all mankind that will but consult it that, being all equal and independent, no one ought to harm another in his life, health, liberty, or possessions; for men being all the workmanship of one omnipotent and infinitely wise Maker.[19]

The postmodern reaction to this line of thought is to argue that reason is not a uniform faculty in all humankind but rather is socially constructed; it is always situated within existing practices and discourses, and it will therefore be biased or slanted in favor of existing power relations.

Foucault: The central issue in philosophy and critical thought since the eighteenth century has always been, still is, and will, I hope, remain the question: What is this Reason that we use? What are its limits and what are its dangers?[20]

Horkheimer/Adorno: The Enlightenment has always aimed at liberating men from fear and establishing their sovereignty. Yet the fully enlightened earth radiates disasters triumphant. . . . [M]ankind, instead of entering into a truly human condition, is sinking into a new kind of barbarism.[21]

Lyotard: There is no politics of reason, neither in the sense of a totalizing reason nor in that of the concept. And so we must do with a politics of opinion.[22]

Rorty: Kant splits us into two parts, one called "reason," which is identical in us all, and another (empirical sensation and desire), which is a matter of blind, contingent, idiosyncratic impressions. [But we should] take seriously the possibility that there is no central faculty, no central self, called "reason."[23]

Given this incredulity toward reason, we can expect that postmodernism will reject any approach to law that claims to be based upon the demands of reason, as if the latter were a neutral court of appeal.

SELF

The modern view of the self reached its apogee in Kant's notion that each individual must be treated as a unique end in himself, inviolable and sacrosanct, never to be used as a mere means. Like other modern thinkers, Kant thought that we might be able to separate the metaphysical, transcendent self from the contingent self, such that the core self can be thought to exist separately from its immersion in a particular culture, language, or history. This attitude has its roots in Cartesian dualism, where the mind was conceived as a substance separate from the body.

> *Descartes:* I have a clear and distinct idea of myself—insofar as I am a thing that thinks and not an extended thing—and because I have a distinct idea of a body—insofar as it is merely an extended thing, and not a thing that thinks—it is therefore certain that I am truly distinct from my body, and that I can exist without it.[24]
>
> *Kant:* Rational nature exists as an end in itself.[25]
>
> *Rawls:* The self is prior to the ends which are affirmed by it.[26]

The postmodern reaction to this line of thinking is to assert that the self is a product of language and discourse, that it is "decentered" (to use Althusser's term), and that there is no core self. The postmodernists seem to concur with Claude Lévi-Strauss' assertion that the Cartesian ego is the "spoiled brat of philosophy."[27]

> *Rorty:* The crucial move . . . is to think of the moral self, the embodiment of rationality, not as one of Rawls' original choosers . . . but as a network of beliefs, desires, and emotions with nothing behind it—no substrate behind the attributes.[28]
>
> *Althusser:* Since Marx, we have known that the human subject, the economic, political or philosophical ego is not the center of history—and even, in opposition to the Philosophers of the Enlightenment and Hegel, that history has no center. . . . In turn, Freud has discovered that the real subject, the individual in his unique essence, has not the form of an ego—*that the human subject is de-centered, constituted by a structure which has no center either.*[29]
>
> *Foucault:* As the archaeology of our thought easily shows, man is an invention of recent date. And perhaps one nearing its end.[30]

Given this view of the self (which is sometimes associated with the so-called death of the subject and the death of the author), one would expect postmodernism to reject any approach based on the assertion that human beings have an immutable nature which predates civil society. The postmodern approach would rule out a social contract theory based upon a "state of nature" or, for that matter, any theory which holds that man is naturally egotistical (Adam Smith) or aggressive (Hobbes). In contrast, postmodernists tend to hold that human behavior is socially constructed, molded by traditions and practices.

TRUTH

The so-called rationalists of the modern epoch (Descartes, Leibniz, Spinoza) thought that philosophy could establish first principles of metaphysics and epistemology. In contrast to the rationalists, the so-called empiricists (Hume, Locke) thought that experience could provide a solid basis for truth. The goal in either case was to find the ultimate nature of reality, to make the real into something rational. The idea of truth as correspondence between language and reality exerted a strong influence far beyond the modern period, holding sway even among twentieth-century philosophers such as Betrand Russell. These thinkers would have soundly rejected the postmodern contention that truth is constructed, changing, and affected by the distorting influences of class, race, and gender.

> *Descartes:* There is a need for a method for finding out the truth. . . . By method I mean certain and simple rules, such that if a man observes them accurately, he shall never assume what is false to be true, but will always gradually increase his knowledge and arrive at a true understanding of all that does not exceed his powers.[31]
>
> *Russell:* Thus a belief is true when it corresponds to a certain associated complex, and false when it does not. . . . What makes a belief true is a fact, and this fact does not (except in exceptional cases) in any way involve the mind of the person who has the belief.[32]

In contrast, the postmodernists are skeptical about the notion of a fixed Truth (with a capital letter). For example, Nietzsche ridicules the notion of Truth and holds instead that the we are faced with alternative interpretations and perspectives; Rorty thinks that the modern focus on Truth has turned up nothing; and Derrida feels that what is typically called "truth" can never find a stable resting place.

> *Nietzsche:* There is something about "truth," about the search for truth; and when a human being is too human about it—"he seeks the true only to do the good"—I bet he finds nothing.[33]
>
> *Rorty:* Truth is not the sort of thing that one should expect to have a philosophically interesting theory about. . . . [I] would simply like to change the subject.[34]
>
> *Derrida:* What is put into question is precisely the quest for a rightful beginning, an absolute point of departure, a principle responsibility. . . . [T]he signified concept is never present in and of itself. . . . Essentially and lawfully, every concept is inscribed in a chain or in a system within which it refers to the other, to other concepts, by means of a systematic play of differences.[35]

> *Foucault:* "Truth" is linked in a circular relation with systems of power which produce and sustain it, and to effects of power which it induces and which extend it. A "regime" of truth.[36]

Given this skepticism, it is easy to see why Truth (as commonly understood) does not play a central role in postmodern legal philosophy. This is not to say that postmodernists disregard questions of truth and falsity, but they purport to be sensitive to the ways in which truth is relative to or shaped by power relations.

GOD/NATURE/SELF-EVIDENCE

The modernists (and their progeny) tended to argue that God had endowed men with inherent rights which could be deduced through the exercise of reason. These rights are innate and self-evident, and they stand as an ideal or standard to which the law should aspire.

> *Jefferson:* We hold these truths be self-evident, that all men are created equal, that they are endowed by their creator with certain inalienable Rights, that among these are Life, Liberty, and the pursuit of Happiness.[37]
>
> *Martin Luther King Jr:* A just law is a man-made code that squares with the moral law or the law of God. An unjust law is a code that is out of harmony with the moral law.[38]

In contrast, postmodernists profess a disbelief in God and reject the notion of self-evident principles of justice and natural law.

> *Nietzsche:* There are still harmless self-observers who believe that there are "immediate certainties"; But that "immediate certainty," as well as "absolute knowledge" and the "thing in itself," involve a contradiction in terms, I shall repeat a hundred times; we really out to free ourselves from the seduction of words.[39]
>
> *Foucault:* It seems to me that the idea of justice in itself is an idea which in effect has been invented and put to work in different types of societies as an instrument of a certain political and economic power.[40]

Given this skepticism toward self-evident truths (and such cherished notions as justice and consensus), postmodern thinkers do not put much stock in common sense or self-evident rules; they are suspicious about the outcomes reached by consensus and popular sovereignty. There is also a commonly held belief—which can be traced to the Marxist Antonio Gramsci—that common sense and reasonableness are determined by existing power relations and reflect biases of class and gender.[41]

WRITERS/TEXTS/MEANING

The thinkers of the modern period tended to assume that the meaning of a text could be reduced to the intention of the author. Texts were interpreted literally and meaning was limited to the document itself. For example, modern-era courts stressed the literal meaning of a contract as controlling, to the exclusion of contextual factors surrounding the execution of the contract. This view continues to exert a particularly strong hold over conservative thinkers and literary critics.

> *Judge Iredall:* Judges deciding constitutional issues should confine themselves to enforcing norms that are stated or clearly implied in the written Constitution.[42]

> *Edwin Meese III:* History and tradition point to an understanding of the Constitution as a document of *fixed meaning,* supplied by those who framed and ratified it.[43]

> *E. D. Hirsch Jr.:* Meaning is that which is represented by a text; it is what the author meant by his use of a particular sign sequence; it is what the signs represent.[44]

For the postmodernists the text is a locus of polysemy, dissemination, and multiple meanings. There is no single "correct" meaning and there is an element of undecidability in the inevitable choice which must be made among different readings. Most important, the whole notion of the author as a locus of meaning is an ideological distortion designed to limit the free play of meaning by anchoring interpretations to a seemingly rigid center of reference.

> *Barthes:* We know that a text is not a line of words releasing a single "theological" meaning (the "message" of the Author-God) but a multi-dimensional space in which a variety of writings, none of them original, blend and clash. . . . Once the Author is removed, the claim to decipher a text becomes quite futile.[45]

> *Foucault:* The author is not an indefinite source of significations which fill a work; the author does not precede the works. . . . The author is therefore the ideological figure by which one marks the manner in which we fear the proliferation of meaning.[46]

> *Derrida:* The central signified, the original or transcendental signified, is never absolutely present outside a system of differences. The absence of the transcendental signified extends the domain and the play of signification infinitely.[47]

Postmodernist thinkers remain skeptical of the idea that a single text (say, the Constitution) is foundational, and they frown on so-called authoritative readings of foundational texts. Furthermore, they argue that interpretations of key texts are always offered from a particular perspective toward a particular end, such that there is no ultimate meaning of a text.

HISTORY/PROGRESS

Modern theorists tended to believe in the ideal of moral progress, the Enlightenment-based belief that as history unfolds, reason lifts us above superstition and moves us toward an increasingly rational political order. Thinkers like Kant and Locke felt that the rise of reason and science during the Enlightenment provided our best hope for the creation of a just society. Later thinkers of the modern era, such as Hegel and Marx, thought that history itself had a inner logic and was moving toward the teleological end point of a better society.

> *Hegel:* The history of the world is none other than the progress of the consciousness of freedom.[48]
>
> *Marx:* Asiatic, ancient, feudal, and modern bourgeois modes of production can be designated as progressive epochs in the economic formation of society. The bourgeois relations of production are the last antagonistic form of the social process of production [and] create the material condition for the solution of that antagonism. This social formation brings, therefore, the prehistory of human society to a close.[49]
>
> *Fukuyama:* Liberal democracy is "the end point of mankind's ideological evolution" and "cannot be improved upon as an idea"; thus, "no further historical change is possible."[50]

The postmodern thinkers respond that history has no necessary internal logic or laws, and that claims of moral progress are unfounded.

> *Nietzsche:* Mankind does *not* represent a development of the better or the stronger or higher in the way that is believed today. "Progress" is merely a modern idea, that is to say, a false idea.[51]
>
> *Lyotard:* Auschwitz refutes speculative [Hegelian] doctrine. This crime at least, which is real, is not rational.[52]
>
> *Foucault:* Humanity does *not* gradually progress from combat to combat until it arrives at universal reciprocity, where the rule of law finally replaces warfare; humanity instills each of its violences in a system of rules and thus proceeds from domination to domination.[53]

Although it would be difficult to summarize the foregoing views of various thinkers associated with postmodernism, it seems clear that a major thrust of postmodern theory is negative: it seeks to question, decenter, relativize, and perhaps undermine our established understanding of truth, justice, rationality, meaning, and moral progress.[54]

A Note on Postmodern Rhetorical Devices

The preceding section illustrates how postmodern theory tries to shake free of the metaphysical and epistemic foundations which lie at the root of the modern approach to ethics, politics, and law. But at the same time, the postmodernists understand that the foundational modernist terms (e.g., selfhood, justice, truth) are in some sense inescapable; in order to talk intelligently about matters of law and justice, we must have recourse to notions of the self, truth, reason, and so on. After all, legal theory must treat people as legal subjects with some degree of freedom and autonomy, and it must make claims which purport to be true, so it will end up using the same type of language which it found so problematic when used by modern thinkers. Postmodern thinkers are thus sensitive to the sense in which our existing language games are steeped in modernist baggage.

Postmodernists deal with this situation by using modernist terms in a wry, almost sarcastic way. Rorty sometimes labels this approach as an "ironic" posture because it necessitates the adoption of a language game (broadly construed) which the ironist acknowledges to be contingent and fallible. The ironist uses a certain set of terms to explain his or her ethical position (e.g., "rights" and "inherent human dignity"), refusing to give these terms the status of a "final vocabulary" closer to reality than those used by others yet willing to switch vocabularies if a more useful one arises.[55] This explains the tendency of postmodernists to pepper their work with quotation marks to signify that terms are being used tentatively or with reservations.

Derrida makes a similar move by using certain words "under erasure." For Derrida, some words and concepts cannot be avoided if we are to speak in a way that can be understood by an audience steeped in the tradition of Western philosophy. These words include basic metaphysical postulates like "soul," "truth," "justice," and "history." Yet while we must use these words as points of reference in order to make discussion possible, we should recognize that these terms carry an effective history with them, a sort of baggage of associations which must be questioned. Derrida, following Heidegger, expresses this double gesture by saying that we cannot avoid slipping into the use of metaphysically loaded terms, so our use of these terms must be playful and ironic, with the result that the traditional meaning of these terms is hedged or erased: "There is no sense of doing without the concepts of metaphysics in order to shake metaphysics. We have no language—no syntax and no lexicon—which is foreign to this history; we can pronounce not a single destructive proposition which has not already had to slip into the form, the logic, and the implicit postulations of precisely what it seeks to contest."[56] One implication of this view is that while we must use such terms as "justice" and "rights," we should be careful to recognize that these words do not have stable meanings and transcendental referents; they come loaded with an effective history that includes distorting factors, to the point where the word itself can be seen as the situs of a power struggle, a contested terrain. For example, the term "rights" has for so long been understood in terms of *negative* rights (i.e., rights to be left alone, as it were) that it sounds strange to talk about rights which are clearly *positive* such as a right to child care, housing, and meaningful employment. Indeed, these might be considered "rights" under a socialist system of government, but we now label them as "privileges," which places them outside the system of rights. Under our present legal system, it seems natural and normal to speak of a right to free speech, but it stretches credulity to speak of a "right to employment." As law professor Mark Tushnet explains,

> Appeals to rights are inherently limited. Such appeals operate within the legal system, or at least within a rhetorical structure shaped in large measure by what the legal system has already done. Some things, such as a right to shelter, simply "go too far" in light of what the legal system has already done. What exactly "too far" means is . . . strongly affected by the sound common sense of the community of professional lawyers.[57]

The basic point here is that the key terms used in the philosophy of law, far from providing a neutral medium for discussing legal issues, are already weighed down by power relations. When we use terms like "justice" or "truth," these words have a history that must be genealogically investigated to detect bias, a method employed in Nietzsche's genealogical investigation of the terms "good" and "evil," as well as in Foucault's genealogical analysis of criminality and punishment.[58] Postmodern thinkers are concerned that our existing language-games tend to become reified to the point where our existing practices and theories seem natural or inevitable, such that every demand for change seems an affront to nature itself and hence inappropriate or even radical.

The use of terms "ironically" and "under erasure" reflects the postmodern supposition that the self is constituted in language-games and discourses, and that these discourses are slanted, biased, and non-neutral. The self is not a Cartesian *cogito* or Kantian transcendental ego which predates the language and the community into which it is thrown. Rather, the self is the result of power networks, disciplines, and discourses (Foucault), a narrative construction which results from the heterogony of language-games in our society (Lyotard).[59] All of this suggests that postmodern theory presents a radically decentered concept of the self and a total rejection of foundations, combined with a skepticism toward the terms and concepts which are found in mainstream legal theory.

In the next chapter I will explore the methodological stance of postmodern legal theory by focusing on its external perspective and its severe antifoundationalism, the two factors which distinguish postmodern legal philosophy from Anglo-American philosophy of law. The question is whether an externally oriented, antifoundational approach can give rise to a normative vision for the law, which is something that may be necessary for a fully operational legal theory.

2 ❧ The Orientation of Postmodern Legal Theory

In this chapter I will examine the general orientation of postmodern legal theory as a collective movement in legal studies. In particular, I will be contrasting the postmodern approach to legal theory with the approach taken in Anglo-American legal theory. One of my goals is to lay the foundation for my subsequent discussion of individual postmodern thinkers, but I am here also concerned to identify two problems that affect postmodern legal theory in a global sense, which need to be addressed straightaway because they are potentially crippling. Since these problems infect postmodern legal theory at a meta-level, they hold true for each postmodern theorist, which is why I have chosen to address them at this point.

My concerns are twofold. First postmodern theory takes an excessively external perspective on the legal system, thereby ruling out insights which are generated from the internal perspective of the participants in the social practice of the legal system. Second, postmodern theory is excessively dubious of any and all foundations in legal theory, thereby dashing any hope of what I have chosen to call "positive jurisprudence," that is, a theory of how the legal system *should* operate in a just state. The key question remains: If postmodern legal theory takes a critical, external perspective on the law, and also remains dubious of all foundations for a legal system, is there any way to salvage a postmodern vision of the just state and the proper legal system ("positive jurisprudence"), or are we consigned to a purely negative, critical theory of law ("negative jurisprudence")? In the balance of this chapter I intend to explore this question by weighing the advantages and disadvantages of the postmodern perspective on law and legal theory.

Internal and External Legal Theory

I have characterized my first concern with the methodology of postmodern theory as *the problem of external perspective*, adopting the latter term from H. L. A. Hart's groundbreaking study,[1] as well as from Ronald Dworkin's seminal works.[2] Hart and Dworkin both stress the possibility of doing legal theory from two perspectives, which they designate as "internal" and "external." Internal theory tends to see the legal system from the perspective of what Hart has called the "officials" of the system (judges and lawyers), while external theory tends to take a third-person (observer's) view of the legal system. As we will see, there are limitations to both approaches; it is especially difficult for a legal theory to take both perspectives into account at the same time.

I might add that the internal/external dilemma is not specific to legal theory, but runs through all areas of social inquiry. The internal perspective in the social sciences has been championed by Peter Winch,[3] who argues that social practice must be understood with reference to the meanings and interpretations offered by the actors themselves. According to Winch, "reflective understanding [of social phenomena] must necessarily presuppose the participant's unreflective understanding."[4]

A radically different view is held by those who adopt an external perspective, which downplays the insights of the participants on the grounds that the internal players are not in a privileged position to understand their own behavior.[5] The external perspective, advanced by sociologists working in the tradition of Durkheim and Marx, holds that the participants in a social practice (such as law) may be deluded about the real impetus for their actions. This means that a theorist who is trying to understand a social practice will invite confusion and distortion by privileging the participants' interpretations of their own behavior.

A quick example may help to illustrate the different approaches. Consider how a professor might attempt to formulate a theory about the role of marriage in America. An internal perspective would take into account the interpretations offered by those who are involved in the marriage ritual. For example, it might focus on the spouses' interpretation of marriage as a sacred ritual of exclusive devotion, or as a necessary step to starting a family. An external perspective on marriage might look to empirical studies on the relationship between marriage and social stability (as measured by crime and suicide rates). The internal perspective might claim that marriage exists in our society because individuals desire exclusive devotion "in sickness and in health," whereas the external perspective might claim that the function of marriage is to stabilize society as a whole, even though the participants don't realize that this is what motivates them to get married. Clearly, an internal view of marriage will differ from an external; the same holds true for internal and external views of the law.

I cannot here address the larger theoretical question of whether the internal or external perspective has proven more valuable in social inquiry; in any event, that question has not been resolved. At this point I merely want to point out that the postmodern thinkers tend to criticize the legal system from an external perspective, that is, from a perspective different from the players who are engaged in the day-to-day operations of the legal system (such as judges, lawyers, and legislators). This external perspective contrasts with the internal approach typically (but not always) adopted by Anglo-American thinkers, who tend to work from within the language games and concepts of those who are officials in the legal system. The question of whether a legal theorist should adopt an internal or external perspective is a fundamental issue of methodology and scholarship coloring the theorist's ultimate conception of law. As we shall see, both Hart and Dworkin—the leading Anglo-American thinkers in the philosophy of law—take an internal perspective which privileges the understandings of those officials who are players in the legal system.[6] Postmodern theory takes an external perspective, remaining dubious about the self-understanding and self-explanations offered by those inside the legal system. This difference in orientation is one reason for the gap (alluded to in the introduction) which seems to divide Anglo-American and postmodern thinkers.

The external strategy of the postmodernists can take place on either of two levels. First, some postmodernists tend to problematize the legal system *as a whole* on the ground that the foundations or fundamental assumptions of the entire system are erroneous, biased, or faulty. This global approach can be seen in Nietzsche's claim that democracy and equal rights constitute a type of "slave morality," as well as in Foucault's claim that the legal system's guarantees of liberty and autonomy are deceptive. These thinkers seem to be saying that the entire legal tradition is rotten, that its basic propositions are faulty or illusory. A second external strategy is to take an established concept *within* legal thought (such as liberty, contract, property, or the public/private distinction) and then deconstruct the concept by showing that its accepted usage harbors hidden ideological distortions. For example, a postmodern analysis of property might demonstrate that a system of private property leads to inequalities and crime, which in turn require governmental enforcement; hence private property has an inescapably public character. These postmodern strategies view the law externally and critically—from the outside, as it were.

In contrast to the external strategy of the postmodernists, Anglo-American philosophers of law tend to focus almost entirely on the act of deciding cases, which they view from the perspective of the judge and the lawyers who are appearing before the court. Thinkers like Hart and Dworkin discuss the meaning and scope of the terms used by those within the legal system (e.g., "due process," "contract," and "liberty"), and they tend to see their project as a way of clarifying but not rejecting the meanings which these terms hold for the officials. Anglo-American thinkers are not interested in the external project of proving that legal concepts are ideologically laden, nor are they interested in demonstrating that legal doctrine is hopelessly indeterminate, sexist, or racist— perhaps because the adoption of these types of positions will be unhelpful to the players inside the legal system whose perspective they have adopted. Analytic legal theorists tend to speak in a language which mirrors the terms used by lawyers and judges; they often adopt this basic framework without subjecting it to external attack, as if the basic terms inside the practice of law were not in need of defense.[7]

Now there is nothing wrong or problematic about adopting an internal or external perspective on the legal system. Indeed, there are advantages and disadvantages to both (these will be discussed in greater detail later in this book). Here I merely want to show that the tendency of the postmodernists to remain entrenched in an external perspective has the effect of limiting the focus and power of their analysis of law in that they fail to make an engagement with the language games and mental states of the actors within the legal system. After all, the law is decided from the inside, so it would be logical for postmodern thinkers to translate their work so that it had some effect on the internal decision-making process.

The distinction between internal and external approaches to law is so crucial that I would like to illustrate it with an example. Consider the following scenario, which has been pieced together from reported cases in the criminal law. A would-be burglar drills a hole through the lock on the door of a small business so that he can gain access to the safe inside.[8] The police arrive immediately after the hole has been drilled but before the burglar has physically entered the building. They charge him with burglary, a felony count. At the court hearing, the defendant's lawyer points out that burglary requires a breaking *and entering*, yet there was no entry in this case because the latter requires complete bodily entry. He insists that the felony count be dropped and that the defendant be charged instead with damage to property, a misdemeanor. The prosecutor responds by arguing that the entry requirement is satisfied when a perpetrator uses any instrument to break the plane of the door—in this case the insertion of the drill through the lock constitutes breaking and entering. Continuing with this hypothetical case, assume that the court accepts the lawyer's argument that complete bodily entry is required for a burglary to take place, and that the court convicts the perpetrator only of misdemeanor property damage, consequently dismissing the felony count.

A critic might attack this decision from an *internal* perspective by saying that the court reached the wrong verdict under the relevant legal doctrines. The internal critic might cite cases from other jurisdictions which have held that bodily entry is not required for a burglary, or he might cite policy arguments for employing a broad interpretation of the term "entering." He might also point out that the requirement of physical entry would have the absurd result that a thief who commits robbery by using a long pole (thereby avoiding bodily entry) would not qualify as a burglar under the court's construction of the law. One can imagine a heated dispute taking place solely on the merits of whether the court followed the correct internal decision-making procedure in this case.

Suppose that a person wanted to criticize the court's decision from an *external* perspective. How would he or she go about doing it? A radical anarchist or Marxist might claim that private property is immoral, such that people arrested for burglary should be understood as freedom fighters in the war on capitalism, battling against an unjust system of exploitation. Therefore the perpetrator in this hypothetical case should not go to jail, should not be tried under a system of illegitimate bourgeois law, and should be set free. A more sophisticated Marxist might admit that the defendant is technically guilty under the law as it presently exists but would quickly add that the latter is a sham, a mere reflection of class rule for the protection of property interests.[9] The Marxist would find the internal debate ("Was it felony burglary or misdemeanor property damage?") too narrow because it wrongfully works from within the framework of the existing legal system without seeing that the entire system is unjust.[10]

In evaluating this criminal case, one should bear in mind that the external critique is rather useless with respect to the debate which takes place inside the practice of judging and, similarly, that the internal debate does not address the issues raised by the external critic. Marxist musings about the immorality of private property don't provide genuine options for the lawyers and the judge working on the criminal case because they cannot realistically release the defendant on the grounds that private property is immoral since this move is not permitted from the inside of the practice. Similarly, the debate which takes place on the inside ("Is the man guilty of burglary or destruction of property?") is irrelevant to the external critic, who thinks that the entire classificatory scheme of the criminal law is unjust.

This is not to suggest that the internal and external approaches constitute separate universes of discourse. In the hypothetical criminal case just sketched, it might be possible for the Marxist to translate his external insight so that it affects the internal workings of the legal system. One way to do this is to convince the internal players that the terms they are using (freedom, criminality, property) are ideologically loaded by demonstrating that certain types of criminality are caused by monopoly capitalism, or that the free will supposed by the doctrine of mens rea (mental state) is a sham. These views might somehow lead to a reshaping of the criminal law, perhaps by creating a defense or excuse for economically motivated property crimes. My point here is that for the external viewpoint to have any impact, it must somehow be translated into the language being used inside the practice, if only to reject the latter or prove that it should be reconstructed.

Postmodern legal theory is similar in orientation to the Marxist stance in that it tends to take place at an external level, to the neglect of the language game going on at the internal level of legal practice. It is therefore subject to the general complaint that it is not couched in the terms used by officials of the legal system, which means that it cannot directly affect the day-to-day practice of law but must effect change in a more subtle and indirect way.

On the other hand, the internal perspective seems to take too much for granted, working from within but failing to rigorously examine the foundations and ground rules of the existing legal system, with the result that there is a formalist and conservative bias built into it. The internal critic tends to privilege the first-person account of those within the system (judges and lawyers), who are disposed to viewing the system as a coherent, ordered set of objective rules. This point of view can easily overlook the outsider's perspective, which is at odds with the official picture from the inside but may be just as illuminating (e.g., there may be something important to learn from a criminal's perspective on the legal system).[11] In later chapters I will be arguing that a good judge (and a good legal theorist) must learn to question the internal perspective by standing outside it and adopting a critical, external perspective.

THE INTERNAL TENDENCY OF ANGLO-AMERICAN LEGAL THEORY

In this section I wish to substantiate my claim that Anglo-American legal theory is largely conducted from an internal perspective, while postmodern theory (like Marxism) takes an external vantage point. Let me begin my analysis of the Anglo-American tradition by citing Hart's book *The Concept of Law*, which is widely regarded as this century's most important treatise on the philosophy of law.[12] Hart's project was to define "law" and to determine the minimal requirements by which a set of social rules could be deemed a "legal system." Hart's project was framed as a response and supplement to the work of John Austin, a nineteenth-century British philosopher who argued that "law" should be understood, roughly speaking, as the coercive command of a sovereign backed by threat of force.[13] For Austin the existence of a law is determined by looking at the behavior of a society. A legal system can be said to exist where there is a series of commands, backed by force, and issued publicly by a sovereign who is habitually obeyed. Austin took this position with the express purpose of distancing himself from the natural law tradition, which dominated jurisprudence at the time. Natural law thinkers such as Augustine and Aquinas held that a command or rule could be a genuine law only if it satisfied the demands of morality; immoral laws were not laws in the genuine or proper sense of the term "law." Austin, writing in the Benthamite tradition of legal positivism, rejected the natural law position by claiming that the existence of law could be determined as a matter of fact by looking at human behavior without reference to whether the purported 'law' was morally sound. In reaction to the natural law claim that 'an unjust law is not a genuine law,'[14] Austin held that "the existence of law is one thing, its merit or demerit is another."[15] Austin was the first major legal philosopher to make the obvious but essential point that an immoral law is still a law.

Hart agreed with Austin's positivism (viz. that the determination of law should be kept separate from questions of morality) but disagreed with his behavioristic, third-person account of law as a function of habits and obedience. Specifically, Hart felt that Austin's third-person account forced him to wrongfully characterize a legal system as a set of sanctions. This characterization (which fits criminal law better than civil law) assumes the perspective of an external observer looking at the legal system from without, like an anthropologist who sees a tribal legal system as a list of punishments enforced by tribal leaders. This approach misses the internal perspective according to which people see a legal system not merely as a set of commands or sanctions issued from above but as a system of rules which enables them to behave in an orderly way. Hart's classic example to illustrate this point is the third-person observer who examines the behavior of motorists at a stoplight. After a short period of observation, the observer will soon be able to make a statement from a third-person perspective about behavioral regularity at the stoplight, such as "There is a high probability that people will stop at the red light, and when they don't they will be chased by a car with flashing lights." Yet this approach misses the internal perspective according to which the participants see the red light as a signal that they ought to stop the car and not merely as a threat that they will be punished if they do not stop. According to Hart, Austin was wrong to see the legal system as a "gunman writ large," issuing warnings to the citizens that they will be sanctioned for particular actions.[16] From the internal perspective, laws are obligatory social rules that have legitimacy because they have been passed by a governing body and are accepted as common standards of behavior.

Hart was insistent that a legal system should not be viewed only according to the model of compliance with sanctions (from the outside, or externally) but also as a system of rules (from the inside, or internally): "A social rule [such as a law] has an 'internal' aspect in addition to the external aspect which it shares with a social habit and which consists in the regular uniform behavior which an observer could record."[17] In keeping with this belief, Hart argued that jurisprudence must take into account both the internal and external viewpoints: "One of the difficulties of any legal theory anxious to do justice to the complexity of the facts is to remember the presence of both these points of view and not to define one of them out of existence."[18] Yet there is reason to doubt whether Hart followed his own advice. Despite his insistence on giving due consideration to the external component of social rules, his discussion of the legal process is almost entirely internal. For example, when Hart discusses the role of judges in the Anglo-American system, he adopts the judge's perspective, untempered by third-person accounts of decision-making offered by sociologists, Marxists, feminists, and others less inclined to view the legal system from the perspective of its officials. In the final analysis, Hart echoes the commonly held judicial belief that the law is coherent, clear, and discoverable in most cases. Specifically, he argues that legal rules are necessarily worded in generalities so that they will apply to a broad variety of cases; this "open texture" quality of rules leaves room for an element of judicial discretion (i.e., legislation) in cases where the law is unclear.[19] In addition to filling in the gaps, judges are called upon to exercise discretion in determining the meaning of vague terms such as "fair rate" or "reasonable," although Hart insists that most cases fall under the clear application of a preexisting rule.

This seems fairly innocuous except for the fact that Hart fails to realize that judges may tend to fill in the gaps according to their own class and gender biases, that they have a stake in perpetuating the status quo, and that they might be deluded about their own actions. He fails to see how the law perpetuates class conflict, sexism, and racism because he is concerned with the mechanics of judging from the perspective of judges and lawyers, who are not charged with seeing the legal system from a critical, external perspective. In addition, he never mentions the ideological function of law as a way of legitimating the status quo. The sole external approach to the law he discusses is Austin's theory, completely ignoring the more powerful external theories offered by Marx, Durkheim, and Weber.

Of course, it was never Hart's goal to provide a sustained critique of the Anglo-American legal system from the external perspective. His goal—to find the key elements which enable us to meaningfully use such terms as "law" and "legal system"—was much broader. Because his book was so influential, its first-person account became the accepted starting point for much subsequent legal theory. This can be seen in the perspective taken by Ronald Dworkin, Hart's successor at Oxford, who is currently the heir apparent to Hart as the leader of Anglo-American legal theory.

Dworkin's theory of law is rather complicated, but a central mission of his work (especially his early work) has been to critique Hart's conception of law.

In his seminal essay "The Model of Rules"[20] Dworkin argued that Hart erred by supposing that judges merely look up the law and apply it to the fact scenarios brought before the court. Dworkin says that judges who are called upon to make legal decisions in hard cases (i.e., cases in which there are precedents supporting both sides of the argument) tend to look beyond the formal rules of law toward overarching principles which stand above and control the application of legal rules. These principles (e.g., "No person may profit from his own misdeed") do not apply in an all-or-nothing manner as do legal rules. A principle may compete for control with various other principles in a single case yet return to challenge other principles in a different case. The law on a given subject is not a "plain fact" that can be looked up in a "rule book" but requires a complicated interpretation of settled rules in light of shared moral principles. The task of the judge is to bring the settled law in line with the overarching shared principles, so that the legal principles *fit* and *justify* the settled law. The judge's restatement of the law as a set of rules guided by principles is labeled the "soundest theory of the law" on any given subject.[21]

Dworkin's more recent work states that the central task of legal theory involves interpretation; the judge must interpret the settled law in light of moral principles and commitments which run through the particular area of law as well as the legal system as a whole. The law is essentially a text that must be reconstituted, and the judge's task is to make this text coherent and consistent, much like an author charged with the task of writing a new chapter for a chain novel. In his magnum opus, *Law's Empire,* Dworkin argues that the law on any given subject is a function of an interpretive act by a judge who is reconstructing the settled law as a coherent doctrine, making it the best it can be in light of our collective commitment to the principles of due process, equality, fairness, and integrity. Dworkin invokes a mythical judge, Hercules, who is able to perform this difficult task. As a judge, Hercules must assume (as a matter of methodology) that the law should be interpreted in its best light, that it is or can be understood to be coherent, and that there is a theory or rationale running through the reported decisions in a particular area of law. Even if the case law is split on a given question, Hercules will make the "right" decision based upon our commitments to integrity, equality, and due process.[22]

Like Hart, Dworkin pays lip service to the need for both an external and internal perspective on the legal system: "Both perspectives on the law, the external and the internal, are essential, and each must take account of the other."[23] Yet he is somewhat shrill in his rejection of external, third-person accounts of the law: "Theories that ignore the structure of legal argument for supposedly larger questions of history and society are therefore perverse. They ignore questions about the internal character of legal argument, so their explanations are impoverished and defective."[24] Dworkin goes on to say that his work "takes up the *internal, participants' point of view.* . . . We will study formal legal argument *from the judge's viewpoint.*"[25] According to Dworkin, this means that third-person considerations of history and class consciousness are generally irrelevant. As a matter of methodology, Dworkin's internal perspective rules out theories which do not privilege the judge's perspective, such as Marxism, radical feminism, Critical Legal Studies, and postmodernism, all of which cannot be applied by judges in their professional capacity as legal arbiters. Dworkin's rejection of external theory confirms my earlier point that internal thinkers tend to see external theory as useless. Predictably, external theorists have responded to Dworkin by saying that his internal perspective is problematic. According to sociolegal scholar Alan Hunt,

> The dominant tradition of contemporary legal theory is epitomized by H. L. A. Hart and Ronald Dworkin, who despite their other differences insist upon the adoption of an internalist perspective. . . . Internal theories exhibit a predisposition to adopt the self-descriptions of judges or lawyers as primary empirical material. . . . There is thus a naive acceptance of legal ideology as legal reality. Internal theory is simply *too close to its subject matter.*[26]

Hunt's point is that the internal approach (exemplified in Dworkin's statement that he is doing legal theory from the perspective of judges) requires a baseline acceptance of the concepts held by the internal players. For example, an internal approach will not have much use for the important sociological finding that the opinions of Supreme Court justices correlate with their political orientations and gender because these insights are external to the judging process; judges do not try to understand their own class and gender biases when deciding cases— although perhaps they should do so now and again.[27] The rejection of sociological data leads to some curious results. For example, given the statistical correlation of Supreme Court opinions with the justices' political orientations and gender, one would think that Dworkin would be wary of writing from the perspective of the ideal, neutral judge (Hercules) who is not affected by his gender or class. It seems obvious to many thinkers that judges' political convictions necessarily affect their decisions on controversial issues such as minimum-wage laws, flag burning, or social-welfare legislation. Of course, from an internal perspective judges are not supposed to be influenced by these factors since the judging process is purportedly a neutral search for the best statement of the law. It should therefore come as no surprise that Dworkin's internal perspective fails to deal with the feminist claim that the law is gendered, nor does he engage at length with postmodernism or Marxism.[28]

Having established that Anglo-American legal theory is internally oriented (at least since Hart's work of the late fifties), I will now examine the ways in which postmodern theory is external. The stage will then be set for a debate on whether legal theory should be internal or external, whether it can (or should) take both perspectives into account, and how such a balance might be achieved.

THE EXTERNAL TENDENCY OF POSTMODERN LEGAL THEORY

In this section I intend to prove my claim that postmodern theory represents an external critique of the legal system by looking at the types of claims raised by postmodern thinkers. As a starting point, consider Nietzsche's claim that the movement toward equal rights is a symptom of "slave morality" and a leveling down of great individuals into the herd, the "bungled and botched."[29] However one chooses to interpret this claim, it is certainly not of much immediate use to the players on the inside of the legal system, who must decide cases and enact laws. Nietzsche's argument may be of some use to legislators in deciding whether to enact, say, welfare laws or affirmative-action schemes (i.e., they may have a Nietzschean conception of the "will to power" at the back of their minds when deciding whether to vote on a particular law), but Nietzsche's claim about "slave morality" is not couched in the language-games typically used by judges and legislators, who speak in terms of constitutional rights, compelling state interests, and balancing tests. Nietzsche, in other words, does not make claims about the rights and remedies available under the Constitution or state laws, so his work cannot be imported directly into those legal controversies (e.g., Nietzsche did not write about the proper role of the judiciary in interpreting documents such as the U. S. Constitution). If Nietzsche's work is to affect the legal system, it must do so in a very roundabout way, perhaps by functioning as a reminder that our push toward equality might have an ugly underside, or by causing legislators to stand back and take a global, critical perspective on the legal system. In other words, Nietzsche's external critique must somehow be *translated* or *mediated* so that it can affect the internal practice of the law, perhaps by forcing a rethinking of the foundational notions (e.g., justice, property, mercy, punishment, and the adversarial system) embedded in the legal system.

For another example of an external claim, consider Lyotard's point that two legal systems can be incommensurate to the point where one is silenced by the hegemony of the other. For example, a claim by indigenous peoples that a mining company should not dig at an ancient burial site (because nobody can own or disrupt a burial site) may fall on deaf ears in a court of law. The legal system excludes this type of "claim" as nonactionable because it is part of a different language-game than the dominant game, which solves property disputes by looking at deeds, easements, and licenses. Lyotard thinks that we should be on the lookout for ways in which a dominant legal discourse silences the claims of certain groups (especially indigenous populations, wage laborers, and minorities) by denying them a hearing, thereby giving rise to what Lyotard calls a "differend," a term which denotes a claim which is valid under a particular political or legal scheme but cannot be heard from the perspective of an alternative scheme. For example, the claim by wage laborers for nonalienating labor cannot be heard within the current legal system (one cannot sue to ensure meaningful labor), so it goes unheard in a court of law.

Lyotard's notion of the "differend" strikes me as illuminating, but from the internal perspective it is just as useless to judges and lawyers as Nietzsche's claim about the pervasiveness of slave morality in the legal system. Lyotard's claim can have no direct effect on the legal arguments offered in courtrooms in the United States and England, especially since a "differend" is by definition a claim that cannot be given a voice under the existing legal system. Lyotard's work, then, cannot affect the law *directly,* though it might lead to a change in the way judges and lawyers think about what they are doing. Again, the postmodernist's external message will have to be translated so that it can have some impact on the internal practice.

Do postmodern thinkers realize their work is somewhat inapplicable to the internal debates of lawyers and judges? It would seem they certainly understand the crucial difference between internal and external perspectives and actually choose to adopt the latter. The best way to illustrate this point is by citing examples of real-life situations encountered by two postmodern thinkers (Foucault and Derrida) and by Marxist lawyers.

My first example is drawn from Foucault's life. As we shall see in chapter 4, Foucault argues that the formal rights which citizens hold in relation to the state in a democratic republic (e.g., liberty, privacy, and property) are something of a smokescreen that distracts attention from the unjust power relations which undercut these formal rights. That is, we live in a society in which people are called "free" yet are subjected to endless coercive practices in schools, factories, hospitals, prisons, and other venues in which they are normalized, classified, disciplined, and punished. Furthermore, people are coerced into accepting "freely agreed upon" work situations (such as telemarketing) in which they are subjected to workplace monitoring, which undermines the subject's rights to privacy and liberty. During a particularly radical phase in his life, Foucault suggested that we should turn away from formal rights toward "popular justice,"[30] and in a televised debate with Noam Chomsky he suggested that "the idea of justice in itself" was an instrument of abuse in the wrong hands.[31] Here is a thinker, then, who wants to question (and perhaps reject) such basic juridical concepts as the right to autonomy, privacy, and property.

Yet a curious thing happened in 1977, when Foucault came to the defense of German lawyer Klaus Croissant, who was hiding in France after being sought by German authorities for illegally passing materials to a left-wing terrorist group. Apparently there was quite an uproar in France over the question of whether Croissant acted immorally in passing information to the terrorists. Given Foucault's political activism, it was no great surprise when Foucault came to Croissant's defense, but what was surprising was the language in which Foucault couched his defense of Croissant: "There exists a right to have a lawyer who speaks for you, with you, who allows you to be heard and to pre-serve your life. . . . This right is not a juridical abstraction, nor is it some dreamy ideal; this right forms part of our historical reality and must not be erased from it."[32] Given his skepticism toward formal juridical concepts, Foucault's insis-tence on basic legal rights was met with incredulity. How could Foucault remain so critical of the legal system as a whole yet, when faced with a con-crete case, invoke the protections offered by this dreaded system?

My second example comes from an incident which has come to be known as "l'Affaire Derrida."[33] In 1987 Derrida was interviewed by the French weekly *Le Nouvel Observateur* on the topic of Martin Heidegger's involvement with the Nazi party. Without Derrida's knowledge, the rights to the interview were later assigned by the French magazine to Columbia University Press so that the inter-view could be included in an anthology entitled *The Heidegger Controversy* being compiled by Richard Wolin.[34] The book was published in late 1991, and shortly thereafter Derrida came across a copy of it in a New York bookstore. For one reason or another, he was very displeased to find that his interview had been included in the collection. Derrida then instructed his lawyer to send a letter threatening Columbia University Press with a lawsuit to enjoin a reprint of the anthology, which was selling well and was due to be released in paperback. In subsequent communications on the issue of whether he was within his legal rights in claiming exclusive control over the interview, Derrida claimed that "any competent lawyer will tell you that I am the only owner of the interview."[35]

What is striking here is not merely the dubious nature of Derrida's claim to ownership of the interview—why should he be deemed the exclusive owner of the interview?—but his invocation of legal concepts such as "authorial inten-tion" and "copyright," which he had spent years ridiculing as "logocentric" fic-tions. The supreme irony of "l'Affaire Derrida" is that Richard Wolin had personally attended seminars held by Derrida in the early eighties in which Der-rida proclaimed the absurdity of the ownership of texts under copyright laws.[36]

Yet when Derrida found himself embroiled in a real-life controversy over a text, he reverted to the formalist legal language which he had previously ridiculed.

A final example is taken from a Marxist-oriented handbook for Critical lawyers.[37] This book contains a series of articles on the question of how Marxist lawyers should structure their legal practice, given the orthodox Marxist position that rights are bourgeois fictions. In general, Marxism advocates the destruction of the legal system, which is seen as a mere vehicle for managing the affairs of the bourgeoisie. Two radical lawyers who contributed a short piece to the handbook pointed out that Marxist lawyers face a double bind. On the one hand, they are committed to what Engels called "the withering away of the law,"[38] yet as lawyers they must operate from within a framework of rights. For them "rights are seen as bourgeois myths, empty promises which are part of the existing hegemony and which place individualistic claims above the needs of the community. Yet the assertion and defense of rights is often the main activity of progressive practitioners."[39] Marxist lawyers, then, must walk a fine line. They must hold that rights are "bourgeois myths" yet they are sworn to protect their clients' rights. Isn't this hopelessly contradictory? How can someone devote his or her life to the protection of rights which are held to be bourgeois myths?

How are we to understand the double gesture employed in these three examples? How could Foucault question the value of rights yet defend Croissant's rights? How could Derrida ridicule the idea of copyright law yet assert his own legal rights to possession of a text? Lastly, how could Marxist lawyers think that rights are myths yet stand up in court and defend their clients' rights? These examples might give rise to the cynical response that these people are hypocrites who advocate one course of conduct in theory but don't follow their own advice in practice.

Another interpretation of their actions places them in a clearer light while also offering a coherent explanation for their behavior. Specifically, one can say that the general theoretical views held by Foucault, Derrida, and the Marxists were *external* viewpoints on the legal system, whereas their particular actions were *internal* responses within the framework of the system. Taking Derrida as an example, one might say that he holds the external view that the entire notion of intellectual property is philosophically untenable. Perhaps he feels that texts are the result of a shared language which cannot be the private property of any single person or entity, or that all texts make reference to other texts and consequently no single text can be "owned" in a literal sense. Yet this external view does not logically necessitate the *internal* response that he should release all rights which he might have to his interview. To be sure, there is something ironic about his simultaneous rejection of copyrights and his assertion of a right to a text, but one should recall that these claims were made in different contexts: the first claim was made in a philosophical forum (before the philosophical community, as it were), whereas the second was made in a legal forum (as a prelude to a court case). A similar double gesture would hold for an anarchist who worked for the postal service: he would insist on his right to a steady paycheck while also believing that his employer (the government) has no right to exist. The examples from Foucault, Derrida, and the Marxists show that a person can hold an external perspective on the legal system and yet switch approaches and appropriate the terms and concepts used by the players inside the system.

The foregoing incidents demonstrate that postmodern theory is largely an external critique, yet on some level the theorists seem aware that there is also an internal side to the law. I say "largely" because there are instances in which the postmodern critique is difficult to classify. For example, there are cases in which a postmodern critique is external to the judging process but has broader implications which can affect the practice of judging. For example, consider Derrida's claim that texts are related to other texts (so-called intertexuality) such that no text is fully closed and self-contained ("there is no outside to the text").[40] If this claim were correct, and if it were adopted by a judge in a contract case, it might allow the judge to disregard or downplay the Parole Evidence Rule (viz. that a written contract cannot be modified by prior or contemporaneous oral communications),[41] permitting him to look beyond the face of the contract and allow evidence of oral communications which predated the contract. In this way, a general theory about language might have an effect on the internal reasoning process of the court. One is dealing here with an external claim that can be translated into the internal practice of the law. Throughout this book I will be performing a similar type of analysis, looking at various external viewpoints offered by the postmodernists and attempting to tease out the internal ramifications of their work.

Foundationalism and Antifoundationalism

Having addressed the subject of postmodern legal theorists' external perspective, I would now like to turn to postmodernists' radical distrust of foundations in ethics, politics, and law.

It is my contention that postmodern legal theory has arisen in response to a perceived crisis of foundations in classical jurisprudence. The crisis stems from a realization that the foundations (i.e., the "grounds" or "first principles") that have been offered in support of the legal system are becoming increasingly untenable. These foundational concepts include neutrality, justice, reason, history, nature, the social contract, God, the rational self, and the inherent autonomy of the individual. Postmodernism wants to problematize (and, in extreme cases, reject) these foundations as if they no longer deserved the sanctity that has been lavished on them over the past few centuries. Therefore, postmodernism is characteristically critical, seeking to expose the foundations of modern jurisprudence as constructs or ideologies which parade as eternal verities. This project involves a sort of decentering and relativizing of such enduring legal conceptions as the legal subject, contract, mens rea (mental state), innate rights, property, consensus, and sovereignty.

The postmodernists are certainly correct in assuming that our legacy in legal and political theory is highly foundational and relies on ahistorical, nonempirical conceptions of human nature, reason, and truth. For example, in the Declaration of Independence Thomas Jefferson justified the American Revolution by alluding to God, self-evident truths, and natural law.[42] Indeed, the founding fathers of our country grounded the U.S. Constitution on the foundation of natural rights set forth by John Locke, including the rights to life, liberty, and property. At about the same time in Germany, Immanuel Kant was arguing that a uniform faculty of reason was held in common by all men, and that this faculty of reason could be used as the basis for a republican government and the rule of law, including rights to liberty and property.[43] Kant's successor, G. W. F. Hegel, as well as Hegel's own successor, Karl Marx, would go on to argue that the laws of history could be used to ground a just political and legal system.[44] Shortly thereafter, in England, John Stuart Mill argued that liberal democracy could be firmly grounded in considerations of general utility.[45]

To this day, the foundational legacy of Locke, Jefferson, Kant, and Marx remains overwhelming. These great thinkers represent our modernist heritage in political and legal theory, and this heritage has an intellectual hegemony so powerful that we automatically assume that legal theory *must* begin with a deep grounding for the state and its laws. The modern, foundational approach demands that philosophers and legal thinkers rest their political and legal visions on absolute, nonempirical, unalterable claims about human reason, truth, natural rights, utility, and/or history.

The beauty of the modern approach is that it provides a secure foundation for legal theory, an end to the nagging problem of infinite regress which haunts all efforts to establish a political or legal platform. To grasp the power of a foundational approach, consider the controversy over fairly recent decisions in which judges ordered the administration of Norplant (a birth-control device) as a condition for granting parole to mothers with a history of violence or drug abuse.[46] These decisions (known as the "Norplant cases") were the subject of public outcry. The basic bone of contention was that the decisions by these judges violated the female defendants' fundamental right to procreate. This sounds fair enough, but the problem of regress raises its head when one asks where the fundamental right to procreate is grounded, given that it is not mentioned in the Constitution. One can answer this question by saying that the right to procreate is an *implied* fundamental right which piggybacks on the rights enumerated in the Constitution.[47] One can press the regress further by questioning what grounds the rights in the Constitution. It is precisely at this point that one seemingly requires some sort of backstop which prevents the endless regress of justifications. And here is where the modern approach steps in to provide the necessary backstop by positing a grounding in human nature or reason which ends the regress. Thus, in the Norplant cases some critics ultimately argued that the judges not only failed to follow the letter of the law but went so far as to violate the foundations underpinning the law, namely, natural rights, inherent human autonomy, and human decency.[48] In other words, the grounding is found in ahistorical notions which are held to anchor the principles of the legal system.

It is no exaggeration to say that this type of foundationalism has guided ethics, political theory, and legal theory for hundreds of years, though there have been notable exceptions throughout the history of philosophy. One can find the ubiquitous modern approach in contemporary liberalism, in John Rawls' early work (which describes a seemingly unencumbered ego in the Original Position), and in Alan Gewirth's attempt to ground liberal principles in basic premises about human agency.[49] At the other end of the political spectrum, one can find the modern approach equally at home in conservatism, such as Francis Fukuyama's notion that liberal democracy represents the culmination and the telos of history, and in the natural law claim that homosexuality can rightfully be outlawed.[50] One can even find the modern approach in radical contexts, as in the Marxist complaint that capitalism destroys man's *inherent* species being.[51]

One might usefully envision the modern approach to law and politics as a house built upon a foundation of first principles. At the lowest level are found the foundational principles of reason, nature, God, utility, history, autonomy, and the soul. At a higher level are the political and legal structure of the just state, which most modern theorists (with the exception of Marx) see as a free-market participatory democracy with basic liberties and rights to due process, equality, and property. Maintaining this analogy, one could turn to any of the modern theorists to see how the foundation allegedly supports the higher structures. For example, Kant held that reason could provide a set of a priori necessary laws which could serve as the basis of the just state;[52] Jefferson held that democracy could be justified by reference to natural law; and Marx thought that historical materialism provided the grounds for believing in the ultimate overthrow of capitalism and the rise of worldwide communism.

But if one no longer believes in the foundations in which one used to believe, doesn't the entire structure built upon the foundation collapse? For example, can one support Jeffersonian democracy if one no longer believes in Jefferson's notion of natural law or God? Can one still hold that the Constitution serves as a foundational text for jurisprudence when one no longer believes that texts have stable meanings? What happens when one questions justice itself as a cause of the oppression which exists in our society, as some postmodern thinkers (e.g., Nietzsche and Foucault) have done? What if one asserts (following Lyotard) that consensus is "terroristic"? Once one loses the old foundations and becomes suspicious about justice and consensus, is there anything left upon which one can build a theory of justice? Postmodern theory is an attempt to call into question the classic foundations and to ask whether we can do without them. Later chapters will reveal whether these thinkers can erect a legal theory without these foundations, or whether some sort of foundations are necessary for legal theory to operate at all.

This, then, is the postmodern predicament: the grounds which had previously been offered in support of liberal democracy and its system of justice are no longer tenable. In the postmodern era, the old foundations seem like after-the-fact rationalizations, ideological constructs, more akin to mythology than science. As Lyotard (perhaps the seminal postmodern thinker) has put it, the condition of postmodernity is a condition of "incredulity toward metanarratives."[53] We no longer buy into the grand stories we have been told about human nature, God, the soul, history, and human emancipation.

The postmodernists discussed in this book adopt different strategies for coping with the loss of foundations. For Nietzsche and Foucault the loss of foundations leads, in varying degrees, to a turn toward aesthetics as a way of supporting political and legal positions, on the assumption that in the absence of fixed moral rules, the self and the state can be created in an aesthetic act. I will subsequently argue that this "aesthetic turn" meets with only limited success. For Derrida, the loss of foundations leads to the adoption of a modified Kantian approach based on Emmanuel Levinas' phenomenological notion of justice, an approach I find equally problematic. Lyotard, too, turns to Kantian theory to explain how we can find universal rules to govern the disparate language-games encountered in a pluralistic society. The most fascinating aspect of postmodern legal theory is the struggle to overcome the loss of foundations without lapsing into nihilism, relativism, or conservatism. The problem of finding a new, nonmetaphysical basis for the law is a perennial problem for all of the thinkers discussed in this book. As Lyotard has asked: "Where, after the metanarratives, can legitimacy reside?"[54]

It should be pointed out that the postmodern attack on foundations is aimed at a group of thinkers (Jefferson, Locke, Kant, Marx) whose approach is becoming less influential in political and legal theory. For example, the cutting edge of Anglo-American theory has distanced itself from the metaphysical foundations once offered in support of liberalism. Rawls' later work stresses that his liberal vision is "political, not metaphysical," in the sense that he purports to articulate principles of justice that apply to a society in which there is already an overlapping consensus in favor of democracy and equality, such as the United States, Canada, or the United Kingdom. His theory is not about the principles of justice which should be adopted by all humans qua participation in humanity, but only for those who are already situated in such a way that these principles are encoded within their basic belief structure. A similar approach is taken by Dworkin, who argues that the law must be determined with reference to political and moral conceptions held by our society at large, but that these political and moral conceptions cannot themselves be tested against some standard of objective morality. Dworkin has even asserted that it makes no sense to speak (as the modern thinkers once did) about the sense in which, say, slavery is *really* wrong for all humans, as if "the injustice of slavery is part of the furniture of the universe."[55]

In a sense, then, the postmodern critique of foundations has already been adopted by a few (but not all) Anglo-American thinkers, who argue that we do not need foundations in the traditional sense of fundamental principles about human nature. These recent Anglo-American thinkers feel that the loss of traditional foundations is not fatal to legal theory because the contingent beliefs of the members of our community provide the grounding necessary for a vision of justice. But for the postmodern thinkers, political and legal theory cannot rest on the contingent foundation of an overlapping consensus or shared moral principles because this consensus is itself problematic. Thus, the postmodernists share a *radical* and deep distrust of *any* foundations, be they metaphysical or contingent. The question arises as to whether this radical skepticism, when combined with the external perspective on the law, can give rise to a normative program for legal reform.

Positive and Negative Jurisprudence

In my assessment of what postmodern legal theory has to offer, I will be making use of the terms "positive jurisprudence" and "negative jurisprudence." The former term refers to any political or legal theory which provides a basis for judicial action in a particular case or situation and/or recommends the basic structures for a just state. Typically, a positive jurisprudence will specify the demands of justice in particular legal controversies, such as abortion, affirmative action, privacy, and the proper extent of taxation. A list of thinkers who offer a positive jurisprudence would include Ronald Dworkin, John Finnis, H. L. A. Hart, and Richard Posner. These thinkers all discuss the nature of law as a social phenomenon, suggesting how decisions should be made in particular cases. Their work is positive in the sense that they offer a normative framework for future action by legislators and judges. Although these thinkers are critical of particular laws and legal decisions, their work displays a normative, constructive component.

By "negative jurisprudence" I wish to designate a theory of law which generates critical insights about the law but does not offer a positive plan for action. The most blatantly negative jurisprudence can be found in the orthodox Marxist position that the state and the courts are merely a conduit for handling the affairs of the bourgeoisie, such that justice cannot be rendered while the current legal system remains intact. Orthodox Marxists favor a situation in which the law ultimately withers away, which means that they cannot offer any pointers for building a better legal system. Most of the thinkers discussed in this book do not adopt such an extreme position, but in one way or another they each eschew (or back away from) a coherent positive jurisprudence.

One might wonder whether a positive jurisprudence is truly necessary for a legal theory. This very question was debated by a group of legal scholars (led by Pierre Schlag) under the rubric of the "Critique of Normativity."[56] At least three salient arguments have been put forth by Schlag and others against the adoption of a positive jurisprudence. In the remainder of this chapter I would like to examine these arguments briefly and then restate why I feel that a legal theory should have a positive jurisprudence and, ultimately, why postmodern theory comes up short for failing to offer such a program.

The first argument is that offering normative prescriptions plays into the ideological distortion that the legal system is a free and voluntary association that will respond to calls for normative change. That is, normative legal theory creates the false impression that theorists (and their readers) have the autonomous decision-making ability and social power to effectuate change.[57] Normative thinkers should realize that our legal system is not responsive to their sermons: legal theorists and their audiences are powerless to steer the system one way or another. The legal system is a vast and unyielding machine which changes only when the power shifts in society at large. Given this reality, the making of normative legal prescriptions creates the distorted impression that our legal system is composed of empowered individuals, when the real mystery is why individuals are so powerless. The best approach is to replace the normative appeals with *description* and *criticism*.[58]

A second, related argument is that normative prescriptions will only replicate the existing social arrangement, thereby lending it additional legitimation.

Lawyers are socialized to accept the existing arrangement as correct and inevitable, with the result that even their prescriptions for change are rote and programmed. Normative theorists typically concern themselves with whether a particular case decision was properly decided or whether a given doctrine should be accepted, rarely grappling with such deeper questions as whether a rights-based framework is appropriate or whether private property and wage-labor should be abolished. By recommending piecemeal reform within a narrow area, normative thought reinforces the status quo and precludes a deeply critical approach to law.

A final argument is that a theory of law should be measured solely according to the insights it generates and not on the basis of whether it provides the framework for a just state or offers solutions to legal disputes. It is better to have a negative jurisprudence which accurately depicts the legal system and generates profound insights (such as Critical Legal Studies) than to have a utopian program which sounds inspiring but fails to take a realistic and critical look at our legal system (such as Dworkin's book *Law's Empire*). Although we have been trained to expect a positive jurisprudence, perhaps this very expectation should itself be questioned.

My initial response to the Critique of Normativity is to acknowledge that it is partially correct. I agree that mainstream scholarship overrates the impact of theory on the actual workings of the legal system and that normative theory often replicates the ideology of the status quo. Yet I still insist that, despite its dangers, a positive jurisprudential program is essential for two reasons.

First, if one wants to critique the existing legal system as a whole or to argue that a particular case was wrongly decided (as postmodernists often do), one can do this only by presupposing some sort of normative conception about what the law *should* be, or at least some fundamental values which the law should be fostering. It is doubtless possible to offer what might be called an "imminent critique of the law" which demonstrates that the law fails to live up to its own expectations (e.g., by showing that the law purports to value fairness but nevertheless enforces unfair contracts, or that it hypocritically protects privacy when it comes to home ownership but not when it comes to sexual preference). But even to adopt this stance (i.e., to deconstruct a legal position, as postmodernists are wont to do) is to suppose that the court's failure is correctable, and that a different legal arrangement could avoid this defect. And to make these claims requires a positive jurisprudence with a normative component. When put on the spot, postmodern legal theorists who profess to reject a positive jurisprudence will grudgingly admit that the decisions in *Bowers v. Hardwick*[59] and *Dred Scott v. Sanford*[60] were morally wrong and should have been decided differently, and they may even employ the foundational normative conceptions they ridicule, such as "autonomy," "equality," "privacy," and "flourishing."[61]

Another reason in support of positive jurisprudence is that legal decisions are usually made inside the legal system by judges and lawyers, not by sociologists and revolutionaries. When it comes to particular issues (like abortion and affirmative action), legal theorists should be able to step inside the law to make arguments that can be understood by judges, lawyers, and legislators who seek reasons for favoring one legal arrangement over another. A purely external critique without a normative or pragmatic component is somewhat useless. To change the law—or even to argue that the law should be changed by someone else—requires a positive jurisprudence of some kind, if only to explain why, for example, abortion should be legal or why affirmative action should be allowed. In this book I will demonstrate that postmodern thinkers typically harbor some sort of positive conception of what the law should be but often suppress this conception for fear that they will be chastised for invoking foundational commitments of the modernist variety. This explains the tension postmodernists experience in rejecting foundations while also requiring foundations to ground their critiques of the law. The solution to this predicament, I will argue, is to adopt fallible, provisional foundations strong enough to support normative claims but not rooted in problematic modernist claims about human nature, reason, and truth.

In this chapter I have attempted to frame the fundamental question of whether postmodern theory can give rise to a positive jurisprudence or, alternatively, whether it must remain an essentially negative jurisprudence. The latter would seem to be the case, given that postmodern theory is externally oriented and radically antifoundational. Perhaps some method of translation can be identified by means of which the external insights of postmodernism can be translated or mediated into constructive proposals which will engage those who are operating on the inside of the law.

In the next chapters I will present an analysis of individual postmodern thinkers, beginning with Nietzsche, the hugely influential thinker Jürgen Habermas recently described as providing "the entry into postmodernity."[62]

3 ❧ Nietzsche's Theory of Law as a Critique of Natural Law Theory

In the past decade there has been a surge of interest in Nietzsche, not only among philosophers and literary theorists but among legal scholars.[1] Nietzsche's growing popularity in legal circles is somewhat surprising, considering that he did not present a systematic philosophy of law[2] and is generally thought to have been a legal nihilist who denied the existence of basic human rights.[3] So how can one explain the sudden interest in Nietzsche?

I contend that this focus on Nietzsche is the result of two burgeoning trends in legal scholarship: an increased interest in postmodernism and poststructuralism, especially in the form of deconstruction, and the focus on nonfoundational, critical, piecemeal approaches to law. With regard to the recent interest in deconstruction, it is useful to remember that the European purveyors of deconstruction are known as "Neo-Nietzscheans"[4] because the method of deconstruction has been traced back to Nietzsche.[5] With regard to nonfoundational approaches, Nietzsche is often touted as the first postmetaphysical thinker and the father of postmodernism.[6] His work seems to support the growing interest in nonfoundational approaches to law, including legal pragmatism[7] and critical legal studies.[8]

While the interest in Nietzsche's overall philosophical program is entirely understandable, legal scholars who are interested in Nietzsche must come to grips with the fact that Nietzsche simply did not write very much on the subject of law. His few references to law and justice are scattered throughout many works, but they are not really synthesized into any organized whole. He generally approached the law in a piecemeal fashion, using scattered aphorisms to address such disparate legal issues as criminal law, equal rights, and debtor/creditor relations. To be sure, there are a few sustained discussions on law-related issues, such as his analysis of the origin of justice in *On the Genealogy of Morals* and his comments on Hindu law and the criminal element in *The Anti-Christ*, but I would estimate that the topic of law (broadly construed) occupies less than one percent of Nietzsche's writings.[9]

The lack of specific textual support on the subject of law leads one to conclude that Nietzsche did not present a systematic legal philosophy. This means that if one wants to formulate a "Nietzschean theory of law," one must pass beyond his limited discussions of law itself and draw from his general approach to such related philosophical issues as his attacks on metaphysics, foundational epistemology, and Christian ideals. Although this takes one somewhat far afield from specifically legal matters, I think it is necessary if one is to formulate something akin to a "Nietzschean theory of law."

My reading of Nietzsche's comments on law and law-related issues is that his approach to law is best understood as a critique of legal foundationalism in general and natural law theory in particular. In this chapter I will attempt to formulate a Nietzschean critique of natural law theory despite the fact that he had comparatively little to say on this topic. I will argue that it is possible to use Nietzsche's few extended comments on law and law-related issues to create a three-pronged attack on natural law theory. First, Nietzsche presents an epistemic skepticism which casts doubts on the possibility of natural law. Second, he presents a linguistic theory that exposes natural law to be a human fiction, a life-preserving and perhaps useful convention. Third, and most important, Nietzsche presents a genealogical analysis of law which denies the notion of inherent rights. Nietzsche's approach to law is primarily though not exclusively critical: he wants to debunk the idea that law can be founded on metaphysical or epistemic claims about nature, pure reason, self-evidence, or Christian morality.

After explaining Nietzsche's critical attitude toward natural law theory, I will explore whether and to what extent it is possible to use Nietzsche's work to generate a positive jurisprudence, that is, a theory of how the law *should* operate in a just state. This is difficult in light of the many passages in which Nietzsche ridicules democracy, the rule of law, the state, socialism, and feminism. Still, I think that it is important to make an effort to see if a positive program is possible for Nietzsche, although I readily admit that such an interpretation is possible only at the expense of discounting and downplaying some of his more outrageous comments on political matters. Using this method of interpretation (which has its detractors), I will put forth the argument that Nietzsche's writings can be interpreted to provide a positive jurisprudence which supports a provisional, rights-based, nonfoundational, and experimental approach to the law. According to such a reading, Nietzsche is not a legal nihilist because he recognizes that there can be (provisional) grounds for choosing one legal scheme over another, namely, the degree to which it is life-affirming and power-generating (in furtherance of the "will to power").

There are, however, some problems with this formulation of a Nietzschean positive jurisprudence. First, such a reading is made possible only by taking Nietzsche's actual work in directions that were probably not anticipated by

Nietzsche himself; this reading of him is therefore somewhat strained. Second, the positive jurisprudence which one ultimately derives from Nietzsche is not very powerful in terms of specifying the parameters of the just state, nor does he provide clear solutions to particular legal problems (e.g., abortion, affirmative action, privacy). I conclude that any theory of law which can be derived from Nietzsche will not be a large-scale, full-blown theory of law but rather a sort of attitude or posture toward law and legal theory. If one sees Nietzsche as offering not a grand theory but a set of reminders for a particular purpose, then one can place his work in a plausible light as making an important but limited contribution to legal theory. This view of Nietzsche is certainly more charitable than the traditional notion that he was a nihilist or, worse, a fascist.

I begin my discussion with an explanation of natural law theory. I then pass to each prong of Nietzsche's three-part critique of natural law. In the final sections of this chapter I flesh out some of the details of a Nietzschean positive jurisprudence and explore some potentially fatal objections to it.

The Basics of Natural Law Theory

Natural law theory typically encompasses three basic positions: (1) there are certain immutable rights and claims belonging to individuals that predate the advent of civil society; (2) these basic rights and claims must be respected whenever people join together to form a civil society because governments are legitimate to the extent that they are a mechanism for the preservation of these inherent rights; and (3) the laws of a just society are commands of nature (or God) that can be determined by reason.[10] For natural law theory, there is a necessary connection between law and morality, such that the test for a "law" is whether it conforms to the dictates of a preestablished, eternally binding morality. An immoral law is simply not a bona fide "law" in the true sense of the term and is thus not morally binding.[11]

The concept of natural law goes back at least as far as Aristotle's distinction between natural and legal justice,[12] but it received its first elaborate treatment in the works of Cicero:

> There is in fact a true law—namely, right reason—which is in accordance with nature, applies to all men, and is unchangeable and eternal. . . . To invalidate this law by human legislation is never morally right, nor is it permissible ever to restrict its operation, and to annul it wholly is impossible. . . . It will not lay down one rule at Rome and another at Athens, nor will it be one rule today and another tomorrow. But there will be one law, eternal and unchangeable, binding at all times upon all peoples, and there will be, as it

were, one common master and ruler of men, namely God, who is the author of this law, its interpreter, and its sponsor.[13]

This early formulation of natural law can be seen at work in the natural law theories espoused by St. Augustine and St. Thomas Aquinas, who added Christian elements to the theory.[14] For many commentators, the definitive version of natural law theory was set forth in Aquinas' *Summa Theologica*.[15] Aquinas saw the natural law as containing an eternal and unchanging set of first principles that were discoverable by reason and applicable to all men regardless of their circumstances. The source of the natural law was divine will, discoverable through God-given reason: "All law proceeds from the reason and will of the lawgiver; the divine and natural law from the reasonable will of God; the human law from the will of men, regulated by reason."[16] Man-made "human law" (what we now call "positive law") was deemed morally acceptable only when it mirrored the natural law, and any attempt to surpass the realm of natural law was deemed immoral. When a man-made law runs afoul of the natural law (say, by imposing unequal burdens or excessive punishments), there are grounds for disobeying the law since a law that is unjust is not really a law.[17] This last point is clearly the chief advantage of natural law theory, namely, that it provides a transcendental grounding for basic civil rights and liberties, thereby creating a standard by which one can reject oppressive laws. In addition, natural law can be used to generate the basic framework for the just state since the latter will be organized such that it respects the fundamental rights of security, freedom, and property.[18]

The natural law position was well entrenched in Nietzsche's time, although it was increasingly couched in terms of social contract theory. The French and American revolutions were greatly influenced by the social contract version of natural law theory, and Nietzsche occasionally spoke about these revolutions.[19] Although Nietzsche did not comment at length on social contract theory, it is clear that he repeatedly rejected the idea that society could be founded on a social contract.[20]

Under the social contract model of natural law theory, people are endowed with certain basic rights as individuals solely by virtue of their status as humans capable of reason. These include (at a minimum) the right to liberty, property, and security. When people come together to form a civil society, each forfeits his natural right to punish others, vesting the state with the exclusive right to punish wrongdoers. In exchange, the individual receives state protection from the violence of others. Since the state is basically a voluntary association, there is a tacit consent to the imposition of law by elected officials, but if the law fails to respect basic rights, it is no longer binding. Under this formulation, the just state is one which most faithfully respects basic, natural (God-given) rights.[21]

This position is clearly at work in the Declaration of Independence, which refers to "the Laws of Nature," "Nature's God," and enumerates certain natural rights: "We hold these truths to be self-evident, that all men are created equal, that they are endowed by their Creator with certain unalienable Rights, that among these are Life, Liberty, and the pursuit of Happiness. That to secure these rights, governments are instituted among men, deriving their just powers from the consent of the governed."[22] As evidenced by the Declaration of Independence, natural law theory tends to be foundational because it presupposes that the natural order has a definite, discoverable teleology. Typically, this implies that God has created the world such that all beings (including man) have an inherent purpose which is discoverable through the exercise of reason. The legal order, then, is founded upon an assumption about (human) nature itself, namely, that it has laws and that these laws can be discovered with certainty once and for all:

> Initially, natural law theories involved more than the simple claim that the legal order was to be understood as essentially connected with the moral order; also involved was a certain claim about the nature of the moral order itself. On this view, the moral order (or at least that part of it not dependent on divine revelation) was viewed as a part of the order of nature—moral duties being in some sense "read off" from the essences or purposes fixed (perhaps by God) in nature.[23]

This means that the specific substantive provisions of the natural law are largely unchangeable because certain rights (freedom, property, security) are derived from an unchanging conception of what it is to be human. As a result, there is a certain static quality to natural law. The natural law claim, then, comes down to this: over and above the physical laws of nature describing how objects in nature actually behave, there is a moral law governing how humans *ought* to behave, and this law can be deduced through reason.

First Critique: The Illusion of Natural Laws

Nietzsche's thoughts on natural law are derived, in part, from his critique of natural *laws* (emphasis on the plural): Nietzsche's rejection of natural laws entails his rejection of natural law. To understand this argument, one should recall that Nietzsche denies the existence of unchanging laws of nature. For him "nature" and "law" are theory-laden interpretations, not ready-made patterns discovered in the world:

> We find a formula to express an ever-recurring kind of succession of phenomena: but that does not mean that we have therewith discovered a "law."[24]

Let us beware of saying that there are laws in nature.[25]

Forgive me as an old philologist who cannot desist from the malice of putting his finger on bad modes of interpretation: but "nature's conformity to law," of which you physicists talk so proudly, as though—why, it exists only owing to your interpretation and bad philology. It is no matter of fact, no "text," but rather only a naively humanitarian emendation and perversion of meaning, with which you make abundant concessions to the democratic instincts of the modern soul![26]

Nietzsche wishes to deny that there is a preexisting natural law written into the universe that only needs to be discovered because for Nietzsche there are no rules to be discovered in nature. As he flatly states, "There is no rule of 'law.'"[27] In his early work *Human, All Too Human* Nietzsche branded laws of nature as "superstition" and "myth":

"Law of nature" a superstition.—When you speak so rapturously of a conformity to law in nature you must either assume that all natural things freely obey laws they themselves have imposed upon themselves—in which case you are admiring the morality of nature—or you are entranced by the idea of a creative mechanic who has made the most ingenious clock, with living creatures upon it as decorations.—Necessity in nature becomes more human and a last refuge of mythological dreaming through the expression "conformity to law."[28]

Nietzsche's central insight is that the seemingly immutable laws of nature do not really exist "out there," as it were, in the ready-made order of things. Such laws are merely an interest-driven interpretation of events, just one among a plurality of competing interpretations.[29] Of course, some interpretations are better than others because they account for the data of experience more fully and are more internally consistent. But even the best interpretation is still a human creation, a life-preserving convention that should not be taken as a perfect mirror of the real: "'Truth' is therefore not something there, that might be found or discovered—but something that must be created and that gives a name to a process."[30] We err when we forget that our interpretations are useful conventions and wrongly project them into the external world. In so doing, we mistake the "map" (the theory) for the "territory" (the real).

Nietzsche also wishes to reject the natural law claim that "nature" can provide a basis for ethics. Depending on how it is interpreted, nature can be used to justify tyranny as well as good behavior:

"Neither God nor master"—that is what you, too want; and therefore "cheers for the law of nature!"—is it not so? But as said above, this is interpretation, not text; and somebody might come along who, with opposite intentions and modes of interpretation, could read out of the same "nature," and with regard to the same phenomena, rather the tyrannically inconsiderate and relentless enforcement of claims of power.[31]

That is, while it is possible for someone like Thomas Jefferson to read natural law out of the fabric of human relations and find a right to life, liberty, and the pursuit of happiness, that is only an interpretation, not a discovery.

The point here is that natural law theorists have interpreted nature in a biased way in order to support their particular ethical and political program. The mistake of reading "nature" according to one's ethical beliefs goes back as least as far as the Stoic admonishment to "live according to nature": "'According to nature'" you want to *live?* O you noble Stoics, what deceptive words these are! Imagine a being like nature, wasteful beyond measure, indifferent beyond measure, without purposes and consideration. . . how *could* you live according to this indifference?"[32] Nietzsche wants to deny that nature provides clues to an immutable moral code, but he also repeatedly warns against reifying one's theoretical models as if they were part of the ready-made order. His concern is that an interpretation will be mistaken for the text itself, so that the interpretation merges with the text and all other interpretations are ruled out. This concern was voiced most forcefully in his comments on the French Revolution: "Noble and enthusiastic spectators from all over Europe contemplated it from a distance and interpreted it according to their own indignation and enthusiasms for so long, and so passionately, that the text finally disappeared under the interpretation—"[33] If Jefferson and other natural law theorists were intellectually honest, they would have to admit that the appeals to "self-evident rights" and "laws of nature" are interpretations, not "text." These regulative ideas are posited by natural law theorists in order to arrive at a justification for their preexisting conception of the just state; "nature" is interpreted in a way that gives support to their political vision. Here the Nietzschean goal is to expose a deception on the part of natural law theory: it purports to derive a legal system from an investigation of (human) nature, yet the reverse is actually true since it is the theory of law that determines the view of nature. The predetermined political vision shapes the epistemic inquiry:

> Indeed, if one could explain how the abstrusest metaphysical claims of a philosopher really came about, it is always well (and wise) to ask first: at what morality does all this (does *he*) aim?[34]

> [Philosophers] are not honest enough about their work, although they make a lot of virtuous noise when the problem of truthfulness is touched even remotely. They all pose as if they had discovered and reached their real opinions through the self-development of cold, pure, divinely unconcerned dialec-

tic . . . while at bottom it is an assumption, a hunch, indeed a kind of "inspiration"—most often a desire of the heart that has been filtered and made abstract—that they defend with reasons they have sought after the fact.[35]

The intellectual dishonesty arises when one thinks one has found a fixed and final interpretation that is the product of cold, disinterested reason. To be honest is to say: "We posit natural rights, despite the lack of evidence, in order to justify the democratic state, and we are willing to revise this postulate if the evidence warrants a revision or if we want to support a different conception of the just state." Instead, the natural law theorist wrongly presumes that the natural order has been decoded once and for all, leaving us with a final authoritative interpretation of human affairs.

If Nietzsche is correct in assuming that there are no laws in nature and that man is constantly revisioning and reinterpreting himself, then basic human rights cannot be grounded in a static conception of nature, reason, or God. Rather, rights can only be affirmed as a human creation, as a necessary, life-affirming postulate. At bottom we do not discover law and morality but *create* it: "We, however, want to become those who we are—human beings who are new, unique, incomparable, who give themselves laws, who create themselves."[36] Yet the responsibility of creating morality brings anxiety and fear, from which we retreat by denying that we create law and insisting that the law must be discovered: "But up to now the . . . law has supposed to stand *above* our own likes and dislikes: one did not actually want to *impose* this law upon oneself, one wanted to *take* it from somewhere or *discover* it somewhere or *have it commanded to one* from somewhere."[37] It is we who create the concept of "natural rights," project this text onto the world (we "naturalize" the text), and finally claim that we have discovered these rights in nature.[38] The best course of conduct is to be aware of this process lest we forget that we have created these conventions out of our own need to preserve life and can alter, change, or abolish them if necessary.

The natural law theorist might respond to all of this by saying that natural law is prescriptive, not descriptive. It is not about the modes of human conduct which can be found in an empirical study of how people do behave but rather specifies how we *should* behave, given our capacity for moral reasoning. Nietzsche would no doubt respond that if the natural law theorist is making this claim (that natural law is prescriptive, not descriptive), then he or she must abandon the idea that natural law can be rooted in an interpretation of human behavior, in which case there is nothing very "natural" about natural law.

I feel that Nietzsche's critique of natural law goes even deeper because he seems to reject the natural law notion that there is an unchanging human essence, or core self, which can serve as the primoridal legal subject. Nietzsche's point foreshadows the postmodern rejection of the humanist idea of a Cartesian *cog-ito* which exists prior to or below social customs.[39] Instead, man is created and constituted as a being who differs from era to era; there is no common "subject" or "self" which can be used to generate a series of necessary moral laws. This is the sense in which man is continually "self-overcoming," such that we have no way of knowing what man will become in the future. There is no way to peel off the layers of culture to find the essence of man beneath the contingent self, no way to find a core of "humanity," an "end in itself," or transcendental self which can ground a system of laws: "Popular morality separates strength from expressions of strength, as if there were a neutral substratum behind the strong man, which was *free* to express strength or not to do so. But there is no such substratum; there is no 'being' behind doing, affecting, becoming; the 'doer' is merely a fiction added to the deed—"[40] Political theory cannot be based upon speculation about how a person (considered as a moral substrate) would have behaved in a state of nature; there is no "moral self" beneath the contingent self to serve as the subject for such an inquiry. In place of the natural law notion of the transcendental subject, Nietzsche proposes to ground the legal order in the fact that man is constantly revising himself and self-overcoming.

To posit natural rights is to think "mythologically"[41] and to mistake one's prejudices for eternal truths: "[Philosophers] are all advocates who resist that name, and for the most part wily spokesman for their prejudices which they baptize 'truths.'"[42] One can safely assume that Nietzsche's main enemy is the refusal to admit that one's postulates are fallible and interest-driven. Yet this, on Nietzsche's reading, is precisely what natural law theory often fails to do.

Second Critique: Natural Law as Linguistic Error

If Nietzsche is correct in assuming that there is no natural law and no irreducible human rights, then he must account for the fact that we speak as if these rights exist. I believe that the explanation for this phenonomenon can be found in Nietzsche's theory of language, which can be augmented with some insights from the current debate over "rights talk." The basic idea here is that rights talk is the result of the sedimentation in language of grammatical and metaphysical errors. The language of rights is mired in bad modes of interpretation and metaphysical assumptions that date back to the beginnings of the Christian era. These time-honored (but mistaken) ways of talking and thinking have led us to believe that the words "natural law" and "natural rights" refer to discoverable entities instead of being expressions of shifting power relations. In other words, our current rights discourse actually makes us think that rights are discoverable things instead of provisional postulates. Rights have become reified.

Nietzsche's thoughts on language are set forth most fully in his unpublished essay "On Truth and Lies in a Nonmoral Sense."[43] In that essay he says that the everyday notion of truth is the result of an agreement, a peace treaty among men resulting from boredom and necessity: "That is to say, a uniformly valid and binding designation is invented for things, and this legislation of language likewise establishes the first laws of truth. . . . It is only by means of forgetfulness that man can ever reach the point of fancying himself to possess a 'truth'."[44] This linguistic legislation creates a shared notion of truth based on a shifting stream of metaphors, metonyms, and anthropomorphisms. This does not mean that there is no such thing as truth or that truth is arbitrary. It only means that truth is not a static end state at which one can arrive, once and for all, but a necessary convention, a "life-preserving error."[45] Inevitably we forget that our truths are conventions, and in so doing we mistake verbal designations for concrete things, that is, we forget that the relation of word to object is only relatively stable, wrongly positing the relationship as fixed and binding. Nietzsche affirmed this point in *Human, All Too Human:* "To the extent that man has for long ages believed in the concepts and names of things as in *aeternae veritates* he has appropriated to himself that pride by which he raised himself above the animal; he really thought that in language he possessed knowledge of the world."[46] But for Nietzsche there can be no static link between word and object, and therefore no fixed basis for human rights, except as a temporary postulate. Therefore, one should not confuse the *usefulness* of rights talk with the *truth* of rights talk: "We have arranged for ourselves a world in which we can live—by positing bodies, lines, planes, causes and effects, motion and rest, form and content; without these articles of faith nobody now could endure life. But that does not prove them. Life is no argument. The conditions of life might include error."[47] So even if one needs to posit the existence of human rights to make life tolerable, there is no reason to elevate this postulate to the level of transcendent reality. Even if one wants or needs to assert the existence of human rights, perhaps on the basis of self-evidence (as in the Declaration of Independence), there is no need to insist that this view is the unchangeable truth. Certainly, intuition and ordinary language provide a starting point for thinking about rights, but they cannot serve as the final authority for the existence or nonexistence of rights.

Nietzsche's point can be illustrated by an analysis of rights talk, which has received some attention recently from legal scholars.[48] In *Rights Talk*, Mary Ann Glendon explains that (at least in America), our linguistic practice is to talk about ever-increasing rights. We talk as if our rights are constantly expanding, and this linguistic convention leads us to believe that these linguistically created rights actually exist: "A rapidly expanding catalog of rights—extending to trees, animals, smokers, nonsmokers, consumers, and so on—not only multiplies the occasions for collisions, but it risks trivializing core democratic values."[49] As she states, our language tends to create rights even when they have no basis in the legal system. For Nietzsche, such talk about rights can be explained as linguistic error; it is an example of mistaking the existence of the word (e.g., "smokers' rights") for the thing (an actual right to smoke in restaurants or airplanes).

This same analysis applies to natural rights discourse. Philosophers, theologians, and statesmen have been talking about natural law for centuries, and we therefore tend to see it as something built into the fabric of human affairs. But the natural law position is essentially a theologically based approach rooted in the mistaken notion that there are immutable laws of moral conduct discernable through reason. Although the belief in God is now eroding, and with it the notion that there is a divine law which gives rise to natural law, we are still stuck with the linguistic conventions premised on His existence. In other words, Christianity dies hard. As Nietzsche has written, "After Buddha was dead, people showed his shadow for centuries in a cave,—a tremendous, gruesome shadow. God is dead: but given the ways of men, there may still be caves for thousands of years in which his shadow will still be shown.—And we—we still have to vanquish his shadow, too."[50] The death of God forces us to realize that human rights are conventions: not 'mere conventions' in the sense of arbitrary designations, but human creations nonetheless.

Further, intellectual honesty requires the admission of fallibility and the willingness to revise or abandon one's interpretation of nature. Nietzsche's emphasis here is upon the notion that there is a range of possible interpretations, such that the process of interpretation is without end, limited only by our needs and interests. There is no point at which interpretation must stop, no point at which truth is reached, no point at which we get to the 'real' or the 'thing in itself': "Rather has the world become 'infinite' for us all over again, inasmuch as we cannot reject the possibility that it may include infinite interpretations."[51] So any workable jurisprudence should be willing to modify, change, or abandon its grounds in the light of interpretations and investigations. To do otherwise is to proclaim an end to interpretation and to critical analysis of foundations.

Third Critique: The Genealogy of Law

Natural law theory typically makes reference to men existing in a state of nature that predates the advent of civil society. Although natural law theorists differ as to whether such a historical condition actually existed, they agree that it is possible to utilize the very idea of such a primordial state in order to determine the legitimacy of the modern state. Book 2 of *On the Genealogy of Morals* contains a critique of the natural law supposition that a prelegal state of "justice" or "natural rights" can exist prior to the institution of positive law. Nietzsche's purpose here is to show (against the views of Locke, Rousseau, and Kant) that it is impossible to even conceive of a state that exists prior to the imposition of law because selfhood is the result of a community which already possesses laws and other social rules. Thus, Nietzsche repeatedly rejects the claim that civil society originated in a social contract:

> Human society is a trial: thus I teach it—A trial, O my brothers, and *not* a "contract." Break, break this word of the softhearted and half-and-half.[52]

> I think that the sentimentalism which would have [the state] begin with a "contract" has been disposed of. He who can command, he who is by nature "master" . . . what has he to do with contracts![53]

Nietzsche's point is not only to deny the existence of a historical contract (this much was conceded by many social contract theorists) but to show that principles of justice cannot be generated by reference to such an idealized state of nature because the latter can only be conceived as a place which is the *result* and not the *absence* of law. That is, people are always situated within one or another legal arrangement, so there is no sense in trying to decide what would have happened in some sort of idealized situation prior to the advent of civil society.

Nietzsche's argument here is genealogical in that he traces the concept of justice back to its primordial sense (in the pre-Christian era) and then argues that the concept of justice underwent a paradigm shift with the arrival of Christianity. His basic point is that our conceptions of "legality," "justice," and "rights" are forever shifting because they are buffeted by a cauldron of power relations:

> Our duties—are the rights others have against us. How did the others acquire these rights? By taking us to be capable of contracts and of repayment, by positing us as similar and equal to them. . . . This is how rights originate: recognized and guaranteed degrees of power. If power-relations undergo any material alteration, rights disappear and new ones are created—as is demonstrated in the continual disappearance and reformation of rights between nations. . . . Where rights *prevail*, a certain condition and degree of power is being maintained, a diminution and increment warded off. The rights of others constitute a concession on the part of our sense of power to the sense of power of those others. If our power appears to be deeply shaken and broken, our rights cease to exist.[54]

Nietzsche argues that there have been two paradigms of law since the beginnings of recorded history. The first epoch of law was based on the discharge of power relations among the strong. This was the original notion of justice as a mutual standoff between equals (those capable of contracts and repayment) and punishment and retribution toward unequals (those who breached contracts). This system was instituted by the aggressive, strong people to govern their relation to those with weaker wills. Justice, then, began as a dramatic tension between equals who sought to trade with each other and preserve themselves by keeping their promises: "Justice (fairness) originates between parties of approximately equal power. . . . [T]he characteristic of exchange is the initial characteristic of justice. . . . Justice naturally derives from prudent concern with self-preservation. . . . Justice is thus requital and exchange under the presupposition of an approximately equal power position.[55] A second epoch of law arrived with the Christian-based ethic of *ressentiment,* in which the weak banded together to oppose the strong and their sense of justice. This reactive approach was fueled by the Christian emphasis on mercy, equality, and fairness toward weaker and unequal parties; the aggressive people were now deemed "evil," while the weak people were deemed "good."

The first paradigm of law roughly corresponds to what Nietzsche calls a "master morality," while the second paradigm corresponds to "slave morality":

> *Dual prehistory of good and evil*—The concept of good and evil has a dual prehistory; *first,* in the soul of the ruling tribes and castes. Whoever has the ability to repay good with good, evil with evil, and also actually repays, thus being grateful and vengeful, is called good; whoever is powerless and unable to repay is considered bad. . . . *Then,* in the soul of the oppressed, the powerless. Here all *other* human beings are considered hostile, ruthless, exploiting, cruel. . . . Our current morality has grown on the soil of the *ruling* tribes and castes.[56]

These two positions have fought for supremacy throughout recorded history, and our present system of justice is a mixed typology containing elements of both paradigms. Nietzsche's larger point here is that the original justice was able to operate without any kind of transcendental grounding because it was a life-preserving, life-affirming practice. Only later, after Christianity, was it supposed (wrongly) that justice had a metaphysical grounding apart from human interests (hence the idea that God mandates certain arrangements of the legal system). A central purpose of Nietzsche's genealogy is to remind us that justice and law were created to serve human interests and needs and should continue to do so despite the Christian tendency to justify laws by looking to God's will.

Nietzsche thinks that there has always been some form of law, if only as a relationship of exchange and punishment among the stronger races. Accordingly, the law cannot have arisen as an infringement on a set of preexisting natural rights:

> "Just" and "unjust" exist, accordingly, only after the institution of law. . . . A legal order thought of as sovereign and universal, not as a means in the struggle between power-complexes but as a means of preventing all struggle in general would be a principle *hostile* to life.[57]

> From a historical perspective, law represents on earth the struggle against the reactive feelings, the war conducted against them on the part of the active and aggressive powers.[58]

Nietzsche's point here is that all legal systems are an expression of power relations. The ancient system of justice was a more overt system of power relations, and it certainly had its excesses and cruelties, but it was largely life-affirming and "yes-saying." The Christian-based legal system is also a system of power relations, but it is a life-denying and *ressentiment*-based system that favors the herd, being based on mythology, fear of change, and hostility towards life. Nietzsche's genealogical analysis would have us question whether the Christian system of justice represents an improvement over the ancient system, although he certainly stops short of advocating a return to ancient law.

Nietzsche's genealogical approach is designed to expose the historical bases of moral imperatives and to reveal moral categories as creations. His goal is to spoil the enjoyment we derive from mouthing "grand words" such as "duty" and "conscience."[59] For Nietzsche, the fundamental question for lawyers should not be "What laws can we discover?" but "What laws should we create, and to what end?" This question paves the way for a positive program of jurisprudence, to which I will now turn. However, one must first ask if Nietzsche's critique of natural law theory is successful.

In answer to this question, I would say that Nietzsche's critique is only partially successful. He presents a strong challenge to the classical view of natural law as something written into the fabric of the universe and discoverable by reflecting on human nature. Nietzsche also seems to successfully challenge the versions of natural law which appeal to self-evident intuitions or transcendental foundations. But there remain a few potential problems that can be traced back to Nietzsche's genealogical approach.

First, Nietzsche offers an explanation of how the concept of natural law arose (as a *ressentiment*-based, Christian reaction to the ancient system of justice), but the fact that it arose under a particular historical situation does not constitute an *argument* against it. Furthermore, the natural rights proponents might agree with Nietzsche that natural rights cannot be predicated on a teleological conception of nature or upon divine commandment, but they could still hold that natural rights are inherent in the human need for cooperation and association, or in the need for communication.[60]

A second problem is that Nietzsche fails to fully appreciate that many theorists in the social contract tradition did not posit a historical state of nature, but instead understand the latter as a postulate that could be used to test the legitimacy of the modern state. The state of nature was considered an idea of reason (or thought experiment) which could be used to determine whether or not the present government is legitimate. Such versions of social contract theory are not based upon historical assertions, so they cannot be directly refuted or challenged by a genealogical inquiry into the origin of law and morality.

These are legitimate problems for Nietzsche, and one can safely say that he did not come to grips with the more subtle points of certain versions of social contract theory (especially Kant's notion of the social contract as a thought experiment or "idea of reason"). Despite this failing, Nietzsche still provided a strong challenge to the idea that natural law could be grounded in self-evidence, reason, God, or nature. In this sense, he provided an early critique that challenged the popular versions of that theory, although one must certainly recognize that his critique is incomplete with respect to more complicated versions of the theory.

The natural law theorist will doubtless respond to Nietzsche's critique by asking what he proposes as an alternative approach to the democratic government and rule of law advocated by natural law theory. The natural law theorist will say that if Nietzsche wants to take a critical stance against natural-law theory, he must propose an alternative legal theory that would be preferable, that is, he must provide some sort of normative criterion by which to assert that one legal system or law is better than another.

This raises the problem of whether Nietzsche is a legal nihilist, that is, whether he holds the view that there is no justifiable basis for choosing between competing legal arrangements. This brings me back to the question raised at the beginning of this chapter: Can Nietzsche's account give rise to a normative theory of law (a "positive jurisprudence") or is he simply offering a critique of traditional approaches to the law? This is where the analysis of Nietzsche's position gets murkier as one attempts to construct a Nietzschean positive jurisprudence. In what follows I will first build this edifice and then criticize it.

Does Nietzsche Offer a Positive Jurisprudence?

I suppose that the cornerstone of a Nietzschean jurisprudence would be the notion that a law (or a legal system) is provisionally acceptable as long as it is life-affirming and power-generating. This simply means that a threshold inquiry must be made to determine if a proposed law seeks justification on the (unacceptable) grounds that it is mandated by nature, God, or tradition, or on the (acceptable) grounds that it is a fair reflection of who we are and who we want to be as free, experimental, and "self-overcoming" individuals. The key would be to maximize the will to power, not in the limited and literal sense of "raw power" but in the sense of self-mastery, human advancement, and self-overcoming.[61] Once we recognize that the legal order cannot be grounded once and for all as a totality in an unchanging conception of human nature or reason, we can move on to the task of molding the law to fit our changing but "all-too-human" needs. The loss of metaphysical foundations, and the accompanying temporary phase of legal nihilism, is a necessary precondition for the responsible creation of a legal order that is free from metaphysical baggage. The Nietzschean approach would not be based on a static metaphysical view of human nature but would try to respect the sense in which man is continually self-overcoming; it would attempt to open up as many avenues as possible for self-exploration and self-mastery.

If this broad outline is plausible, then Nietzsche escapes the charge of legal nihilism (viz. the view that no arrangement of law can be morally superior to others) because he provides a criterion for choosing one legal arrangment over another. First, we must reject all laws or legal systems which are tied to problematic notions of (human) nature, self-evidence, or God. Second, for a law to be acceptable, it must be rooted in our present conception of ourselves as free and creative individuals and must allow maximum room for power-generation and self-mastery.

I have just interpreted the will to power as a *private* project; by reading it in this way, one avoids the charge that the *state* must obey the will to power, which might entail some sort of fascism or elitism. This reading of Nietzsche makes him a legal nihilist only in the weak sense that (like Rawls and Dworkin) he rejects the possibility of an ultimate and unchanging grounding for the legal order. But he is not a legal nihilist in the strong sense because he *does* think that some legal systems are better than others.[62]

Thus configured, a Nietzschean theory of law would not necessarily require an immediate and radical change in the legal system (though such measures are not incompatible with Nietzsche's theory). I would suspect that Nietzsche's theory could be used to justify a legal order similar to our own legal system (including full rights provisionally proscribed). The key difference would be that we should obey the law because we *created* it, not because we *discovered* it or because it was laid down by God. The law would then be seen as liberating because its changeableness would allow for the "law of life"—the self-overcoming of man through his private projects.[63] In fact, Nietzsche alludes to this new type of law: "What is required: the new law must be made practicable—and out of its fulfillment, the overcoming of this law, and higher law, must evolve. . . . Laws as the backbone. They must be worked at and created, by being fulfilled. The slavish attitude which has reigned hitherto towards law!"[64] According to this approach, a superior system of law would honestly admit that rights are human conventions that can be granted, repealed, or amended for our life-preserving ends.[65] We follow a rights-based system of law because it affords the greatest opportunity for control, mastery, and power in the sense of self-fulfillment and self-overcoming:

> We, however, want to become those who we are—who give themselves laws, who create themselves.[66]
>
> What does your conscience say?—You shall become that you are.[67]
>
> All great things bring about their own destruction through an act of self-overcoming: thus the law of life will have it, the law of the necessity of "self-overcoming" in the nature of life.[68]

Thus formulated, Nietzsche's position has the advantage of freeing us from the difficulties of foundations, a freedom described by Joseph Singer as follows: "The absence of secure foundations or decision procedures should be experienced not as a void but as an opportunity. . . . It is not a matter of finding a foundation on which to stand, or of finding the truth. It is a matter of conviction. We have to take responsibility for making up our minds."[69] The idea here is that the loss of foundations should pave the way for new, positive directions in law.

Having sketched the broad outlines of a Nietzschean approach to law, I wish to consider how it might fare when applied to a few well-known cases. First, consider the Georgia law criminalizing sodomy that was upheld by the Supreme Court in *Bowers v. Hardwick*.[70] A Nietzschean jurisprudence would reject the assertion that sodomy can be outlawed as an offense against God or nature, or simply because our Christian tradition has historically outlawed sodomy. A Nietzschean analysis would ask whether the kind of society we want to create is one which tolerates the free choice of others to engage in consensual sex. In short, does a society which tolerates such behavior lead to greater or lesser power, in the sense of greater opportunities for self-mastery and self-overcoming? I think that a Nietzschean would strike the Georgia statute on the grounds that the government should allow individuals to exercise as much autonomy as possible in their effort to become who they want to be, to create themselves.

Of course, this is only a rough sketch of a single decision, but the basic reasoning process can be extended to other contexts. For example, I could imagine a Nietzschean attack on the natural law notion that private property is an inherent right, which might have the result of leading us into alternative arrangements such as state ownership of the means of production or restrictions on the right of inheritance. Also, Nietzsche's emphasis on self-mastery would seem to provide the basis for allowing women the right to choose to have an abortion. Using this type of thinking, it is possible to draw the rough outlines of a Nietzschean approach to law, including a justification for a legal framework that includes liberal democracy, the rule of law, and minimal state interference with self-regarding behavior. In this legal system each person would be free to pursue, as a private matter, the version of the good life which he or she finds most life-affirming. This political and legal structure lacks an *immutable* foundation and must only respect man's capacity for self-overcoming, that is, the "law of life." The downside to all of this is that since Nietzsche is not a rights-foundationalist, there can be no absolute guarantee that a Nietzschean jurisprudence will *always* lead to liberal democracy; as I will suggest, it might lead to fascism if this is the direction that the will to power takes. But for now liberal democracy can be justified on the Nietzschean grounds that it permits the greatest expression of power, understood as a life-preserving and life-affirming force.

Perhaps a more difficult case to support on the basis of the Nietzschean theory of law would be *Brown v. Board of Education of Topeka.*[71] At first glance this decision would seem to go against those passages in which Nietzsche says that order and rank are important, and that slavery may be necessary in order to produce a higher type of man.[72] Yet I think that it is possible to see how Nietzsche's approach could be used to justify the decision in *Brown,* perhaps on the argument that freedom from segregation is necessary for meaningful self-overcoming to take place by African-Americans. In other words, we must eliminate all barriers to human realization, including racist laws (or homophobic laws, as in *Bowers*). The idea would be to create a *public* sphere that permits maximum self-overcoming in the *private* sphere. This interpretation bears a strong resemblance to Rorty's depiction of a Nietzschean politics: "To see one's life, or the life of one's community, as a dramatic narrative is to see it as a process of Nietzschean self-overcoming. . . . *Privatize* the Nietzschean-Sartrean-Foucauldian attempt at authenticity and purity."[73] This view of Nietzsche is no doubt wildly different from the traditional view, which holds that he would praise the political and legal system that authorized the maximum release of force and raw power, which would probably lead to a class society ruled by an aristocratic elite. A common belief is that Nietzsche sought a return to the Greek "master morality" and would never grant the existence of human rights. This view is explained by Andre Mineau:

> Nietzsche does not accept the human rights founding principle that all men are values in themselves simply because they are human. It is natural differ-

ences that are relevant here, and his hope for the revival of the spirit of Archaic Greece entails, in a certain sense, a desire to return to ancient law based on statuses, and expressing differences that were considered more significant than men's common humanity.[74]

This interpretation has ample textual support—indeed, it has enough support to cast serious doubt on my own reading of Nietzsche as a thinker who might be persuaded to embrace democracy and the rule of law.[75] Nevertheless, the traditional view is somewhat misleading because it fails to see that Nietzsche's comments on law are not critical of democracy and law per se but only of the pretense that law can be fully and finally grounded, whether in reason, humanity, or God. He is critical of any static approach to law, any method whereby interpretations come to an end. So Mineau's reading of Nietzsche, while supported by relevant passages, avoids the central problematic, namely, that Nietzsche was disdainful of *all* foundations for law, including Greek foundations. What attracted Nietzsche to the Greek form of law and morality (and what distinguished it from the Christian tradition) is that it was less deceptive and less pretentious about its origins in human needs, less tied to universalist claims about laws of nature and universal human rights. Nietzsche does not so much advocate a return to Greek law as a turn away from the Christian tendency to seek the origin of law outside of human needs and human will. It is not the *substance* of ancient law which is superior to Christian law but the lack of masks and disguises offered to support it.

To summarize, a Nietzschean jurisprudence would be nonfoundational (because no principle of law is so sacred that it cannot be revised if necessary) and experimental (because new laws could be adopted and repealed to satisfy our changing conception of ourselves). This would be a piecemeal jurisprudence skeptical of any totalizing, static conception of justice, and it would follow Nietzsche's plan as set forth in *The Will to Power:*

> Proud aversion to reposing once and for all in any one total view of the world. Fascination of the opposing point of view: refusal to be deprived of the stimulus of the enigmatic.[76]

> No limit to the ways in which the world can be interpreted . . . plurality of interpretations a sign of strength. Not to desire to deprive the world of its disturbing and enigmatic character.[77]

Based on the passages and inferences I have set forth, there are strong reasons to suppose that Nietzsche is not a legal nihilist.

It might be objected that Nietzsche remains stuck in a variant of foundationalism because he proposes to judge legal systems according to whether they foster the human capacity for creating and overcoming the self (i.e., whether they respect the will to power, understood as a quest for self-mastery). This jurisprudence, like natural law theory, would still be founded on a conception of human nature, albeit on the rather unorthodox version put forth by Nietzsche, which is static only in the sense that it sees human nature as inevitably caught up in the quest for self-mastery and self-creation. In a sense, this objection is correct because Nietzsche is a foundationalist to the extent that he rejects the law of nature only to embrace "the law of life."[78] Yet one might argue that this is not a truly foundational approach because it allows the law to continually overcome itself and change as our self-conception changes, unlike natural law theory, which is rooted in an unchanging conception of the self. If Nietzsche is a closet foundationalist, his version of foundationalism is sufficiently unorthodox to raise the question as to whether the term "foundationalist" can be meaningfully applied in this context.[79] But there is some truth to the charge of foundationalism because (like Aquinas, Hobbes, and Smith) he begins with a view of human nature and then designs a political and legal platform around that conception; unlike those thinkers, though, Nietzsche allows for this nature to change.

One potential danger of a Nietzschean jurisprudence is that it denies the existence of fundamental, unchanging human rights. The main cause for concern is that a change in man's self-conception (i.e., the rise of a violent and destructive notion of "power" or "self-mastery") may take the law in unexpected and unsavory directions. For example, suppose that our changing concept of self leads us to believe that a single elite group of individuals should exercise prior restraint over the publication of books and newspapers, that this is demanded by the will to power. For a Nietzschean, there is no possibility of vitiating this result by appealing to a fundamental right of free speech based on a God-given or self-evident right of autonomy. A Nietzschean jurisprudence *could* lead to a Nazi state if such a state were truly the most life-affirming and power-generating state that we thought possible. But it is doubtful whether this need be the case so long as a liberal state continues to afford its citizens the best opportunities for self-mastery and experimentation. That is, the existing constitutional democracy can be justified on the Nietzschean grounds that it creates a public realm that maximizes the possibilities for a private life which is life-affirming and power-generating. For these reasons I think that Nietzsche escapes the oft-recited charges of nihilism and fascism, though he offers no foundational backstop which would rule these arrangements out of court.

Problems with a Nietzschean Positive Jurisprudence

At the beginning of this chapter I said that one of my goals was to explore the claim that Nietzsche's theory can be used to generate a positive jurisprudence.

This claim is difficult to prove precisely because it lacks overt textual support and must be constructed from scattered aphorisms that touch only indirectly on the topic of law. This is a questionable mode of interpretation because it downplays much of what Nietzsche actually said about the legal and political affairs of his day. One could easily adopt the opposite strategy: by focusing on Nietzsche's specific comments on legal and political matters, a reader might reasonably conclude that no positive jurisprudence (or political theory) can be generated from Nietzsche's writings other than a sort of anarchism or elitism, because there are so many passages in which Nietzsche ridicules such ideals as democracy, feminism, and equal rights. The charge of anarchism or elitism would seem to rest on the following passages, which occur with alarming frequency in Nietzsche's work:

> At least, it seems to be all over for a species of man (people, races) when it becomes tolerant, allows equal rights and no longer thinks of wanting to be master—[80]

> In the age of universal suffrage, i.e., when everyone may sit in judgment on everyone and everything, I feel impelled to re-establish order of rank.[81]

> Every enhancement of the type "man" has so far been the work of an aristocratic society—a society that believes in the long ladder of an order of rank and differences in value between man and man, and that needs slavery in some sense or other.[82]

> "The emancipation of women"—this is the instinctive hatred of the physiologically botched—that is to say, barren—women for those of their sisters who are well constituted.[83]

> I am opposed to: 1. Socialism, because it dreams quite naively of "the good, true and beautiful" and of "equal rights" . . . 2. Parliamentary Government and the press, because these are the means by which the herd animal becomes master.[84]

> Only where the state ends, there begins the human being who is not superfluous.[85]

> Injustice never lies in unequal rights, it lies in the claim to "equal" rights.[86]

These passages seem to indicate that Nietzsche was essentially apolitical and aristocratic. This reading is supported by Nietzsche's frequent antidemocratic diatribes against the "herd" and the "bungled and botched." It is no wonder that some thinkers have seen these types of statements as conclusive evidence that it is not possible to build a Nietzschean justification for democracy, the rule of law, equal rights, and pluralism.[87] This is certainly the most cautious interpretation of Nietzsche because it does not take the difficult step of extending Nietzsche's program beyond his particular comments on the political affairs of his day.

Yet this interpretation fails to appreciate the more general political and legal implications of Nietzsche's work. In order to construct a coherent Nietzschean view of law, one must try to go beyond such vitriolic passages and formulate a jurisprudence that is consistent with Nietzsche's *entire* philosophical enterprise, including his experimentalism, his fallibilism, and his genealogical focus.[88] Yet when one does this, when one tries to derive a broader Nietzschean theory of law (perhaps even a "Nietzschean liberalism") by examining his more general philosophical comments, one inevitably finds it difficult to square this theory with what Nietzsche actually said about the affairs of his day. This leads to an impasse in the quest for a positive jurisprudence.

Throughout this chapter I have tried to view Nietzsche's theory in its best light, to see it as a coherent and plausible attempt at creating a positive jurisprudence. This project is not without its difficulties; every time that one tries to find a Nietzschean argument for democracy and the rule of law one is confronted by a quote in which Nietzsche ridiculed these very concepts. This means that any "Nietzschean theory of law" will contradict many of his actual opinions on law and politics, with the result that one will often be theorizing Nietzsche against himself, as it were.

The main problem is that Nietzsche does not provide enough theoretical material to support a coherent vision for the legal system in a just state, nor does he provide consistent answers to legal problems. One can use his overall philosophical work to justify, say, gun control, but one can just as easily find passages which could support the opposite position. His work stands so far outside the existing legal system (i.e., the critical distance is so great) that it is difficult to use Nietzsche's work to step back inside the system and advocate particular solutions to legal problems. To obtain specific solutions from Nietzsche requires a major stretch. Perhaps one should take this as a sign that his work was not meant to be stretched in this way.

Nietzsche's antifoundationalism and experimentalism is best viewed not as a general theory of law but as a set of reminders or cautions that we should acknowledge when doing legal theory. For example, we should be cognizant of our fallibility, our tendency to reify rights talk and to confuse interpretations with reality. Nietzsche also reminds us to be open to experiments in the law, to be aware of the genealogy of basic concepts of legal theory, and to be wary of discovering immutable laws of human nature. Most important, Nietzsche demonstrates that our current paradigm in legal theory (which is largely based on the Christian "slave morality") is contingent.

What one gets from Nietzsche, in the final analysis, is the foregoing set of methodological tools and "reminders for a particular purpose."[89] These insights are not couched in the language of mainstream legal theory, nor can they be used to dictate particular outcomes in court cases (though they might be of limited use to legislators). Nietzsche's work is *external* in the sense discussed in chapter 2; his work is of limited use in the internal debates currently raging over abortion, affirmative action, privacy, government takings, and so on. Nietzsche's writings on law are worthwhile, yet they fall far short of providing the positive jurisprudence that one seeks.

I am sure that this view of Nietzsche will satisfy neither postmodernists nor mainstream legal thinkers. Some postmodernists will insist that Nietzsche's work *can* support a full-blown legal theory of the just state and the ideal legal system, although I have shown that there are reasons for doubting that this can be done. Similarly, some mainstream thinkers will argue that Nietzsche's work is wholly useless for legal theory and is a mere distraction from genuinely pressing questions in the law. I have narrowed the gap between these views by demonstrating that although Nietzsche's work is important when viewed as a check against some of the chief postulates and assumptions of mainstream legal theory, it cannot support a rich, full-blown positive jurisprudence.

4 ❧ Foucault on Law:
Modernity as Negative Utopia

The purpose of this chapter is to provide a charitable yet critical reading of Michel Foucault's remarks on law. Ultimately one must conclude that Foucault's work on law depicts the existing legal system as a "negative utopia," a seemingly humane but ultimately coercive product of Enlightenment rationality gone awry. To my mind, Foucault's approach is similar to the critique of modernity set forth in Aldous Huxley's *Brave New World* or George Orwell's *Nineteen Eighty-Four*. Like Huxley and Orwell, Foucault warns us about a future that may have already arrived, a future in which inhuman laws are heralded in the name of humanity. Like them, Foucault depicts the underside of certain disciplines which have their roots in the Enlightenment.[1]

Over the last five years or so, legal scholars have become increasingly interested in Foucault's work. This is somewhat surprising, given that the topic of law was not a central concern for Foucault, nor did he write a book-length study of law. Perhaps it is precisely Foucault's lack of focus on the topic of law which allows his work to be taken in so many disparate directions. For instance, some commentators have taken Foucault to be a legal historian who made empirical claims about the evolution of legal systems, namely, that the premodern legal system was based on coercive law but eventually evolved into a modern (and postmodern) legal system governed by disciplinary normalization.[2] Other commentators, downplaying Foucault's historical claims, have instead explored the way in which Foucault's writings can ground a feminist approach to legal theory.[3] Still others have explored the similarities and differences between Foucault and Marx's comments on law.[4] Some writers have tried to tease out the ways in which Foucault's poststructuralist stance might generate new insights for legal theory.[5] Finally, Foucault's ideas have been applied to particular legal issues, such as the right of privacy, the ownership of intellectual property, and punishment.[6]

On my reading, Foucault's contribution to the study of law is threefold. First, he wishes to challenge the presumption of progress in law, the idea that the law is becoming increasingly humane and less coercive. Foucault's point here is that the legal rights to privacy and autonomy have been undercut by a quasi-legal system of coercion and discipline. Second, he wishes to expose and challenge a theoretical framework which, he argued, continues to dominate jurisprudence and political theory, namely, the "classical juridical theory" which arose with the social contract theorists. This approach sees power solely in terms of *state* power and ignores the ways in which power is exercised from noncentral locations ("at the capillaries," to use Foucault's phrase). Third, Foucault wishes to show how law has become increasingly tied to the rise of the so-called disciplines, meaning that law has become increasingly regulatory, administrative, and normative (instead of merely coercive and repressive).

To best understand Foucault's comments on law, one must first examine the view that he rejects, namely, the so-called classical juridical theory. In the first part of this chapter I will present this "classic juridical model," followed by a discussion of Nietzsche's attack on this model, which anticipates Foucault's critique. In the second part I will present Foucault's writings on law as a continuation and extension of the Nietzschean critique of the classical juridical model. I will discuss the relationship between law and discipline and provide a detailed explanation of Foucault's critique of contemporary political and juridical theory. In the third part I will turn to a critical assessment of Foucault's project, pointing out how Foucault failed to appreciate the beneficial aspects of modern law and lacked a normative ground from which to condemn the role of law in modernity. Finally, in the last part of this chapter I conclude that Foucault's comments on law do not provide the grounds for a full-blown positive jurisprudence, nor does he have much of a program for liberation. Despite the lack of a positive jurisprudence, Foucault provides us with a type of negative utopian vision of mainstream political and legal theory—and negative utopias of this sort are useful in a limited but important sense.

The Classical Juridical View and Nietzsche's Critique

CLASSICAL JURIDICAL THEORY

Foucault does not have a "theory of law" in the strict sense. Rather, he seeks to problematize a dominant approach (or paradigm) in jurisprudence and political science, a view which Foucault refers to variously as the "classical juridical," "sovereign-juridico," "sovereignty," and "contract oppression" view.[7] The classical juridical view derives from the social contract theorists of the sixteenth through eighteenth centuries (Hobbes, Locke, and Rousseau), but the assumptions and basic framework of this view are still very much in evidence today. The hallmark of the traditional view is that power should be analyzed in terms of the relationship between the state and the individual. It holds that the individual is free in all areas of life except those in which he or she is subject to the power of the state; where the state is silent, the individual is free to enter into contracts with others and pursue individual projects. According to the classical theory, power is *state* power and is *repressive*. As we shall see, Foucault points out that this conception of power is more fitting for a premodern than a modern society because modern forms of power are not necessarily aligned with state power but are a complex web emanating from disparate sources. The classical juridical focus on state power tends to obscure the ways in which the individual is dominated by other forces (e.g., schools, hospitals, the military, psychiatry).

Foucault associates the classical liberal view with the social contract tradition that arose at the end of the medieval period, especially Thomas Hobbes' *Leviathan*.[8] The central problematic of social contract theory is the legitimation of state power over the individual, in other words, whether there can be a rational justification for the state. Social contract theory answers this question by supposing that the state can be justified as the product of a free choice among individuals in the state of nature. The basic idea is that each individual in the state of nature is endowed with certain natural powers, such as the rights of self-preservation, self-defense, liberty, contract, and property. Individuals cannot peacefully coexist in the state of nature, so they agree to alienate some or all of their natural rights in order to create a neutral, sovereign state to protect them. On this model, the state is the result of a contract, so the state is legitimate to the extent that it satisfies the mandate of the individuals who participate in the contract. As Foucault explains,

> In the case of the classic, juridical theory, power is taken to be a right, which one is able to possess like a commodity, and which one can in consequence transfer or alienate, either wholly or partially, through a legal act or through some act that establishes a right, such as takes place through cessation or contract. Power is that concrete power which every individual holds, and whose partial or total cessation enables political power or sovereignty to be established.[9]

This point can be seen in Hobbes' claim that the parties in the state of nature come together to cede their power to the sovereign, agreeing that the sovereign shall be solely responsible for the exercise of power in the state. Thus, only the sovereign can punish, make laws, and coerce the subjects. On this model, "power" must be understood only in terms of the *state* over the *individual;* in all other realms, according to Hobbes, the individual is free:

> In cases where the Sovereign has prescribed no rule, there the subject has the liberty to do, or forbear, according to his own discretion. . . . The liberty of the subject lies therefore only in those things which the Sovereign has permit-

ted; such as the liberty to buy, and sell, and otherwise contract with one another; to choose their own abode, their own diet, their own trade of life, and institute their children as they themselves think fit, and the like.[10]

Foucault points out that Hobbes saw power as purely repressive, as something which is instituted from the top down, from the state to the individual. According to Hobbes, where there is no state action or interference, the individual is totally free: "Liberty, or freedom, signifies (properly) the absence of opposition."[11] The basic idea is that the individual need not submit to any forces or powers which he or she has not authorized through voluntary consent. The individual can exist in a sphere of individual liberty, a zone of self-regarding conduct in which he or she is free to live according to personal dictates.

Another theme running through the classical juridical theory is the notion that the creation of a democratic state and the adoption of a system of formal law represents moral progress. That is, the modern state signals the end of tyranny, the end of rule by divine right or brute power, and the establishment of a legitimate government based on the dictates of reason. This belief was held so firmly by Hobbes and Kant that they refused to recognize a right of rebellion against the modern state, since the civil state represents a tremendous advance over premodern modes of government. For the social contract theorists, it is through the triumph of reason that we were delivered from a government according to the rule of *men* into a government according to the rule of *law*.

NIETZSCHE'S CRITIQUE

Nietzsche took issue with three aspects of the classical juridical model: the idea of a social contract, the idea of a neutral "subject" existing below and beneath social conventions, and the idea of moral progress. Since all of these themes were picked up by Foucault, it is important to stress his connection to Nietzsche on these points.[12]

As was demonstrated in chapter 3, Nietzsche rejected the basic premise of social contract theory, namely, that there could be a prelegal state of "justice" or "natural rights" prior to the institution of positive law.[13] Nietzsche wanted to prove (against the views of Locke, Rousseau, and Kant) that it is impossible to even conceive of an individual who exists prior to the imposition of law but is nevertheless capable of consenting to the creation of the state. Nietzsche rejected the notion of a social contract among preexisting individuals because it is only possible for a person to be an individual within the confines of an already existing state.

The interesting point here is that Nietzsche was attempting to eliminate the

Kantian appeal to a transcendental subject which predates the imposition of power relations:

> For just as the popular mind separates the lightning from its flash and takes the latter for an action, as the operation of a subject which is called lightning, so popular morality also separates strength from the expression of strength, as though behind the strong man there existed some neutral substratum, which enjoyed a caprice and option as to whether or not it should express strength. But there is no such substratum, there is no "being" behind doing, working, becoming; "the doer" is merely a fiction added to the deed.[14]

But Nietzsche's critique went even further. He argued that the classical juridical theory erred by supposing that the imposition of civil law would establish a condition of perpetual peace in which individuals are free of power relations. For Nietzsche there is no such thing as a realm in which the individual is *exempt* from power relations. To be sure, power relations may shift (e.g., from a Pagan exercise of power to a Christian system), but there is no escaping power itself. At every stage and in every facet of one's life, one is confronted with and constituted by power relations: "This is how rights originate: recognized and guaranteed degrees of power. If power-relations undergo any material alteration, rights disappear and new ones are created. . . . Where rights prevail, a certain condition and degree of power is being maintained, a diminution and increment warded off."[15] Nietzsche's point is that a civil state which exists under the rule of law obtains its stability by virtue of the dramatic tension of power relations among individuals. A situation that seems to be rule-governed and devoid of power relations is actually steeped in the latter. Nietzsche would claim that our smoothly running society is itself held together by a dramatic tension between claims of power, with the forces of "slave morality" struggling against the last vestiges of "master morality." According to Nietzsche, democracy, no less than fascism, is a system of power relations.

FOUCAULT'S DEBT TO NIETZSCHE

Foucault's debt to Nietzsche can hardly be overemphasized. Foucault picks up on each element of Nietzsche's critique of social contract theory. Just as Nietzsche argued against the existence of the "subject" as a substrate beneath the subject's attributes, so Foucault heralded the "death of the subject."[16] Like Nietzsche, Foucault thought that we should get rid of the notion of a pre-existing subject who serves as the substrate (or "prime matter") that is molded by the imposition of law and discipline. The individual does not pre-exist the imposition of power, but rather it is power which creates the individual in the first instance. As Foucault explains:

> My objective . . . has been to create a history of the different modes by which, in our culture, human beings are *made subjects.*[17]

> The individual is no doubt the fictitious atom of an "ideological" representation of society; but he is also a reality fabricated by the specific technology of power that I have called "discipline."[18]

Foucault wants to focus on how the individual is produced and turned into a subject by a series of disciplines, especially those which are not allied with the state, such as schools, hospitals, the military, and the prison system. As we shall see, Foucault insists that the traditional understanding of power (as *state* power over the individual) is radically one-dimensional because it wrongly assumes that power must be *repressive* (as opposed to *productive*). The classical model fails to capture the ways in which the individual is shaped by powers other than state power, primarily in the form of the "disciplines."[19] The "self" or "subject" is merely what *results* from these forces, not something apart from them; there is no Cartesian *cogito*, no Kantian "transcendental ego," as had been supposed by social contract theory.

Foucault is also heir to Nietzsche's incredulity toward the claim of moral progress.[20] Nietzsche argued that Christian morality did not bring about the end of abusive power relations but was itself an expression of a particular type of power, namely, the power of the herd, the weak, the "botched and bungled."[21] That is, power seeps through all facets of human behavior, such that even the most pious Christian morality is built upon an indirect exercise of power turned upon itself (*ressentiment*). Just as Nietzsche uncovered the hidden power relations behind Christian morality, Foucault wants to uncover the hidden power relations at work in the creation of the modern legal system, which is touted as an advancement over the premodern state. If Nietzsche and Foucault are correct, then one cannot confidently claim that humanity has progressed from an age of domination to one of liberty. Rather, humanity has moved through different stages of domination; our present system is merely a high-tech and decentralized version of the centralized brute power which obtained during the premodern period. Foucault explains this point in great detail:

> It would be false to think that the total war exhausts itself in its own contradictions and ends by renouncing violence and submitting to civil laws. On the contrary, the law is a calculated and relentless pleasure, delight in the promised blood, which permits the perpetual instigation of new dominations and the stagings of meticulously repeated scenes of violence. . . . *Humanity does not gradually progress from combat to combat until it arrives at universal reciprocity, where the rule of law finally replaces warfare; humanity installs each of its violences in a system of rules and thus proceeds from domination to domination.*[22]

This anti-Enlightenment position questions the possibility of progress in law and politics. Whereas Nietzsche was concerned with the genealogy of Enlightenment-era (Christian) morality, Foucault was concerned with the genealogy of the classical juridical theory. Foucault thought that he could unmask the classical theory by exposing its roots in a genealogical analysis: "My general project over the past few years has been, in essence, to reverse the mode of analysis followed by the entire discourse of right from the time of the Middle Ages. My aim, therefore, was to invert it."[23]

Foucault on Law and Discipline

Foucault's central contribution to legal theory is of a critical nature: he argues that the dominant paradigms in political theory and jurisprudence commit a grave and fundamental error by focusing solely on the power relations between the state and the individual.[24] A genealogical analysis of the classical approach shows that its focus on state power is due to the fact that this model arose as a method for legitimating state coercion over the individual.

GENEALOGY OF THE CLASSICAL MODEL

Foucault wants to force us to reject the classical juridical model by exposing its origins; that is, by showing that this model purports to set limits to state power but actually arose as a way of legitimating and extending state power. The Hobbes–Locke–Rousseau project of seeking a philosophic justification for the state arose as a way of granting the state the right to control the individual. Foucault thinks this genealogical insight will change the way we view social contract theory. Specifically, we will realize that social contract theory is not primarily concerned with individual freedom but with social control: it purports to protect the individual from the state but has the perverse effect of extending and rationalizing state control over the individual.[25]

Foucault points out that the social contract model did not spring full-blown from the minds of political theorists but arose at a particular time for a particular purpose. Specifically, it arose at the end of the Middle Ages, during the decline of feudalism and the rise of monarchical European empires. The coming together of large populations at this time gave rise to the unique problem of how to govern a large collection of individuals by means of a centralized authority. Here is where social contract theory proved useful as a way of rationalizing the sovereign's need to organize large numbers of people. Under the social contract model, the sovereign could reason that the individuals living within his borders had voluntarily consented to state rule and had willed their own submission to the government.

As we have seen, the classical juridical model conceives of power as a right originally held by individuals, typically in the form of natural rights held in a state of nature. According to this model, the individual vests the government with the authority to establish civil and criminal laws, set up schools, put together an army, build roads and bridges, and so on. The free social contract sets up a centralized government that restrains its citizens through criminal laws, taxation, and conscription. Foucault claims that this social contract model (with its focus on a centralized state government) served the interests of the monarchs, who espoused the model in conjunction with a revival of Roman law. This package (viz. social contract ideology and a Roman legal system) served the monarchs well because it provided a basic framework for the management of a large, centralized state. By adopting the Roman legal system, the monarchs manufactured or produced a new system of thought ("juridical science") which spoke in neutral terms about justice, rights, liberties, contracts, and freedom. Paradoxically, this was a discourse that was adopted, produced, and generated in support of the monarchy. So the resulting law betrays a double gesture: it speaks of individual freedom but tends to legitimate the exercise of state power. That is, the legal system purports to protect the individual but has become the mechanism for state control over the individual: "Western monarchies . . . were constructed as systems of law, they expressed themselves through theories of law, and they made their mechanisms of power work in the form of law."[26] The social contract model of classical juridical theory has undergone many permutations, but its various formulations have been put in the service of state interests:

> This . . . juridico-political theory of sovereignty of which I spoke a moment ago . . . had four roles to play. In the first place, it has been used to refer to a mechanism of power that was effective under the feudal monarchy. In the second place, it has served as an instrument and even as a justification for the construction of large-scale administrative monarchies. . . . Finally, in the eighteenth century, it is again this same theory of sovereignty, re-activated through the doctrine of Roman law, that we find in its essentials in Rousseau and his contemporaries, but now with a fourth role to play: now it is concerned with the construction of . . . parliamentary democracy.[27]

Foucault's claim here is that the discourse of rights arose—and continues—as a way in which the individual can be coerced or dominated by the state. The liberal state is a mechanism whereby large numbers of people can be rendered docile so that they are willingly classified, organized, and dominated, not only by the state but by private interests.

Foucault's claim is completely contrary to our present way of thinking, in which rights are seen as trumps against state interference; that is, we believe that the system of rights protects us from state power.[28] But Foucault claims that the legal system as a totality arose as a way of legitimating the use of state power: "The system of right, the domain of the law, are permanent agents of these relations of domination, these polymorphous techniques of subjugation. *Right should be viewed, I believe, not in terms of a legitimacy to be established, but in terms of the methods of subjugation that it instigates.*"[29] The "domain of the law" is itself a form of domination and a smokescreen for domination, according to Foucault, and should not be understood as a system which protects the individual from state domination (as was supposed by Hobbes and Locke and, more recently, by Ronald Dworkin's notion that rights are trumps against state coercion).

THE RISE OF "GOVERNMENTALITY"

Foucault argues that at the end of the Middle Ages, large nation-states began to replace the myriad feudal estates, raising the problem of "governmentality."[30] Formerly there had been no question of the legitimacy of the state since the latter was seen as divinely authorized. But with the decline of religion during the Enlightenment, and the emergence of large, centralized populations, the monarchs needed a method of extending state power. So there was a shift from concern over how the king should run his own affairs to how the state could be managed as an independent enterprise. In other words, the state began to emerge as an entity in its own right. As proof of this shift in emphasis, Foucault points out that political treatises during the Middle Ages took the form of guidebooks containing "advice for the prince" about proper behavior (e.g., Machiavelli's *Prince*), but from the sixteenth to the eighteenth centuries, we see the rise of treatises concerned with the "art of government." It was at this time that the question of state control over the population became problematized. In the political treatises of the seventeenth and eighteenth centuries, we see the rise of the contractual model as a way of explaining how subjects can be contractually (and morally) bound to obey a powerful, centralized government. These treatises raised a series of legal and political problems which are still central today in jurisprudence and political philosophy, among them the problem of natural rights, the enforcement of contracts, the bounds of legitimate government action, and the right to disobey the law. But these are all problems from *within* a framework of law that was a tool for monarchs to extend their power in the premodern era. Foucault wants to dispel the notion (which he sees as endemic in political theory) that these problems are eternal ones that plague all approaches to law and politics. In contrast, he sees these as specific problems that arose for specific reasons.

As sovereignty emerged as an important issue in the sixteenth through the eighteenth centuries, treatises were being developed that extended the concept of "governance" to all aspects of life. This led to the emergence of a series of disciplines which proved useful for organizing and regulating large numbers of people. The new fields of statistics, economics, public health, geography, and political districting all signaled the beginning of a new set of tactics whereby the centralized state began to exercise subtle control over its citizens. These disciplines were aimed at centralizing and extending the power of the state over its subjects, on the analogy of the "pastoral power" of the shepherd over his flock. In short, the seventeenth and eighteenth centuries witnessed the convergence of the Enlightenment, the rise of the centralized state, and a concern with sovereignty and government. Given these factors, one can understand the central role played by social contract theories in the seventeenth and eighteenth centuries: these theories dealt with the problem of how large numbers of people could be regulated and brought under the control of a centralized state. By the late nineteenth and twentieth centuries, however, it was no longer the state that was the exclusive source of control and regulation; power had become diffuse ("capillary"), issuing from various sources.

Foucault makes the important observation that classical juridical theory focuses on the coercive relationship between the state and the individual, which was a genuine problem during the seventeenth and eighteenth centuries—*before* the rise of the disciplines. But the rise of the disciplines has created new forms of power which cannot be understood according to the social contract model. In other words—and this is Foucault's central insight on law—there is a time lag between the way in which we conceptualize power relations and the way in which we are actually confronted by them. In our political theory, we remain largely mired in a premodern notion of power as repressive force by the state, wrongly assuming that the absence of state power translates into freedom for the individual. Foucault's comments on law are designed to force a rethinking (or rejection) of the contract-oppression model and to show that law is now tied to the disciplines. The contract-oppression model may have been appropriate for the seventeenth century, but it is inappropriate for the modern state: "We must eschew the model of *Leviathan* in the study of power. We must escape from the limited field of juridical sovereignty and state institution, and instead base our analysis of power on the study of the techniques and tactics of domination."[31] That is, the sovereign-juridico model cannot explain the myriad ways in which modern individuals are shaped by the disciplinary system. Political philosophy tends to revolve around the issue of state sovereignty, but the state alone is no longer the only apparatus which dominates the individual: "But in the seventeenth and eighteenth centuries we have the production of an important phenomena, the emergence, or rather the invention, of a new mechanism of power possessed of highly specific procedural techniques . . . which is also, I believe, absolutely incompatible with the relations of sovereignty."[32] Since the juridical model sees power as the force of the sovereign, it cannot grasp other ways in which individuals are constrained, especially in nonpolitical contexts such as hospitals, schools, and factories. So the classical juridical approach is not so much "wrong" as "outdated" in that it fails to explain how the individual is coerced by forces other than the centralized state. The picture of the free individual offered by the classical theory is belied by the way in which individuals are coerced and manipulated by the disciplines in the modern era. Our concern should no longer be with *repressive* laws (e.g., state punishment, taxation, conscription), but with the way in which the individual is turned into a subject by *productive* laws and regulations (e.g., public health codes, zoning restrictions, public aid regulations, registration requirements, social security): "We must cease once and for all to describe the effects of power in negative terms: it 'excludes,' it 'represses,' it 'censors,' it 'abstracts,' it 'masks,' it 'conceals.' In fact, power produces; it produces reality; it produces domains of objects and rituals of truth. The individual and the knowledge that may be gained of him belong to this production."[33] I now turn to an examination of the disciplines, which constitute the central way in which power is exercised in the modern state.

THE DISCIPLINES AND LAW

The classical juridical theory (which Foucault rejects) views the state as the source of power. This may have been reasonable in an era when kings ruled with an iron hand, but with the rise of the disciplines there is no centralized source of power. Rather, power is diffuse, being exercised at the "capillaries." So the problem with the juridical model is that it locates power in a single source (the state), while ignoring other sources: "Rather than ask ourselves how the sovereign appears in his lofty isolation, we should try to discover how it is that subjects are gradually, progressively, really and materially constituted through a multiplicity of organisms, forces, energies, materials, desires, thoughts, etc. . . . *This would be the exact opposite of Hobbes' project in* Leviathan."[34] The Hobbesian project was to ask how free, sovereign individuals could transfer their power to a centralized state. The problems raised in the Hobbesian model are typical of the problems addressed in Anglo-American jurisprudence, which concerns itself with rights, contracts, reason, fairness, violence, and the issue of state interference with liberty. For Foucault, this way of thinking is based on a model of society that is premodern:

> To conceive of power on the basis of these problems is to conceive of it in terms of an historical form that is characteristic of . . . the judicial monarchy. . . . And it is true that the juridical system . . . is utterly incongruous with the new methods of power whose operation is not ensured by right but by technique, not by law but by normalization, not by punishment but by control, methods that are employed on all levels and in forms that go beyond the state and its apparatus.[35]

In essence, Foucault calls for a shift away from the juridico-political theory of sovereignty to a study of the way in which individuals are shaped by nonjuridical forces: "What we need is a political philosophy that isn't erected around the problem of sovereignty, nor therefore around the problems of law and prohibition. *We need to cut off the King's head: in political theory that still has to be done.*"[36] Foucault offers two explanations for why the theory of sovereignty persists even though it is outdated. First, he thinks that it serves an ideological function, namely, to offer a sort of smokescreen which prevents us from seeing the disciplines as loci of power relations (i.e., if power is understood on the sovereign-juridico model, we will fail to recognize alternative types of power, which in turn allows these new forms of power to flourish). Second, since our legal codes are based on the paradigm of state power, we cannot easily conceive of power outside state power (i.e., political theorists do not see hospitals, schools, and factories as sources of "power" because they tend to think of the latter as "control by the state").[37] The theory of sovereignty is an ideological gloss of the actual ways in which disciplinary practices work to shape the individual. Foucault's project forces a shift in focus toward "nonsovereign power," which he terms "disciplinary power."[38]

THE SHIFT FROM STATE POWER TO POWER AT THE CAPILLARIES

For Foucault, the new forms of disciplinary power consist of normalizing techniques issuing from a plurality of sources: "The discourse of discipline has nothing in common with that of law, rule, or sovereign will. . . . The code they [the disciplines] come to define is not that of law but that of normalization. . . . It is human sciences which constitute their domain, and clinical knowledge their jurisprudence."[39] So a dual picture of law begins to emerge from Foucault's analysis. Our current legal system arose as an ideological framework for allowing European monarchs to develop techniques for controlling their subjects. The classic example of law in this period was the criminal code, consisting of a set of prohibitions issued from the state to the individual. But in the modern era a system of discipline has arisen to complement the old system of law, and this new system is far more intrusive than the premodern repressive legal system. This new network of power relations is a seamless web that never leaves the individual alone but actually constitutes the subject as a subject: "In fact, power produces; it produces reality; it produces domains of objects and rituals of truth. The individual and the knowledge that may be gained of him belong to this production."[40] To understand the ways in which the individual is affected by power, one must look not only to the system of codified laws but to the system of disciplines which supplement the law: "Law is neither the truth of power nor its alibi. It is an instrument of power which is at once complex and partial. The form of law with its effects of prohibition needs to be resituated among a number of other, non-juridical mechanisms."[41] To understand the way in which the older forms of repressive state action have been complemented by the disciplines, one can turn to Foucault's study of the evolution of the prison system. In *Discipline and Punish* Foucault chronicles the paradigm shifts in punishment since the eighteenth century. At that time punishment took the form of direct action by the sovereign against the individual. Punishment was a species of torture, a show of excess in which the sovereign demonstrated his absolute power over the individual. At the beginning of the nineteenth century, punishment became less of a spectacle and was tailored to fit the crime; the key for this paradigm was the representational function of punishment (e.g., cutting off a finger for theft, putting a drunkard in stocks). But in the middle-to-late nineteenth century, new forms of knowledge were brought to bear on the body (and the mental life) of the offender, which caused another shift in the method of punishment to the model we presently use, namely, confinement, isolation, regulation, examination, and normalization.

These changes in the methods of punishment parallel the decentralization of the state as a locus for the disciplining of subjects. Indeed, many of the various disciplines (including statistics, economics, political and military science) arose primarily as methods for governing large populations yet are now employed in a variety of nongovernmental contexts. The disciplines do not flow from the state alone; indeed, they seem to have no particular "source" as that term is typically used. Rather, there is a sort of endless loop of disciplinary strategies in which we are caught, and the loci of these disciplines includes schools, hospitals, factories, prisons, and the military.[42]

The rise of the disciplines took place against the framework of the system of liberal rights. One might say that the disciplines were the "underside" of the juridical system, inasmuch as the latter guaranteed the sanctity of individual liberty and privacy, whereas the disciplines were busily eroding such rights: "The general juridical form that guaranteed a system of rights that were egalitarian in principle was supported by these tiny, everyday, physical mechanisms, by all those systems of micro-power that were essentially non-egalitarian and asymmetrical that we call the disciplines."[43] While the jurists were busy establishing the formal rights of equality, liberty, and fraternity, the disciplines were eroding these formal liberties by creating a carceral society, a "panopticon" in which each person is watching the other: "The [social] contract may have been regarded as the foundation of law and political power; panopticism constituted the technique, universally widespread, of coercion. . . . *The 'Enlightenment,' which discovered the liberties, also invented the disciplines.*"[44] Foucault goes on to characterize the disciplines as "counter-law" and "anti-law" since the law purports to set a limit beyond which the individual cannot be coerced, yet the disciplines pass beyond this limit, invade individual autonomy, and thus pervert the letter of the law.[45] The disciplines are neither an "infra-law," nor a system of microlaws but an "underside of the law [which] undermines the limits that are traced around the law."[46]

The rise of the disciplines allowed subjects to be controlled without utilizing the force of the sovereign. By creating a system of "subsidiary judges," the disciplinary era fragmented the legal system into a constellation of mini–punishing tribunals. Thus, schools, military barracks, and factories came to resemble prisons—they all shared a common interest in disciplining and shaping the subject. But whereas the premodern law worked by virtue of *sanction,* the disciplines and their regulatory apparatus work through *normalization.* The disciplines shape the person in a way that the law is incapable of doing, namely, by continually subjecting the individual to normalizing modes of regulation. If Foucault is correct, then we must rephrase the classical question "What are the legitimate limits of state power?" to read "What are the ways in which I am presently a product of power relations and disciplines over which I have no control, whether these are imposed by the state or otherwise?"

Foucault is *not* arguing that the law is fading away and being replaced by the disciplinary system. Instead, he is arguing that the law is beginning to conform to the disciplinary system (and vice versa), such that the disciplinary system is now encoded in the form of laws and regulations: "I do not mean to say that law fades into the background or that the institutions of justice tend to disappear, but rather that the law operates more and more as a norm, and that the juridical institution is increasingly incorporated into a continuum of aparatuses (medical, administrative, and so on) whose functions are for the most part *regulatory.*"[47] That is, the law is becoming increasingly regulatory and administrative and consequently less punitive. One is no longer subject to the commands of the all-powerful sovereign, but to the mini-judgments of the secretary of state, the Department of Motor Vehicles, the Internal Revenue Service, the local zoning board, and the municipal code. While the law is becoming more disciplinary, the disciplines are becoming more "legalized."

SOME EXAMPLES OF LAW AND DISCIPLINE

Foucault provides many striking examples of the relationship between law and discipline. Perhaps the best illustration involves a trial that took place in France in 1978, where an admitted rapist refused to respond to questions by the judge concerning his motive for committing the crimes. That is, he admitted that he was guilty of the offenses and was willing to accept punishment, but he refused to reveal his motives. In this case everything seemed to be in order: the law was clear, the evidence was uncontroverted, and the accused admitted his guilt. But the judge and jury wanted a confession and an admission of depravity. When the accused refused to respond, a juror cried out, "For heaven's sake, defend yourself!"[48] The need to get inside the head of the criminal in order to regulate and normalize his thoughts is a product of the combined disciplines of psychiatry and penology, which became intertwined in the nineteenth century. Foucault feels this case proves that the sovereign-juridico model (where the state is a purely punishing or repressive force) cannot account for the way in which power is presently exercised because according to this model all the elements of the offense had been satisfied and the judge and jury should have been happy. But the sovereign-juridico model no longer fits our society because the disciplines have moved to the forefront: law is no longer merely the punishment of *external* behavior (though, of course, this remains essential) but now also consists of exposing and regulating the *internal* thoughts of the perpetrator. In this case the judge and jury wanted more from the criminal than the mere admission of guilt. As Foucault explains, "Much more is expected of him [the criminal]. Beyond admission, there must be confession, self-examination, explanation of oneself, revelation of what one is. The penal machine can no longer function [solely] with a law, a violation, and a responsible party."[49] We now have new forms of domination which are more subtle and insidious than the blunt repression once doled out by the all-powerful sovereign. These new forms strike at the body of the subject (and hence constitute a "bio-power" and "anato-politics"), but they also strike at the subject's internal world. The new form of domination is both repressive and constitutive of the individual, that is, it creates at the same time that it prohibits. In the present example, the criminal law does not merely punish, it constitutes the criminal as a criminal, a person who possesses criminal thoughts, longs to confess, and is mentally disturbed. In this sense the criminal-justice system does not merely *punish* criminals, it *creates* them.

For another instance of the increasing intersection of law and discipline, consider an example that Foucault mentions briefly in *Discipline and Punish:* the workplace contract.[50] Under traditional legal theory, the workplace contract is seen as the result of a free choice between employer and employee: the individual freely gives of his or her time and labor, and the employer assumes responsibility for payment of wages, work assignments, and so on. From a legal perspective, the employer–employee relationship is regulated by common-law principles of contract and by state and federal regulations affecting work environments.

But—and here is Foucault's key point—this *legal* framework only goes so far in capturing the power relations at work in the employer–employee relation. To fully understand the employer–employee relationship, one needs to examine not only the terms of the employment contract and the governing statutes but also the various ways in which the worker is normalized, subject to control and regulation, classified, ranked, and penalized. To see the full range of microregulation of the employee, one need only turn to the employee handbook to find a complex web of micropunishments and petty rules governing everything from the proper use of office equipment to the allowable number of bathroom visits. The employee is "free," but his or her every step is monitored and assessed. In addition, one finds a growing use of surveillance devices by which supervisors can eavesdrop on workers, bosses can monitor managers, and workers can spy on each other. Furthermore, managers have access to software which can minutely chart employee work hours, profitability, and efficiency. The combined effect of such microregulation is to create an unfree work environment despite the fact that the workplace contract is deemed a free contract from the legal perspective. In this way Foucault's approach can be used to explore the way in which a seemingly free work contract is weighed down with invasive mechanisms which rob the individual of freedom. Where the law is silent, the individual is not necessarily free. In such cases the disciplines take over by assuming the form of laws and regulations. These new regulations are not to be confused with the clearly coercive premodern laws ("pay a tenth of your money to the state or you will thrashed"), but they are nonetheless coercive in a more subtle way. Unlike the repressive laws of the old regimes, the new system of discipline and quasi-law is all-pervasive, monitoring thoughts and behaviors which the repressive law could never control.

Does Foucault Offer a Positive Jurisprudence?

Paradoxically, Foucault's central point is that jurisprudence should not focus so heavily upon law, that is, upon laws enacted by legislatures and case decisions rendered by judges. Rather, it should focus on the way in which the premodern type of (repressive) law has been melded together with the disciplines, and how modern law has enabled the expansion of the disciplines (and vice versa). Foucault's overall approach to law and discipline is perhaps best exemplified in *Discipline and Punish*, where he argues that the premodern system of punishment involved an excessive display of sovereign power, whereas the modern system involves isolation, normalization, regimentation, confession, and moral reeducation. What holds for punishment also holds for law: the law has become less repressive yet more regulatory, less severe yet more pervasive, less coercive yet more administrative. The danger in this movement is that the individual's thoughts and behaviors have been increasingly regimented, such that there is no longer any private space (no outside) from which the individual can resist or rebel. And since power is so diffuse, there is nothing against which to rebel.

Certainly, Foucualt's analysis generates insights into the law, but can it provide the normative grounds for a program of legal reform? In what follows I will argue that Foucault does not have a program for a positive jurisprudence, and therefore should be understood chiefly as a social critic who points out the failure of the Enlightenment to live up to its own emancipatory pretensions. In other words, I see Foucault as offering a critical perspective on modern law (from an external vantage point), but I don't see him as offering a program of legal change within the system of modern law.

Much of Foucault's work seems to play out the Nietzschean theme that "the highest values devalue themselves."[51] Foucault wants to show that what seemed like progress in politics (the arrival of democracy, the power of reason, and the humanitarian reform of the prison) is in fact an excuse for repression and discipline. That is, the social changes made in the name of humanity (as well as freedom, truth, and liberty) have led to the creation of a society which is just as coercive as the barbaric practices from which humanity was trying to liberate itself, although it is barbarism of a subtle sort. Foucault points out that the civil state of the eighteenth century was heralded as the delivery of the individual from brute power, yet it has handed the individual over to another type of power which is more diffuse, decentralized, and involves constant monitoring and normalization. Foucault's overarching theme is that there is a "dark side" to the Enlightenment.[52] As he explains, "My point is not that everything is bad, but that everything is dangerous."[53] Foucault's questioning of "everything" extends to a problematization of the very use of "reason," which thereby calls into question the Enlightenment notion that reason is a neutral court of appeal. Instead, we should see reason as a tool, a tactic, employed for specific ends: "I think that the central issue of philosophy and critical thought since the eighteenth century has always been, still is, and will, I hope, remain the question: *What* is this reason that we use? What are its historical effects? What are its limits, and what are its dangers?"[54] Not only is reason suspect, but justice is suspect as well: "I will be a little bit Nietzschean about this. . . . [I]t seems to me that the idea of justice in itself is an idea which in effect has been invented and put to work in different types of societies as an instrument of a certain political and economic power or as a weapon against that power."[55] Judging from these comments, Foucault's approach to law can be seen as questioning such basic ideas in jurisprudence as neutrality, objectivity, reason, freedom, and justice. We automatically view these as the building blocks of jurisprudential theory and seldom see them as problematic in and of themselves. For example, we employ legal reasoning as a way of reaching a just decision in a legal case, but we seldom bother to ask the following questions of legal reasoning itself as a "discursive practice": When was it first employed? For what purpose? Who determines the parameters of acceptable legal reasoning and to what effect? These are important, critical questions that can (and should) be asked of traditional jurisprudence.

But in order to make the claim that the new methods of discipline are "bad" or "morally impermissible," Foucault will need to employ the time-honored (but discredited) concepts of reason, neutrality, and inherent dignity. In short, he must have recourse to some sort of normative ground in order to anchor his critique of the carceral society. Foucault's hidden normative agenda rises to the surface time and again, as evidenced in the following call for struggle against the seemingly neutral institutions of the modern state: "It seems to me that the real political task in a society such as ours is to criticize the working of institutions which appear to be both neutral and independent: to criticize them in such a manner that the political violence which has always exercised itself obscurely through them will be unmasked, so that one can fight them."[56] But if Foucault doesn't like the way in which the disciplines and the law are headed, then he needs some mechanism whereby he can critique them as immoral. It is hard to see how Foucault's positivistic, descriptive analysis of modern law could give rise to a value judgment that this law has been erected at the expense of mankind. Most important, who is this "man" (if he exists for Foucault) who has been harmed by modernity? It seems that Foucault's theory implies—and needs to imply—a particular view of man which he never outlines or discusses but simply adopts as the victim of disciplinary society.

And here is precisely where Foucault's theory leads to problems. In order to generate a program for legal change, Foucault must provide some test to measure whether a law is good or bad, moral or immoral, just or unjust. This can only be done if there is some notion of the "man" or "self" who must be liberated, yet Foucault is curiously silent on the status of this "man" or "soul." This is a problem for Foucault. If the soul is merely a historical construct (and not a deep structure with an innate yearning for freedom), it isn't clear how the soul (or mankind) is injured by the trend toward the disciplinary society and the carceral network.[57]

Traditionally one looks to the Constitution and the legal system to provide some limits on the extent to which the individual can be controlled and dominated. Unfortunately, Foucault thinks that one cannot contest the disciplinary network by invoking inherent rights against oppression because he has rejected the framework of innate rights as being part of the problem in the first place—it was precisely under cover of such notions that humanity ended up in a carceral society. Foucault thinks that one cannot look to the legal system for protection but must seek an alternative escape from domination: "If one wants to look for a non-disciplinary form of power, or rather, to struggle against disciplines and disciplinary power, it is not towards the ancient right of sovereignty that one should turn, but towards the possibility of a new form of right, one which must indeed be anti-disciplinarian, but at the same time liberated from the principle of sovereignty."[58] What Foucault is saying here, oddly enough, is that since the juridical notions of emancipation (freedom, privacy, autonomy) are themselves merely devices which facilitate power relations, there is no point in using these notions as protection against an abuse of power: "It is not through recourse to sovereignty against discipline that the effects of disciplinary power can be limited, because sovereignty and disciplinary mechanisms are two absolutely integral constituents of the general mechanism of power in our society."[59] Foucault's point is that one cannot use juridical principles (e.g., the law) as a defense against discipline because the law is, in fact, part of the disciplinary network. The disciplines are coercive, but so are the laws which purport to protect the individual from the disciplines. Given this situation, it is hard to envision an escape from domination; Foucault can only point toward the possible emergence of a "new form of right" that is neither disciplinary nor based on juridical principles.

To flesh out this "new form of right" that struggles against the disciplines, one might turn to Foucault's final works on the history of sexuality. In these Foucault explored the possibility of an ethics of self-mastery in which the subject could create him or herself through an aesthetic process. As Foucault explained: "From the idea that the self is not given to us, I think that there is only one practical consequence: we have to create ourselves as a work of art."[60] Presumably this project would have political ramifications in that the just state would allow this type of aesthetic transformation. Ostensibly this would require a "new form of right" divorced from the classical juridical model; unfortunately, Foucault cannot tell us very much about this new form of right, apart from some vague statements about the need for new forms of subjectivity:

> The political, ethical, social, and philosophical problem of our days is not to try to liberate the individual from the state, and from the state's institutions, but to liberate us both from the state and from the type of individualization which is linked to the state. We have to promote new forms of subjectivity through the refusal of this kind of individuality which has been imposed on us for several centuries.[61]

It seems that Foucault is calling for the creation of new forms of right and subjectivity, yet he fails to specify the parameters of such new forms. Frankly, he seems to be fumbling around in his effort to envision a more desirable political and legal system. He admittedly says that at each point at which power is exercised there is the possibility of resistance, but it is unclear how Foucault could generate an overarching program which explains *why* we must resist, *who* is resisting, and *where* and *when* resistance should be offered. Foucault may have his reasons for abstaining from these types of claims, but they are precisely the questions that need to be answered if we want to generate a positive jurisprudence.

Here, I think, one must finally admit that Foucault cannot generate a positive jurisprudence. By arguing that one cannot look to the juridical notions of privacy and autonomy as a defense against the disciplines, Foucault eliminates the possibility of an emancipatory program of jurisprudence. For it is these juridical notions of autonomy and privacy, however jaded, which are the only available way to challenge the disciplinary network. Even though the law can be faulted for enabling the disciplines (it was under cover of the law that individuals were subjected to discipline), the law remains the best way to resist the disciplines on the grounds that they violate basic constitutional rights. For example, the best way to challenge inhumane police tactics is to claim that they infringe on privacy, that they are cruel and unusual, or that they violate the right against self-incrimination. It may be a cliché, but our rights are the last line of defense against inhumane treatment.

Foucault cannot make this move because he thinks that these rights are mere chimeras which have, in fact, furthered the domination of the individual. By making this move, Foucault paints himself into a corner: he decries the disciplines and the legal system, refusing to see the law as an avenue for protection of the individual. This nihilistic attitude may strike some as overly defeatist. As Colin Gordon writes "Readers of Foucault sometimes emerge with a dismaying impression of a paranoid hyper-rationalist system in which the strategies-technologies-programs of power merge into a monolithic regime of social subjugation."[62]

This analysis points up a major problem with Foucault's understanding of law, namely, that he focuses too closely on the genealogy of modern law and therefore fails to appreciate the way in which the modern legal system (especially constitutional law) has *protected* individuals against coercion. Even if one grants Foucault's genealogical point that the judicial system arose as a way of exploiting the individual, this does not mean that it continues to have this function. In the United States, for example, the First Amendment rights to a free press, privacy, and association are intended to prevent the individual from being forced to think in a particular manner, to protect the individual from domination and normalization. Furthermore, the Fifth Amendment "takings clause," the Third Amendment prohibition against quartering soldiers, and the Fourth Amendment right against search and seizure are all designed to protect the individual against intrusions. It would seem that any plausible program of liberation must incorporate these rights.

Foucault might respond by agreeing that these constitutional rights appear to set limits on state interference, but they are powerless to stop more subtle abuses of power, such as workplace monitoring, involuntary confinement for mental disorders, and moral reeducation in our schools. That is, liberal jurisprudence focuses too closely on the elimination of state power over the individual instead of focusing on the way in which the legal system permits other forms of domination. There is some truth to this observation, but this way of thinking doesn't leave Foucault with many options for changing or reforming the legal system. Foucault sees power relations as so pervasive that there is no coherent possibility of escape: "there is no outside" to the "carceral network," condemning us to the ever increasing microphysics of power relations.[63] The modern age represents an inexorable march toward more highly developed modes of discipline, increased surveillance, mass normalization, and the eroding of subjectivity. Foucault often talks as if this trend should be resisted, yet without a normative foundation of some kind, without a belief in fundamental rights, it is hard to see how Foucault's critique could amount to a positive program for change. At best one can read Foucault as advocating a system in which power relations are no longer rigid but rather allow the individual an opportunity to resist: "The important question is not whether a culture without restraints is possible or even desirable but whether the system of constraints in which a society functions leaves individuals the liberty to transform the system."[64] The idea here is that power relations are not per se immoral or illegitimate but can become objectionable if they rigidify to the point where they cut off all resistance and become transformed into relations of domination.[65] The problem with this approach, however, is that it refuses to specify the grounds upon which resistance can be justified, remaining silent about the type of society that must be created to counteract the dominant regime of power relations.

Foucault as Negative Utopian and Enlightenment Critic

Given these comments, one can safely say that Foucault lacks the grounds for a positive theory of legal reform. This means that even if his understanding of the legal system generates critical insights, he nevertheless fails to provide a plan for making the system more just or ethically sound. Instead of looking to Foucault for a full-blown legal theory or a program of legal reform, one should probably view his comments on law as making the somewhat modest (but important) claim that the law has undergone an important shift from being primarily repressive to being primarily regulative and normative, and that power has shifted from being primarily negative (prohibitory) to being primarily positive (or constitutive). He also makes the excellent point that jurisprudence as a discursive practice is a self-perpetuating way of *producing a truth,* a discourse which purports to protect the individual but can (if mishandled) have the opposite effect of legitimating the abuse of the individual. Foucault also shows that political theory continues to focus on problems of state legitimacy when the more pressing issue of our time is the extent of nongovernmental forms of power.

By offering these types of insights, Foucault provides a much-needed critical perspective on our legal system. He shows us the underside of our practices and forces us to rethink the assumption that jurisprudence can be a neutral science. Furthermore, he shows us how legal subjects are not found in the ready-made order of things but are constructed by power relations. Most important, he problematizes the use of reason and shows us that the laws and practices developed in the name of humanity often result in new forms of tyranny more insidious and intractable than the practices they were designed to remedy. This casts doubt on the idea of moral and legal progress.

The secondary literature on Foucault is divided on whether Foucault's work can be understood as providing a normative basis for a political (or activist) program or, alternately, whether Foucault is better understood as a critical theorist who offers a "way of seeing," a sort of jaundiced look at contemporary society.[66] With regard to his writings on law, I would put Foucault in the latter category. Foucault's work is essentially an external (historical) critique of the legal system which fails to take a stance on internal issues within legal doctrine.[67] Whereas Foucault's work does not force an immediate change in the legal order, it *does* change the way that one thinks about the legal system. After reading Foucault, one somehow thinks skeptically about the law, and that alone is worthwhile, if only as a counterbalance to some of the more mainstream approaches in political and legal theory.

5 ❧ Derrida: Borrowing (Illicitly?) from Plato and Kant

Jacques Derrida is a highly controversial but undeniably influential French philosopher whose method of "deconstruction" is beginning to make itself known within legal theory.[1] Derrida has been active in French philosophy since the mid-sixties, but his early work was not overtly political. A gradual turn toward social issues began when Derrida offered a deconstruction of the Declaration of Independence in honor of the 1976 U.S. bicentennial.[2] In the mid-eighties Derrida wrote about Nelson Mandela's struggle for justice in apartheid South Africa and about Kafka's famous parable "Before the Law."[3] This movement toward social issues reached its height in 1989, when Derrida was the keynote speaker at a Cardozo Law School symposium entitled "Deconstruction and the Possibility of Justice."[4] It was during this talk that Derrida outlined his approach to law and justice, which is the subject of the present chapter.

Derrida's speech was entitled "Force of Law: The 'Mystical Foundation of Authority.'"[5] As the title of the symposium indicated, the conference was organized to address—and perhaps quell—the widely held impression that deconstruction lacks a coherent conception of justice. Derrida's lecture is a bold response to those critics who have charged deconstruction with political nihilism, irrationalism, and conservatism.[6] Surprisingly, in "Force of Law" Derrida comes very close to setting up a full-scale theory of justice and an accompanying account of law. Given that Derrida's more recent work affirms the account of justice set forth in "Force of Law," his lecture merits close scrutiny.[7]

Although I provide a lenient reading of Derrida's lecture on law and justice, I ultimately conclude that Derrida's conception of justice is largely problematic because it ironically carries metaphysical and epistemic claims which Derrida had elsewhere rejected. Specifically, Derrida's conception of justice borrows quite heavily from Plato and Kant, thereby retaining much of the "logocentric" metaphysics of presence which he had found objectionable in these and other thinkers. In the first part of this chapter I provide a charitable and thorough explanation of Derrida's position on law and justice. In the second part I show that Derrida's approach to justice is heavily indebted to Plato's notion of justice as a transcendent idea (or form), as well as to Kant's notion of justice as a regulative idea. I also point out that Derrida's rejection of traditional metaphysics and epistemology does not permit him to hold the quasi-transcendent view of justice he appropriates from Plato and Kant. In the third part I further elaborate on the notion that Derrida's position on law and justice has a hidden "metaphysics of presence" and is therefore undercut by his own epistemic and metaphysical skepticism. Finally, in the last part I conclude that Derrida's ultimate goal is laudable, namely, to set forth a concept of justice that demands a tireless, impossible, and incalculable vigilance to ensure that justice is done to the other. However praiseworthy this position may be, it nevertheless carries metaphysical baggage that must be rejected based on Derrida's own critique of "logocentrism." This means that Derrida's recent writings on justice and law are inconsistent with his earlier, more deconstructive pieces.

In order to lay the groundwork for this conclusion and to provide the reader with a complete overview of Derrida's work, I will begin with a short discussion of Derrida's method of deconstruction. This should help the reader to understand how Derrida's recent work on law and justice differs in style and content from his more deconstructive work.

Derrida's method of deconstruction grows out of an intellectual movement dating from the early part of this century known as "structuralism," which is why Derrida is often termed a "poststructuralist." Structuralist thinkers such as Ferdinand de Saussure, Freud, Marx, and Claude Lévi-Strauss held that social and psychological phenomena were best understood as a struggle or tension between component structures which derive their meaning in relation to other components. For example, Freud showed that the seemingly unitary Cartesian "self" or "ego" consisted of three separate structures (an id, an ego, and a superego) in perpetual conflict. Marx demonstrated that capitalist society was internally divided between two antagonistic classes, each existing by virtue of the other. Most important, the Swiss linguist Saussure showed that words, sounds, and concepts get their meaning only in relation to other words, sounds, and concepts. Saussure pointed out that meaning is made possible by slight differences: the sound "bat" gets its meaning by contrast with terms like "cat" and "mat"; a concept such as "dog" derives its meaning only by contrast with related categories such as "wolf" or "hyena." The sound "bat" and the concept "dog" have no meaning in isolation, but they make sense when understood relationally, as parts within a structural system of sounds and concepts.

Derrida extended Saussure's structuralist insight by claiming that since words get their meaning relationally, a term or concept will always implicate other terms and concepts. From this Derrida concludes that meaning is never fully present and enclosed within rigid boundaries since each term leaves "traces" in related terms. Accordingly, meaning is diffuse, "disseminated," open-ended. In a famous essay Derrida claimed that all terms get their meaning by "differing" from other terms, so meaning is always "deferred" (here Derrida is playing on the terms "differ"/"defer").[8] As a result, meaning is always in flux or "play": "Essentially and lawfully, every concept is inscribed in a chain or in a system within which it refers to the other, to other concepts, by means of the systematic play of differences."[9] For Derrida there can never be closure to a "text" (this term is used broadly by Derrida to include, for example, the "text" of Western philosophy). Instead of closure we have a condition of "intertexuality" in which texts refers to other texts; hence Derrida's famous claim that "there is no outside to the text." While the full meaning of a term can never be completely present, most theorists continue to act as if this can be accomplished by setting up rigid definitions and hierarchies. The belief that a concept can be made fully present so that it can be enclosed and mastered is chastised by Derrida as the "metaphysics of presence."

Derrida sometimes uses the term "logocentrism" (from the Greek *logos*, meaning order, or reason) to describe the Western tradition's obsession with a metaphysics of presence, the idea that we can grasp the Truth completely by naming it with the right terminology.[10] Derrida chastises logocentrism as a search for a "transcendental signified," an absolute end point where the free play of meaning is anchored forever. He thinks that logocentrism is flawed because meaning can never be made fully present; hence we must be content to recognize the free play of signs without closure, or at least to concede that any closure we achieve is fallible, temporary, and "deconstructible." Derrida is also at pains to point out that words and concepts are repeatable ("iterable" is the term Derrida prefers), so they can appear repeatedly in different contexts, giving rise to new meanings. For example, the term "dog" can appear literally ("My dog is a poodle"), metaphorically ("He is a dog"), and in other contexts which extend the meaning of the term in new ways ("He was doggedly determined"; "I'll be doggone"). So the concept "dog" can be played out in new and shifting contexts, making it hard to enclose and grasp once and for all.

These general theoretical ideas take on a practical dimension in the method of textual analysis known as "deconstruction." Derrida argues that the logocentric project of searching for the transcendental signified is implicated whenever a theorist tries to build a theory around rigid boundaries and binary oppositions. Inevitably one term of the opposition is given pride of place, while the other term is denigrated as derivative and secondary. The Western tradition, according to Derrida, is built upon a series of such hierarchies: subject/object, male/female, speech/writing, interior/exterior, rational/irrational, public/private, appearance/essence, and so on. Such opposing concepts form the basis upon which most theories (perhaps *all* theories) are *constructed*. The project of *deconstruction* involves a close reading of texts to show that the foundational hierarchies set up by the author collapse upon closer scrutiny; in deconstruction, a text is read against itself, as it were, to show that the boundaries which it constructs cannot be maintained. According to Derrida, structural hierarchies must be challenged because "we are not dealing with the peaceful coexistence [of binary terms] but rather with a violent hierarchy. One of the two terms governs the other . . . or has the upper hand. To deconstruct the opposition, first of all, is to overturn the hierarchy at a given moment."[11] Derrida's most famous (and perhaps also his most controversial) deconstructive reading deals with the hierarchy of speech/writing. Derrida claims that the Western tradition has valued speech over writing for at least two reasons. First, it was assumed that writing was derivative of speech because some societies possess speech without writing but not vice versa. Second, speech allows the speaker to pretend that the meaning of a term is fully present when the word is spoken ("phonocentrism"), whereas in writing the "speaker" is absent, so his or her meaning is always deferred, cloudy, and subject to interpretation. In a highly controversial move, Derrida argues that a type of writing ("arche-writing") actually predates speech, thereby inverting the speech/writing hierarchy running through the Western tradition. A similar inversion of hierarchies has been attempted to deconstruct the boundaries between fiction/nonfiction, metaphorical/literal, rational/irrational, and so on. In addition to deconstructing conceptual hierarchies, it is also possible to deconstruct metaphysical entities. For example, the Cartesian *cogito* (or the Christian notion of the soul) can be deconstructed by showing that the self is never fully present, never transparent to itself, always engaged in a struggle of repression, conflict, and disassociation. These two projects (the deconstruction of hierarchies and the deconstruction of metaphysical entities) lie at the center of the deconstructive enterprise. Accordingly, most deconstructive essays involve an attempt to dissolve a hierarchy or to debunk a metaphysical position.

As deconstruction gained support in academic circles, legal theorists began to realize that the deconstructive method could be applied to some of the traditional hierarchies and oppositions in legal doctrine. Soon innovative legal thinkers were using deconstruction to question or subvert distinctions such as public/private, law/politics, internal/external, and text/margin,[12] as well as to analyze particular legal decisions.[13] For example, a legal theorist could deconstruct the law/politics distinction by showing that while judges profess to follow the law as if it were an autonomous set of neutral principles divorced from politics, their interpretation and application of legal principles is typically based upon their political affiliations, thereby erasing any rigid boundary between law and politics.

Just as the deconstructive project was gaining popularity in the late eighties, it was announced that Derrida would be giving a lecture on law and justice. There was an assumption that Derrida would take the opportunity to advance a deconstructive reading of particular cases or legal doctrines. But, to the surprise of many, Derrida instead gave a lecture that was notable for its *constructive* features in terms of the positive things it had to say about justice. It is to this lecture that I now turn, bearing in mind that the thrust of Derrida's earlier work was primarily deconstructive and critical.

Derrida on Law and Justice

Several important themes emerge in Derrida's "Force of Law": (1) deconstruction is not politically nihilistic (on the contrary, it recognizes an unceasing call to do justice to the other at all costs); (2) there is a distinction between law and justice in that justice is *not* deconstructible while law *can* be deconstructed; (3) deconstruction reminds us that law can never reach a stage of complete justice since justice is transcendent and never wholly imminent; (4) justice takes the form of an experience of three *aporias*; and (5) justice requires a commitment to traditional emancipatory ideals and the recognition of marginalized groups. I will address each of these points in turn.

DECONSTRUCTION AS ANTI-NIHILISM

The central undertaking of Derrida's lecture is to defend deconstruction against the mischaracterization that it is indifferent to political and ethical issues.[14] Derrida thinks that this misunderstanding of deconstruction may have been caused by the fact that deconstruction does not operate from within the dominant discourse of law and justice, in the sense that it does not engage in specific internal debates over particular rights, duties, and laws. Nevertheless, deconstruction is centrally concerned with matters of law and justice, albeit from an external or critical perspective, whereby it calls into question the justice of the entire legal apparatus. Deconstruction seeks to problematize the notion that a system of laws can be said to be "just" at a given moment in time. Deconstruction points to a "reinterpretation of the whole apparatus of boundaries within which a history and a culture have been able to define their criteriology."[15] Derrida insists that deconstruction does not correspond to a "quasi-nihilistic abdication before the ethico-politico-juridical question of justice."[16] Deconstruction is not nihilistic; on the contrary, it posits the greatest, most unattainable, infinite duty to do justice to the other. Unlike traditional jurisprudence, which errs by conflating positive law with justice, deconstruction views justice as being "beyond" the legal system. Derrida argues, against the legal positivists, that justice is something over and apart from the rights and remedies available under the existing legal system. Specifically, justice is an ethical relation that cannot be fully encoded in the form of statutes, rules, and legal precedents.

Derrida claims that deconstruction has only *appeared* to avoid the issue of justice when, in fact, it has been discussing justice all along, although he concedes that his previous interrogation with justice has been somewhat oblique. The reason for this indirect engagement with justice, according to Derrida, is that justice cannot be approached directly without making the mistaken claim that "this [law] is just," a move Derrida finds problematic since justice is unpresentable and cannot be identified with particular decisions.[17] Whereas Derrida's earlier writings addressed justice somewhat indirectly, "Force of Law" represents Derrida's most direct engagement to date.

JUSTICE VERSUS LAW

Derrida makes a fundamental distinction between "justice" and "law" (by which he means positive, man-made law). Since this distinction is crucial for his theory, it is worth examining at length. Derrida seems to think that justice is outside the law; it is a relation or debt from one person to another, an irreducible and incalculable duty to act without thought of repayment. Derrida thinks of justice as something that "exceeds" the law and can perhaps even contradict the law in extreme cases. Justice is deemed an "experience that we are not able to experience" and involves *aporia*.[18] Although these comments seem cryptic, Derrida's main point is that justice, properly understood, should not be confused with positive law.

Some clues to Derrida's notion of justice can be gleaned from his comments that justice is an "incalculable" demand to treat the other on the other's terms. Derrida exemplifies this demand in his delivery of the lecture in English, which evidences his attempt to speak the language of the other: "To address oneself in the language of the other is, it seems, the condition of all possible justice."[19] Justice takes the form of an unconditional duty to recognize the other. This debt is incalculable, excessive, such that one can never fulfill it and it cannot be measured because it is infinite. This means that justice is a duty to the other which can never be satisfied yet must be attempted. Hence the *aporia* of justice: "I think that there is no justice without this experience, however impossible, of aporia. Justice is an experience of the impossible. A will, a desire, a demand for justice whose structure wouldn't be an experience of aporia would have no chance to be what it is, namely, a call for justice."[20] This formulation of justice (as a "call" to the other) has unmistakable Levinasian overtones. Indeed, Derrida cautiously acknowledges his debt to Levinas, especially on the issue of the infinity and incalculability of the debt to the other.[21] In addition, Derrida's discussion of justice as an *aporia* seems to parallel his continuing interest in aporetic structures, most notably his recent work on gift without exchange, in which he tries to articulate a gift which does not entail a reciprocal return.[22] Like a one-way gift without exchange, justice demands that we fulfill our duty without repayment, that we perform without expectation of reciprocity: "The deconstruction of all presumption of a determinant certitude of a present justice itself operates on the basis of an infinite 'idea of justice' because it is irreducible, irreducible because owed to the other, before any contract, because it has come, the other's coming as the singularity that is always other."[23] The call to justice reveals a responsibility without limit, a sort of bottomless duty to the other.[24]

In contrast to justice, the "law" is a system of determinate rules. Law involves a process of calculating between claims, a determination of proper adherence to rules, and the subsuming of particular cases under general rules. Derrida's understanding of law follows Pascal (who, in turn, was following Montaigne) in the notion that the legal system is not founded upon reason or justice but upon an act of interpretive violence. Montaigne recognized that law is *nomos* (convention), and hence derives from custom, which is itself arbitrary and groundless. Of any particular law it can be asked, "What is the authority for *this* law?," which leads to the question, "What is the authority for *this* authority?" By tracing the chain of authority backward, one must eventually acknowledge that the law is not "based" on anything beyond arbitrary custom backed by state violence. Because there is no rational point of origin for the law, it is self-grounding, according to Montaigne.[25] That is, the founding law (typically, a constitution or charter) is itself merely a construct, a fiction installed by an act of force. This realization led Montaigne to hold that "custom is the sole basis for equity, for the simple reason that it is received; it is the mystical foundation of its authority. Whoever traces it to its source annihilates it."[26] Montaigne's point is that the law is mired in practices and customs and hence is not a system that has been constructed to meet the demands of justice: "And so laws keep up their good standing not because they are just but because they are laws."[27]

Derrida wishes to focus on Montaigne's notion that law is a "construct" because it follows from this that the law is *de*constructible. Derrida thinks that the law is self-grounding in that it arises by means of an "autobiographical fiction," a performative act which is a "coup of force."[28] In other words, at the moment of the foundation of the legal system, there must be an originary act of violence which sets up an initial standard of legality.[29] Since this standard is itself the criterion for other laws, it cannot be measured against any external standard of legality (e.g., the U.S. Constitution was not authorized under the prior Articles of Confederation, so in a certain sense the founding of this country was "extralegal"). Using this logic, Derrida claims that the origin of law is beyond law, that is, it is neither legal nor illegal but creates the category of legality: "Since the origin of authority, the foundation or ground, the position of the law can't by definition rest on anything but themselves, they are themselves a violence without ground. Which is not to say that they are in themselves unjust, in the sense of 'illegal.' They are neither legal nor illegal in their founding moment."[30] Derrida has elsewhere pointed out that the origin of law is an autobiographical fiction that has been forgotten over time; the birth of the state is achieved through a creative act that is forgotten, such that a higher moral justification is presumed to underlie the founding of the state.[31] In other words, people begin to believe that the law is grounded in a higher order (God, reason, natural law), instead of realizing that the law is largely a fictional creation which self-perpetuates (in the sense that laws derive their authority from other laws in a circular system of self-referencing support). There is thus a tendency to collapse justice into positive law, which results in a sort of naive legal positivism, the view that there is no justice apart from the rights and remedies available within the existing legal system. In order to combat this position, Derrida adamantly insists that justice *cannot* be collapsed into law. One can never say, in good conscience, that "the law is [completely] just."[32]

The key difference between law and justice is that justice is not deconstructible, whereas law can be deconstructed since it is inherently a construct.[33] Presumably, the "deconstructibility" of law means that it is possible to trace the chain of authority back to an originary act of founding, an original positing of placeholders which enable the legal system to operate but which are themselves not justified by the legal system which they enable. In other words, one ultimately reaches an origin of the legal system which, paradoxically, grounds the system of authority but is itself ungrounded and hence self-justifying. The deconstruction of law shows that the legal system is a giant construct without ground; in other words, its foundation is groundless and "mystical": "Here the discourse comes up against its limit: in itself, in its performative power itself. It is what I here propose to call the mystical. Here a silence is walled up in the violent structure of the founding act."[34] Unlike law, justice is not deconstructible because it is a fundamental category of experience, not a construct. As such, it cannot be fully coded in the legal discourse of specific rights, duties, and obligations without losing its irreducible character. One is called to do justice toward the other, yet this justice is excessive, incalculable, unreachable. There is no point at which it can be said that justice has been reached, nor is there a point at which one can say definitively that a decision is "just."[35] Paradoxically, justice seems to appear as present because it insinuates itself as a call to the other and thereby affects legal decisions. Even if there is no justice, *"there* is justice."[36] Hence justice (however infinite and unpresentable) emerges as a standard against which one can interrogate the legal system.

THE NON-PRESENCE (YET PRESENCE) OF JUSTICE

Derrida feels that justice cannot be fully present and can only be experienced as something other than itself. That is, its presence is always deferred, always "to come." While justice can never be truly "done," one is still called to do justice. So it follows that justice presents itself as an *aporia,* a blocked passage, an "experience of the impossible."[37] But while justice cannot be laid out as a system of rules, the law can be presented as a system of rules, and for this reason the law is often confused with justice. Some thinkers (especially extreme legal positivists) have argued that the realm of law is coterminous with that of justice. For these thinkers justice is completely served when a decision has been rendered in accordance with existing law, since these thinkers refuse to recognize any justice outside the existing system of positive law.

Derrida is adamant in his rejection of legal positivism, arguing that under no circumstances should the law be mistaken for justice. Although justice and law are separate, they necessarily converge at the instant of the judicial decision. At the moment when a case must be decided or a law enacted, one is called to justice and forced to do the impossible: to encode infinite justice into a finite decision. This fundamental *aporia* can be divided into three separate *aporias* which arise when a decision must be reached. The *aporias* arise from the simultaneous need for justice to be rendered immediately in the form of a legal decision and the competing need for justice to be infinite, beyond calculation.

JUSTICE AS THE EXPERIENCE OF THREE APORIAS

The first *aporia* is the "epokhe [suspension] of the rule."[38] This *aporia* arises because a judge must follow the law (in the form of legal precedent) yet must also decide each case on its own terms and must be free to overturn or reject (or distinguish) the precedents which impinge upon him or her. If the judge merely applies the rules mechanically, as might be the case if he or she read the law literally or searched for an original intent, then the judge would be acting in accord with the law but would be blind to the possibility that the law was itself immoral or wrong. On the other hand, if the judge suspends the law altogether and decides the case *de novo*, he or she effectively "invents" the law in derogation of the duty to follow the law. To be just, the judge must follow the law but must also stand ready to overrule it. This means that he or she will be regulated yet unregulated—must "conserve the law and also destroy it."[39] Thus, for a judge to do what is "legal" may involve making a decision that is unjust; and to do what is just may require a decision that has little or no legal support. In this way, justice runs up against the limitations of law, and law runs up against the impossibility of justice.[40]

The second *aporia* is "the ghost of the undecidable."[41] Derrida's focus here is not merely that a legal case can be decided in favor of either party, depending on the precedents. Rather, Derrida is concerned with the fact that there must be a rapprochement between justice (incalculable, infinite, excessive, and unconditional) and law (calculable, determined, contingent, and rule-governed). Justice resists formulas, so one can never say that a particular formulation of law is "just" in the sense of rendering complete justice to the other. At the same time that justice resists encapsulation, there is a need for a decision to be made. While there is no justice prior to a decision ("for only a decision is just"), no decision can completely capture justice. Derrida also wishes to stress that even though there is an encounter with justice inherent in each decision, this encounter is forgotten after the case has been decided. Once a decision has been rendered, the case becomes a "precedent" and is part of the law, such that the judge's struggle with justice is forgotten.

The third *aporia* is "the urgency that obstructs the horizon of knowledge."[42] Justice must be rendered immediately, but to satisfy the infinite demand for justice, one would need infinite time and knowledge. Derrida quotes Kierkegaard to this effect: "The instant of decision is a madness."[43] In other words, the necessity of reaching a decision will bring a premature ending to the process of rendering infinite justice to the other. Derrida wants to stress that justice "has no horizon of expectation" and is always "to come" in the sense of being deferred: " 'Perhaps,' one must always say perhaps for justice. There is a 'to come' for justice and there is no justice except to the degree that some event is possible which, as event, exceeds calculation, rules, programs, anticipations and so forth. . . . [J]ustice exceeds law and calculation."[44] But even though justice is incalculable, one is forced to calculate, in the sense that one must weigh the claims of the parties before the court. Jurisprudence requires an impossible and overwhelming task: to translate incalculable justice into calculable rules, to "codify" an obligation that is beyond codes. Hence the *aporia* of justice: there is a need to do justice to the other, yet this can never be accomplished in the form of legally prescribed rights and duties.

AFFIRMING THE CLASSICAL EMANCIPATORY IDEAL

Derrida seems to think that his notion of justice, properly conceived as a "call to the other," can provide the basis for what he refers to as an "ethico-juridico-political" position. The deconstructive project is not meant to produce new legal codes or to fill in the gaps in the law; instead, it requires a "re-doing things from top to bottom."[45] That is, one should try to show that the *foundations* of a legal concept are illegitimate, as, for example, when the term "man" is used in founding documents (such as the Declaration of Independence) in a way that is limited to white males, or when the term "family" is deemed to exclude homosexual couples. The deconstructive project is to "reinterpret the very foundations of law such as they had previously been calculated or delimited."[46] Presumably this involves an expansion of those who are granted standing (and a voice) in the legal system, to achieve ever-widening circles of inclusivity. Perhaps it is for this reason that Derrida affirms the process of liberation characteristic of the Western democratic tradition: "Nothing seems to me less outdated than the classical emancipatory ideal. We cannot attempt to disqualify it today, whether crudely or with sophistication, at least not without treating it too lightly and forming the worst complicities."[47] At the end of his lecture Derrida also suggests that deconstruction ought to remain concerned with the recognition and liberation of marginalized groups, presumably including gays, minorities, the homeless and disabled, and animals.

Having completed my summary of Derrida's lecture, I should point out that the view of justice and law set forth in "Force of Law" has been affirmed by Derrida in his most recent texts. For example, in his 1993 lectures on Marx, Derrida speaks of an "idea of justice" which is "irreducible to any deconstruction" and is "not yet there."[48] One can conclude that Derrida's "Force of Law" sets forth a view of justice he will continue to hold.

In "Force of Law" and the more recent *Specters of Marx*, Derrida seems to be laying the groundwork for an approach to jurisprudence which insists upon an almost dialectical struggle between law and justice. That is, justice and law differ *in kind;* justice is transcendent or (quasi-transcendent) and is not deconstructible, while law is imminent and deconstructible. Justice cannot be formulated as law without losing its infinite qualities, whereas law cannot reach a point of unity with justice, since law is inherently deconstructible. But—and here is my main point—the law can be changed so that its foundations more clearly reflect the demands of justice. Justice must be vigilant toward the law; it must interrogate and haunt the law. Most important, deconstruction must remind us that the law should not pass itself off as justice, since there is no possible legal arrangement which could do full justice to the other. At the very least, the deconstructive project forces a shaking or trembling of the legal order such that its foundations are put into question.[49]

If my interpretation is correct, namely, that Derrida is setting up a system in which justice can be used to interrogate the ethical status of the law, then this would place him in a long line of thinkers who draw a (sharp) division between law and justice. The two thinkers whose ideas exerted the most important influence on Derrida are Plato and Kant. In what follows I will argue that Derrida's view of justice borrows heavily (but illicitly) from Plato and Kant.

Platonic and Kantian Influences

From Plato, Derrida borrows the notion that justice is something ideal and unattainable in our existing practices (in essence, a form that stands apart from the various attempts to render justice within the existing legal system).[50] From Kant, Derrida borrows the notion that justice is a regulative idea, a horizon that cannot be reached but serves as a goal toward which we should strive. What I am suggesting is the following: Derrida wants (and perhaps needs) to borrow from the Platonic and Kantian tradition, yet he cannot do so because these positions carry metaphysical and epistemic warrants that are untenable for him. As a result, Derrida adopts a kind of metaphysically stripped-down Platonism and Kantianism which (to my mind) renders his position untenable. Paradoxically, Derrida ends up espousing a position which carries the very type of metaphysical assumptions he has found problematic in other thinkers.

Let me begin by exploring the seemingly Platonic elements in Derrida's account of law and justice. Plato distinguished between the form of justice, which is justice *in itself* as an intelligible idea, and the various instantiations of justice in the material world. The various "just" things in the world are deemed so by virtue of their participation in the form of justice.[51] Plato distinguishes between absolute "Justice itself" versus particular just actions.[52] Absolute justice (which can be understood only by a philosopher-king trained in the art of dialectical thinking) can be used as a measuring rod to determine whether particular social arrangements (or particular persons) can be described as "just." Plato defines *social* justice as a harmony among the social classes, with each class performing its respective function in the just state; he defines *personal* justice as an inner harmony of the soul. By setting up a standard of justice as harmony in the state and individual, Plato can then assess whether a given state or person measures up to the transcendental form of justice.

It is not difficult to see how Derrida might be accused of Platonism. He speaks of justice as something which is never reached, never fulfilled, but manages to present itself as an immediate demand. Furthermore, he seems to feel that justice stands outside the law as a stable ideal when he comments that deconstruction "operates on the basis of an infinite 'idea of justice' [which] seems to be irreducible."[53] Derrida's separation of justice and law at times seems to border on a distinction between a form (justice) and various attempts at instantiating that form (law): "Law is not justice. Law is the element of calculation, and it is just that there be law, but justice is incalculable, it requires us to calculate with the incalculable."[54] Of course, the analogy with Platonism is not complete and total because there are obvious differences between Plato's and Derrida's notions of justice. Derrida has spent a good portion of his career attacking Platonic notions, such as the idea of a fully present and fully knowable truth, the possibility of complete and total mastery of a text, the existence of a stable self, and so on. But while the analogy between Plato and Derrida is not perfect, it is nevertheless illuminating; the description of Derrida's work as Platonic seems accurate, at least at some basic level.[55]

While Derrida's conception of justice sometimes appears to take on a quasi-transcendental Platonic status, at other times he seems to envisage justice as a Kantian regulative idea.[56] For Kant regulative ideas are produced by reason yet have no corresponding empirical object. These ideas prove useful in the realm of *practical* reason. In the context of deciding issues in ethics and politics, one must make use of ideas which have no possible object of experience but which nevertheless serve as a horizon or goal toward which one must be oriented.[57] For example, in the realm of practical reason, one must act upon maxims which could bring about a kingdom of ends for all rational beings, yet there is no way to experience such a kingdom of ends. Similarly, freedom must be presupposed in order to make ethics possible, yet this freedom can never be empirically verified. As Kant explains: "Freedom, however, is a mere Idea. . . . Thus the Idea of freedom can never admit of full comprehension, or indeed of insight, since it can never by any analogy have an example falling under it. It holds only as a necessary presupposition of reason in a being who believes himself to be conscious of a will."[58] Kant uses the concept of the "limit of moral inquiry" to claim that regulative ideas (freedom, God, kingdom of ends) point to a realm beyond the phenomenal world (i.e., the noumenal world) even though we cannot say anything about this world.

Kant's notion of a regulative idea seems to underly Derrida's claim that justice is a demand or "call" to the other that can never be fully realized.[59] Like

Kant's regulative ideas, which are never substantiated in the phenomenal world, Derrida's "justice" does not correspond to any event or decision in the realm of existing law, yet it intervenes in every legal decision. One can never say "this is just" or "justice is done" about events in the empirical world,[60] yet one must heed the call of justice in any event. There seems to be little difference between Derrida's "call to justice" and Kant's notion of justice as a regulative idea. To be sure, Derrida would reject such Kantian metaphysical postulates as the phenomenal and noumenal worlds and the transcendental subject, but there remains something essentially Kantian about Derrida's notion that justice is a call to the other, an ultimate responsibility that can never be attained or experienced.[61]

Given these Platonic and Kantian elements running through Derrida's lecture on law and justice, it is easy to see how he might be viewed as a legal Platonist who posits justice as a Kantian regulative idea. This interpretation has been advanced by Merold Westphal in a thoughtful review of Derrida's "Force of Law." Westphal argues that Derrida's distinction between justice and law bespeaks a Platonist notion that justice is a "higher law to which every human code is answerable."[62] This makes Derrida a natural law theorist because he distinguishes between a higher law (natural law) and positive law (human law). In Derrida's terminology, "justice" would be the unattainable higher law, while "law" would be the human code constructed in the shadow of the higher law. Westphal construes Derrida to be saying that justice "intervenes" in the judicial process. That is, justice makes itself present as a transcendent (yet occasionally imminent) standard by which one can judge positive laws.

Westphal believes (correctly, I think) that Derrida envisions this Platonic justice as a Kantian quasi-regulative idea. Westphal understands that Derrida cannot accept the metaphysical baggage of either Platonism or Kantianism, and that this puts him in a bind: he must affirm certain elements of two views which he has previously decried as "logocentric," that is, tied to an unacceptable "metaphysics of presence."[63] The Derridian project, as far as justice is concerned, is to set forth a Platonic and Kantian notion divorced from the metaphysical and epistemic warrants in which these views have been mired.

Westphal is optimistic that Derrida can successfully weed out the unwanted metaphysical claims and bring forth a workable, nonmetaphysical notion of justice. Justice so conceived would be quasi-transcendental: it does not exist wholly apart from various contexts, yet it remains categorically binding and somehow infiltrates itself into the act of judging:

> Still, the idea of justice in itself functions as a quasi-regulative idea for Derrida. It is not something that exists outside of every human context, and it is

not an ideal essence to which we can give a fixed and final meaning. It is a bit like what Kierkegaard had in mind when he spoke of "thoughts which wound from behind." Though we cannot get them out in front of us where they are fully present to us and we can master them, they nevertheless insinuate themselves into our thinking, disturbing its complacency in ways that we can neither predict nor control. They ambush our absolutes. On Derrida's view it is precisely as deconstruction that the idea of justice in itself wounds our legal systems, both as theory and as practice, from behind.[64]

Westphal thinks that deconstructive justice takes the form of a Kierkegaardian "thought which wounds from behind." To my mind, this interpretation is an ingenious attempt to rescue Derrida from a serious problem: he borrows Platonic and Kantian notions of justice, yet these notions are wedded to metaphysical baggage that cannot be removed without deneutering the accompanying concepts of justice. Westphal identifies but then avoids the key problematic in Derrida's text, namely, that Derrida wants to posit what he cannot defend: a Platonic notion of justice as a Kantian regulative idea. That is, Derrida wants to reappropriate the ethical thoughts of Plato and Kant (ironically, thinkers Derrida has "deconstructed" in the past) while removing the metaphysical warrants of these thinkers by equivocating on the exact metaphysical and epistemic status of "justice." This puts Derrida in a double bind that plays itself out in his comments on justice: he wants to say that justice is transcendent, yet not in a Platonic sense; similarly, he wants to say that justice is a regulative idea, but not in a Kantian sense. In the end, he picks up the metaphysical language of Plato and Kant while simultaneously denying that he is putting forth a metaphysical viewpoint.

This simultaneous appropriation and distancing from Plato and Kant is most clearly evidenced in Derrida's 1988 afterword to *Limited Inc.* Notice, in the following passage, how Derrida first relies on the Platonic notion that justice is independent and transcendent (outside of all contexts), then takes back this assertion by saying that justice is not present outside of particular contexts, and finally reverts back to the idea that justice is transcendent:

> [Unconditional responsibility] is *independent* of every determinate context, even of the determination of a context in general. It announces itself as such only in the *opening* of a context. *Not that it is simply present* (existent) elsewhere, outside of all contexts; rather, it intervenes in the determination of a context from its very inception, and from an injunction, a law, a responsibility that *transcends* this or that determination of a given context.[65]

It is unclear to me how Derrida can hold that justice is "independent of every determinate context" yet "not outside of all contexts." The problem is that he wants to say that justice is transcendent, but he cannot make this claim because it would involve him in a logocentric metaphysics of presence. Derrida does a similar double take with respect to Kant, at first borrowing from him and then realizing that he cannot do so:

> I have on several occasions spoken of "unconditional" affirmation or of "unconditional" "appeal." . . . Now the very least that can be said of uncon- ditionality (a word that I use not by accident to recall the character of the cat- egorical imperative in its Kantian form) is that it is independent of every determinate context. . . . *Why have I always hesitated to characterize it in Kant- ian terms? . . . Because such characterization seemed to me essentially associated with philosophemes* [sic] *that themselves call for deconstructive questions.*[66]

This double gesture shows that Derrida *needs* a metaphysical basis for his con- ception of justice yet cannot hold a metaphysical position without contradict- ing the deconstuctive efforts of such antimetaphysical earlier works as "Differance," "Structure, Sign and Play,"[67] and *Of Grammatology.* This leaves him with little support to fall back upon, as I will further explain in the next section.

Problems with a Derridean Positive Jurisprudence

As I indicated earlier, Derrida tries to reappropriate Platonic and Kantian notions of justice while simultaneously distancing himself from these same thinkers. The result of this double gesture is that the reader is left wondering about the exact status of justice. Derrida never expressly states what he means by "justice," but it appears that (following Levinas) he offers a phenomeno- logical account of justice. This means that justice is derived from the inter- subjective relation of self to other; it is an "ethical relation" built into all encounters with the other. It specifies that one owes an incalculable debt to the other, an excessive and ultimate demand to heed the call of the other. This interpretation is bolstered by Derrida's repeated references to Levinas,[68] and his quotation of Levinas' statement, "the relation to others—that is to say, jus- tice."[69] Since this relation is primordial, basic, and foundational, it cannot be encoded in legal statutes and case decisions, but must always remain outside of such encoding, as a 'beyond' to which the legal system points. In this way justice interrogates the legal order and allows the latter (which is a construct, an act of fiction) to be *de*constructed. The call to do justice to the other is what spurs the deconstructive process into action, and hence the very process of deconstruction is a process of seeking justice: "Deconstruction is justice."[70]

This sounds inspiring, but questions concerning the metaphysical status of this "justice" immediately arise. I see no problem with positing a call to do justice to the other, but it is not clear how this call is to be understood outside of metaphysical assumptions about stable subjects, meanings, and contexts for ethical communication, and undistorted relations between oneself and others. These assumptions seem to be just as top-heavy as the minimal metaphysical assumptions Derrida finds so problematical in, say, Gadamer's hermeneutics or Austin's speech-act theory. Furthermore, Derrida's notion of justice seems to assume a stable and continuous subject who is called upon to do justice, this despite Derrida's earlier rejection of a stable metaphysical subject.[71] Apart from the metaphysical assumptions in Derrida's notion of justice, there are hidden epistemic claims. The greatest of these is simply that the demands of justice can be known (at least to Derrida himself) and then used as a sort of litmus test for whether legal decisions and laws are "just." But to posit a stable and knowable "justice" which emerges from an unvarying relationship between stable and knowable subjects seems to carry more metaphysical baggage than Derrida ought to tolerate.

Even if the metaphysical and epistemic problems are bracketed, Derrida must come to grips with another problem, namely, the difficulty of explaining the specific demands of justice. How can a system of justice be laid out if, as Derrida claims, justice cannot be encoded, is always "to come," and is "unpresentable"? This problem becomes more apparent when one turns to specific issues. For example, does justice require a system of private property or collective ownership of the means of production? Is it consistent with both, or is Derrida bracketing this issue? Again, justice to the other would seem to require freedom of speech so that the other can be heard, but does justice require freedom for *hate* speech and pornography? What about a mutual sadomasochistic society? Should there be a death penalty? What about surrogate parenting, the rights of future generations, and affirmative action? It would seem that Derrida's notion of justice cannot provide a sufficiently determinate ground for deciding these issues. To be sure, these are difficult questions for any theory, yet it seems that they are especially difficult for Derrida, as opposed to, say, Rawls or Dworkin.[72] This is because Rawls and Dworkin think that justice can be encoded into specific principles and put to work in our practices and institutions.[73] By denying that justice can be formulated into concrete principles, Derrida gives justice a transcendental status that is too far removed from the everyday world in which justice must be rendered.

Furthermore, Derrida's formulation of justice lacks a practical strategy for determining the demands of justice; he lacks a decisional procedure such as Rawls' "original position" or Habermas' "ideal speech situation." The lack of a decisional procedure makes arbitration difficult when a dispute arises between competing parties. For example, if there is a dispute on the issue of rent control between a landlords' consortium and a tenants' rights association, how is one to use Derrida's theory to decide whether a rent-control statute is "just"? What, exactly, does "openness to the other" require in this scenario, and how does one arbitrate a dispute when both parties claim that they are being open to the other? Certainly, openness to the other will require that all sides to a dispute be heard, but at some point a decision must be reached, and one needs *grounds* for such a decision and a procedure for resolving the dispute. Derrida's notion of justice seems too slender a reed to serve as a workable framework for reaching decisions in hard cases.

It might be argued that Derrida's notion of justice is not directed at particular matters of justice but at the foundations of legal systems as a whole. This is the interpretation provided by Drucilla Cornell. According to her, deconstruction "exposes the quasi-transcendental conditions that establish any system, including a legal system as a system. This exposure, which in Derrida proceeds through what he calls the 'logic of parergonality' demonstrates how the very establishment of a system as a system implies a *beyond* to it, precisely by virtue of what it excludes."[74] She is correct in that Derrida often focuses on the foundations of legal systems *as systems.* This approach is more apparent in Derrida's piece on Nelson Mandela, where he points out that when the South African constitution proclaimed the formal equality of all men, this proclamation was a performative act of fiction because all men were *not* equal in South Africa. As such, the South African constitution could be deconstructed as an unjust fictional act based on a lie about the universality of rights and the equality of all (white) men.[75]

On Cornell's reading, Derrida is trying to set forth a notion of justice aimed at the level of legal *systems* and not at the level of particular laws. He is trying to show how entire categories of legal thought should be deconstructed. This interpretation is consistent with Derrida's statement that "a deconstructive interrogation . . . starts . . . by destabilizing, complicating, or bringing out the paradoxes of values like those of the proper and property in all their registers, of the subject, and so of the responsible subject, of the subject of law, and the subject of morality. . . . *A problematization of the foundations* of law, morality, and politics."[76] This implies that Derrida is concerned with justice at a level deeper than that currently discussed by, say, Rawls, who seeks to provide explicit principles to be used for arrangements of distributive justice. On this reading, Derrida's discussion of justice is "transcendental" in the Kantian sense: he is exploring the conditions for the possibility of justice.

But this reading can only be taken so far. Derrida is not concerned solely with problematizing the foundations of entire legal systems, because he mentions particular problems that need to be solved, such as AIDS, the homeless, racism, and animal rights. He does, in fact, seem to have his eye on justice at the level of actual issues. This is where one runs into difficulties in the application of Derrida's concept of justice. The call to do justice to the other, as an incalculable demand to speak to the other in the other's language, is simply too minimalist to serve as the basis of a jurisprudential program. Certainly Derrida provides grounds for saying that slavery, discrimination, and animal testing are unjust because they fail to do justice to the other; but he does not provide a mechanism for deciding other questions of law, the most important of which is the economic structure of the just state.[77]

It might be objected that even Kantian theory is itself vague on particular legal matters. All things considered, Derrida's notion of justice is perhaps no more unwieldy than Kant's categorical imperative, which has proved difficult to apply in hard cases. This response has some merit, but it only goes so far, since Kant at least made the effort to extend his theory to particular legal issues, such as the structure of the just state, inheritance laws, civil disobedience, the death penalty, and so on. I believe that Derrida will encounter serious problems in fleshing out his theory (more so than Kant), given his critical writings on "logocentrism" and, particularly, his critique of classical metaphysics and epistemology.

To start with, since Derrida rejects transcendental entities as "logocentric" fictions and decries the "metaphysics of presence," it is unclear how he can accord justice with the status of a "call" or "ghost" which stands in judgment of law. What, exactly, is the metaphysical and epistemic status of this "justice"? How can it be "present" in all contexts when Derrida has elsewhere said that nothing is ever fully present in and of itself?[78] I suppose that Derrida would say that justice is neither a material thing nor a form but (following Levinas) an "ethical relation," a way of being. This perhaps circumvents the metaphysical problem, but it raises the epistemic issue: How can one know when one has approached justice? Given two interpretations, which interpretation is more just? Who should decide which interpretation is better? Furthermore, is there a single "justice" for all people, wherever they may be situated, or does justice vary with history and tradition?

More important, how is it possible to even broach the issue of justice when the latter is the experience of the impossible? Derrida holds that justice is elusive: "It is possible, as an experience of the impossible, there where, even if it does not exist (or does not yet exist, or never does exist), *there* is justice."[79] Derrida feels compelled to make justice this elusive because, as I have pointed out, he wants to uphold a Platonic and Kantian theory of justice while disclaiming the Platonic and Kantian baggage typically accompanying their conceptions of justice. But a justice thus severed from all epistemic and metaphysical warrants is not sufficiently strong to support a coherent legal or political program. There is simply not very much one can say about Derrida's justice except that it is the type of thing of which very little can be said, since it can never be codified or set down as a group of principles. One can only affirm this type of justice at the cost of having very little to say about it. When viewed in this way, it is understandable why Derrida holds that justice cannot be addressed directly: he has so enervated the concept of justice that there is literally nothing left to say about it: "Justice as the experience of absolute alterity is unpresentable."[80] But an "unpresentable" justice which has been so removed from our existing practices and principles is hardly useful in hard cases.

A final problem is that Derrida seems to speak of justice as a *universal* call to the other, an event beyond events which permeates every context: "Justice as the experience of absolute alterity is unpresentable, *but it is the chance of the event and the condition of history.* No doubt in an unrecognizable history, of course, for those who believe they know what they're talking about when they use this word, whether its a matter of social, ideological, political, juridical or some other history."[81] This seems perilously close to a claim that justice has a single meaning that holds constant throughout history as the ground or condition for history itself.[82] The claim that justice has a *fixed* meaning as the "condition of history" would seem unwarranted given Derrida's insistence that "there are only contexts without any center of absolute anchoring."[83] It is not clear how Derrida can say that justice is "the condition of history" which "transcends this or that determination of a given context" and then turn around and criticize other philosophers as mired in a logocentric metaphysics of presence.

Toward an Assessment

I have argued that Derrida's notion of justice borrows heavily from the Platonic and Kantian tradition yet removes the metaphysical and epistemic baggage that made these theories powerful in the hands of Plato and Kant. As a result, Derrida's notion of justice is somewhat empty. Apart from internal inconsistencies, there are problems of vagueness in application. So, how is one to assess Derrida's project?

On the one hand, I can see how it might be argued, strangely enough, that Derrida's approach is attractive precisely because it imposes a seemingly supererogatory demand to do justice to the other even though this justice can never be fulfilled. This is the interpretation of Derrida offered by Drucilla

Cornell, who argues that deconstruction reveals that every legal system points beyond itself, beyond law, and hence triggers a "quasi-transcendental analysis."[84] For Cornell, deconstruction resists the collapse of justice into positive law and therefore provides a program for transforming the legal order. In this sense deconstruction is "utopian":

> Deconstruction keeps open the "beyond" of currently unimaginable transformative possibilities precisely in the name of Justice. And so we are left with a command, "be just with Justice," and an infinite responsibility to which we can never close our eyes or ears through an appeal to what "is." . . .
> Derrida's account gives greater attention to the necessary "utopian" moment in the vigilant insistence on the maintenance of the divide between law, established norms, and Justice.[85]

If this is the proper interpretation of Derrida's position, then deconstruction can hardly be accused of nihilism or irrationality in jurisprudential matters because it imposes eternal vigilance in the service to the other and is therefore more demanding than most ethical theories. Derrida does, in fact, speak of justice as an impossible demand, an incalculable duty to speak to the other in the other's language, to give to the other without expectation of return. So in a certain sense one can rightly say that Derrida provides a deeply rigorous ethical theory. Although he relies on Plato and Kant, he tries to avoid the logocentric metaphysics which he finds so problematic in these and other thinkers (including, surprisingly, Gadamer and Austin).[86]

I hesitate to allow Derrida to have it both ways: he cannot retain the deconstructive critique of foundational systems which runs through his earlier works and then turn around and erect a seemingly foundational notion of justice that works as a quasi-transcendental idea. He cannot decry the metaphysics of presence and the Cartesian *cogito* and then say that justice is grounded in the relation of incalculable indebtedness from one subject to another subject qua participation in humanity. I would suggest that there is something highly paradoxical—even contradictory—about Derrida's double gesture of deconstructing Western metaphysics and then lauding the "classical emancipatory ideal" which relies upon Western metaphysics.

The basic problem for Derrida is simply this: all ethical positions require some metaphysical or epistemic commitments. The commitments may be great (as in Plato's forms and Kant's noumenal world) or they may be weak (as in Habermasian ideal speech-act conditions), but there must be some constraints for an ethical theory to get off the ground. It seems to me that Derrida's notion of justice (as something which transcends the law but is never reached and cannot be encoded) carries metaphysical and epistemic baggage that is equal to or greater than the warrants required on, say, Gadamer or Habermas' approach. Derrida wishes to reject alternative approaches as metaphysically weighed down yet fails to see that his own theory presupposes quite a few metaphysical claims, including a quasi-transcendental justice that has a stable and univocal meaning through time. My suspicion is that Derrida's long-standing deconstructive efforts in other areas of philosophy have rendered him incapable of holding a workable position in the area of ethics and politics. Ultimately something has to give: either he learns to live with the metaphysical assumptions necessary to ground an ethical and political theory or he learns to live without these types of theories. I suspect that Derrida will need to posit the following: the existence of a reasonably unified and stable self who hears the call to justice; the primacy and universality of an ethical relation between two subjects; the inherent value of each subject and each "other" to whom a duty is owed; and the existence of justice as a stable idea that impinges on every ethical decision. Finally, Derrida will have to grant that there are better and worse interpretations of the demands of justice, that some laws are a better approximation of justice than others. But the moment Derrida admits all of this, he will be contradicting his earlier, more deconstructive work.[87]

Derrida's "Force of Law" is a bold entry into the political arena, and it successfully challenges the widespread belief that deconstruction lacks a conception of justice. But it creates a new problem in that it announces a notion of justice which rests upon the types of metaphysical claims which Derrida has found problematic in other thinkers. Derrida's overall approach will need to be rethought in order to make room for his emerging conception of justice. As things stand, Derrida does not offer enough to generate the positive jurisprudence one seeks.

6 &✦ Lyotard: Postmodern Gaming and a Plurality of Justices

In this chapter I will examine and critique Jean-François Lyotard's writings on law and justice. One of my reasons for including Lyotard in this book is that his work is frequently cited but rarely discussed in detail by legal scholars, who are doubtless put off by his obscure and often difficult texts. However, a familiarity with Lyotard's work is essential for anyone who wants to understand postmodernism; indeed, most studies of postmodernism begin with Lyotard's seminal book *The Postmodern Condition,* which has come to define the genre. Because Lyotard is perhaps *the* central figure of postmodernism, devoting an entire chapter to teasing out his position on justice and law seems warranted.

Lyotard is somewhat unique among so-called postmodern and poststructuralist philosophers in that he does not shrink from a direct discussion of issues in ethics, law, justice, and politics. But while Lyotard devotes considerable attention to questions of justice, his approach is highly complicated—even convoluted at times—drawing upon esoteric and obscure strains in continental philosophy, speech-act theory, Greek philosophy, and aesthetics. In what follows I will try to render Lyotard's notion of justice intelligible and coherent to a lay audience of Anglo-American legal scholars. In the first part of this chapter I discuss Lyotard's general theoretical approach to justice and law. After viewing Lyotard's position in its best light and explaining its attractions, I then subject it to a searching critique. Ultimately I conclude that Lyotard's work on law serves as a useful check against some of our basic liberal values (including consensus, tolerance, and neutrality), but his conception of justice is largely unworkable. From reading Lyotard one gains an increased respect for the cultural differences which should not only be tolerated but encouraged; Lyotard makes a strong and moving plea for tolerance under the law because he understands the subtle ways in which minorities are silenced and disempowered. Ironically, Lyotard's antifoundationalism provides no firm basis for insisting that the law should be tolerant in the first place. My conclusion, then, is that Lyotard provides insight into some of the problems inherent in our existing system of justice, but he fails to erect a convincing system of his own, that is, he articulates a negative jurisprudence but fails to erect a positive one in its place.

Lyotard on Postmodern Law and Justice

Lyotard has been an important contributor to the philosophical scene in France since the sixties, but he has come to worldwide prominence only during the last ten years or so, which was about the time his focus shifted to issues of justice, especially the problem of reaching justice in a multicultural society that is deeply divided by race, class, and gender.[1] These questions are treated at length in three of Lyotard's works, each of which is required reading in order to get a good idea of his conception of justice: *The Postmodern Condition* (1984 [originally published in French in 1979]), *Just Gaming*, with Jean-Loup Thébaud (1985 [1979]), and *The Differend* (1988 [1983]).[2] Although Lyotard has continued to address issues of law and justice in his more recent work, I wish to focus initially on these three works, augmenting my analysis periodically with selections from his later writings.[3]

THE POSTMODERN CONDITION

The Postmodern Condition ostensibly reported on the status of knowledge in advanced industrial societies, a state of affairs which Lyotard terms "postmodern." Lyotard thought that "the sciences" (understood in the European sense to include all academic disciplines from physics to sociology to philosophy) have historically sought legitimation from "metanarratives" which served as justifications for the scientific endeavor. These narratives arose as ways of legitimating science, purportedly answering the questions, "Why do we engage in physics, sociology, philosophy, economics, or political science?" and "What are we moving toward or hoping to find?" According to Lyotard, the two dominant narratives that justified the pursuit of knowledge were the *emancipatory narrative* and the *speculative narrative*. The emancipatory narrative supported the scientific enterprise by supposing that the pursuit of knowledge would lead to emancipation and increased liberty. This narrative can be traced back to Kant's claim that the Enlightenment represents man's escape from tyranny though the use of reason and public debate.[4] The speculative narrative, which has its roots in Continental thinkers such as Hegel, supported the scientific enterprise by supposing that all knowledge could someday be unified into a coherent, totalizing scheme, a sort of unified field theory that would bring unity and order to all human endeavors, from affairs of state to everyday life.[5]

An example of the emancipatory narrative would be the claim that political scientists can discover the best political and economic structure for a just state in which the citizens voluntarily and autonomously give their assent to the law and are thereby free and emancipated. Certainly, this narrative finds a home in Jefferson's notion that the government should foster a coming together of citizens to deliberate in a public forum about the laws that will govern them. The emancipatory narrative is also at home in the Marxist claim that science will provide the proletariat with the skills to emancipate themselves.[6]

The speculative narrative is perhaps less common in Anglo-American countries than it is on the Continent. Lyotard exemplifies this narrative by referring to Heidegger's claim (during his days as a university rector and Nazi supporter) that the Nazis would unify the German state in line with the demands of the Germanic race and spirit.[7] The speculative narrative can be found in any claim which supports science as a way of serving the greater good of, say, the "national spirit" or the "American way."

According to Lyotard, these types of grand narratives are no longer believable: "The grand narrative has lost its credibility, regardless of what mode of unification it uses, regardless of whether it is a speculative narrative or a narrative of emancipation."[8] Part of the reason for the loss of credibility is that these narratives have not made good on their promise: the emancipatory narrative did not lead to liberation, and the speculative narrative did not bring unity of purpose. After two hundred years in furtherance of these narratives, we seem to be no closer to emancipation or rational government:

> Auschwitz refutes speculative doctrine. . . . Berlin 1953, Budapest 1956, Czechoslovakia 1968, Poland 1980 (I could mention others) refute the doctrine of historical materialism. . . . May 1968 [the Paris student riots] refutes the doctrine of parliamentary liberalism. The passages promised by the great doctrinal syntheses end in bloody impasses. Whence the sorrow of the spectators in the end of the twentieth century.[9]

In other words, history has proved both liberalism and communism to be less than stellar, or at least less than what was promised. We are moving neither toward emancipation nor toward a rational society. This had led to our present state of suspicion in the face of grand claims about the promise of human emancipation and unity. In the eyes of many people living in Western democracies, the scientific knowledge we have accumulated (especially sophisticated computer technology) appears to be enslaving and oppressing rather than liberating or unifying.

For Lyotard, the breakdown of grand narratives can be used as a criterion to separate the epochs known as *modern* and *postmodern*. A given endeavor or pursuit (e.g., a political platform, a motion picture, a university's mission, a constitution) can be termed modern if it relies on a grand narrative, whereas it can be deemed postmodern if it relies on smaller, more localized narratives.

That is, modernity and postmodernity are not defined in strictly historical terms but rather in terms of the types of legitimation they offer:

> I will use the term *modern* to designate any science that legitimates itself with reference to a metadiscourse of this kind making an explicit appeal to some grand narrative, such as the dialectics of Spirit, the hermeneutics of meaning, the emancipation of the rational or working subject, or the creation of wealth. . . . Simplifying to the extreme, I define *postmodern* as *incredulity toward metanarratives.*[10]

Lyotard thinks that the breakdown of grand narratives has left in its wake a diffuse and complicated web of micronarratives (sometimes referred to as "petite" or "small" narratives). These small narratives are relatively self-contained in that they hold jurisdiction over a small segment of life and do not aspire to govern all other areas of life. Unlike grand narratives, small narratives do not seek hegemony over other narratives. One can understand each small narrative as a sort of game having "moves" which differ from those in other small narratives. With the loss of grand narratives, "all we can do is gaze in wonderment at the diversity of discursive species [of localized narratives]."[11]

Lyotard thinks that each person lies at the intersection of dozens—or perhaps hundreds—of these small narratives and games. Indeed, the "personhood" of the individual is *created* by these narratives: the self is a narrative construction. Lyotard often refers to these small narratives as "language-games" (adopting the term from Wittgenstein). He sees the individual as constructed by his or her participation in these language-games. The individual does not use language and language-games as a tool but rather is played by the games themselves, with the latter determining the individual: "There are many different language-games—a heterogeneity of elements. They only give rise to institutions in patches—local determinism. . . . Each of us lives at the intersection of many of these."[12] Examples of these games might include my participation as a tenant in the game of landlord–tenant relations, my role as a young lawyer struggling with older members of the bar, or my position as a Jew in a country that is mostly Gentile. No single legitimating formula applies to all of my endeavors (as a student, a son, a worker, a Jew, and so on). Rather, each of these games has its own set of rules, and no set of rules ought to apply beyond the scope of its own local game. For example, it would be wrong for me to take the rules that bind me as a worker and apply these rules to my relationship with my girlfriend. Furthermore, within the boyfriend–girlfriend relationship game, I might undergo a series of shifts, sometimes playing the role of addressor and sometimes addressee, each time using different rules to govern my behavior. For Lyotard each game has its own rules and its own conception of justice in accordance with those rules. For example, in my relationship with my parents it may be necessary and just that I reveal my secret hopes and dreams, but this would not be just in the game which I play with the Internal Revenue Service. For Lyotard justice is local and imminent within each game, such that there can be no overarching and transcendental principle of justice which applies to all people all of the time in all of their affairs.

But if our experience is informed by a series of radically incommensurate and heterogeneous language-games and justice is only local, how can we find a rule for regulating the complex web of language-games through which we pass? That is, how can we find a *political* structure which governs the various language-games in which we find ourselves? Lyotard poses this very question at the beginning of *The Postmodern Condition*: "Where, after the metanarratives, can legitimacy reside?"[13] His answer, which will be analyzed in detail, is that we should abandon hope for a single hegemonic principle of justice (e.g., a categorical imperative or a Rawlsian decision procedure) and instead embrace the idea of a "multiplicity of justices, each one of them defined in relation to the rules specific to each game."[14] Paradoxically, as we shall see, the multiplicity of games is ensured by a single overarching principle of justice (analogous to a Kantian categorical imperative) which forces us to keep the various games distinct and autonomous.

It is crucial to understand that Lyotard sees classical liberalism (of the type espoused by Locke, Kant, and Jefferson) as a particularly *modern* approach because it relies on a grand narrative, in this case the narrative that autonomous subjects can come together freely to reach consensus on the rules which will govern them; hence the liberal sees the workplace, personal relationships, and politics as the product of agreement or consent among autonomous individuals. This idea that consensus among free peoples is the global solution to all of our problems is characteristic of a modern approach in which a single formula is used to regulate the rules of disparate language-games. Lyotard feels that the imposition of a single standard on all aspects of life (the standard of "consensus") results in a kind of terrorism: "Consensus does violence to the heterogeneity of language-games."[15] Furthermore, given the fact that each of us occupies different roles in a complex web of games, consensus in the liberal sense is an "impossibility" because any consensus will be "manufactured."[16] In layman's terms, consensus is a legitimating myth that has been used as an excuse for state tyranny, a way of rationalizing the accumulation of knowledge that only enslaves us but does not lead to the emancipation promised.

For Lyotard the social bond is constituted as an aggregate of disparate language-games, such that "the social subject itself seems to dissolve in this dissemination of language-games."[17] No single game is more legitimate than any other since each carries its own unique mode of legitimation. As a result, there is no overarching principle by which the games can be ordered and regulated, "no possibility that language-games can be unified or totalized in any metadiscourse."[18] Yet it is precisely the goal of liberal society to subject all discourses to a master principle of consensus, whereby all people are deemed capable of creating and assenting to the rules which will bind them. Consensus involves a tyranny by the majority through which Western democracies impose a single set of values on the disparate language-games, silencing some of the players in an act of terrorism: "By terror I mean the efficiency gained by eliminating, or threatening to eliminate, a player from the language-game one shares with him. He is silenced or consents, not because he has been refuted, but because his ability to participate has been threatened."[19] This means that consensus is "outmoded" and "terroristic" because it silences minorities and other marginalized groups by denying them a role as a player in the political game. Thus, Lyotard rejects the idea of a single standard of justice in favor of a series of microjustices, each tied to a localized small narrative, which will give a voice to those who are excluded:

> The answer is: Let us wage a war on totality; let us be witness to the unpresentable; let us activate the differences and save the honor of the name.[20]

> There is no genre whose hegemony over others would be just.[21]

> Every one of us belongs to several minorities, and what is important, none of these prevails. It is only then that we can say that the society is just.[22]

In other words, let us give a voice to groups which have been excluded by the dominant culture, to positions which have gone unrepresented.

At this point the reader should realize that while *The Postmodern Condition* is subtitled *A Report on Knowledge,* the book quickly turns into a position paper on justice and legitimation in the postmodern age, themes treated more fully in *Just Gaming*.

JUST GAMING

Most of the themes introduced in *The Postmodern Condition* can be found in *Just Gaming*, although Lyotard adds a few interesting twists that should be explored. Lyotard begins with the now familiar claim that consensus is impossible, that is, manufactured.[23] He then argues that political theory has moved through three paradigms: the *classical* approach, the *modern* approach, and the *pagan* (postmodern) approach.[24] In the classical approach, exemplified by Plato, the philosopher begins with a model of the just society and then attempts to manipulate the existing society so that it matches the model. Justice is understood only by the philosopher or statesman who announces a master plan for the state. In Plato's model, each person is assigned a role in the service of the state and is not free to experiment with new roles or invent new lifestyles; society is static and immobile. According to this system, a single form of justice is imposed from above to govern every aspect of the citizens' behavior.

In the modern approach, exemplified by Kant and Rousseau (and, I would add, Hobbes and Locke), justice is derived from the free choice of autonomous individuals who come together to express their consensus in a social contract. According to Lyotard, the modern approach is the dominant paradigm today, holding that "justice lies in the self-determination of peoples. In other words, there is a close relation between autonomy and self-determination: one gives oneself one's own laws. And so we get the idea of autonomy that has dominated, and still dominates, the modern problematic of politics and justice."[25] Lyotard argues that the modern approach (the autonomy model) must be rejected on the grounds that people are *not* free and autonomous but are instead determined by the narratives in which they are situated. In a fascinating series of passages, Lyotard compares people in our society to members of the Amazonian Cashinahua tribe, whose lives are framed by a series of shared narratives. When a member of the Cashinahua tribe tells a narrative, he reveals his name *after* the story. For Lyotard this is very significant because it shows that the story comes *before* the individual; in other words, the self is created and constituted as a product of the collectively shared narrative. Lyotard thinks that our situation is similar to that of the Cashinahua in that we, too, are created by narratives. Individuals in our society are "named" by the stories they hear, which means that they are not autonomous:

> This implies the very opposite of autonomy: heteronomy. It also implies that, *ultimately, it is not true that a people can ever give itself its own institutions.*[26]

> In paganism [postmodernism], there is the intuition, the idea . . . that no maker of statements, no utterer, is ever autonomous. On the contrary, an utterer is always someone who is first of all an addressee, and I would even say that one is destined.[27]

Individuals are free to make changes (experimental "moves") within the context of their narratives, but they get their identity through the narrative itself, which means that people are not free and autonomous in the deeper sense that they might be able to create a government from gound zero through the use of reason. One can subvert the narrative in which one is situated by inventing new moves, but there is no way to step outside the narratives altogether in order to be truly and deeply autonomous.

Lyotard parlays this analysis into the claim that there can be no "metadiscourse" which grounds political and ethical decisions.[28] This leads to the third approach to justice, namely, the pagan (postmodern) model, in which one abandons the mistaken search for a fail-safe conception of justice. The pagan approach does not specify a model or paradigm for the just state; rather, it points out the dangers of adopting a large-scale model. In other words, there are no ultimate grounds for choosing, say, capitalism over communism, and therefore the choice must be based on opinion instead of reason. The error of modern thinkers lies precisely in their supposition that questions of justice revolve around issues of truth and reason.[29]

Lyotard concludes from this line of thinking—wrongly, I feel—that when a person makes a normative judgment, he or she judges *without criteria*.[30] Part of the claim here is that there is an unbridgeable gap between a *descriptive* claim (e.g., Hobbes' claim that "mankind is naturally aggressive") and a *prescriptive* claim ("we ought to create a Leviathan"). For Lyotard a prescriptive claim ("we ought to do X") cannot be grounded in a descriptive claim (i.e., a claim about ontology):

> There is a change of language-game [from descriptive to prescriptive]. One describes a model of strategy, of society, of economy, and then, when one passes to prescriptions, one has jumped into another language-game. One is without criteria, yet one must decide.

> I believe that one of the properties of paganism is to leave prescriptives hanging, that is, they are not derived from an ontology.[31]

Lyotard thinks that the law (the legal system) represents a futile attempt to legitimate prescriptive claims on the basis of descriptive claims about human nature, consensus, or autonomy. For any given piece of legislation, even if it is true descriptively that the elected representatives voted in favor of the legislation, it does not follow prescriptively that we ought to obey it, nor that the particular law is thereby just or binding.[32] There is an unbridgeable gap between the descriptive claim that "this law has the assent of the people" (a claim which Lyotard denies, in any event) and the prescriptive claim that "you ought to obey this law because it has the assent of the people."

Lyotard concludes from this that there is no valid overarching principle of justice: "There is no just society."[33] We cannot have recourse to models of justice (Plato) and we cannot rely on autonomy and consensus (Rousseau and Kant). That is, we cannot tie law to ontological claims about "human nature," human destiny, autonomy, or consensus. What's worse, we can't seem to get beyond justice at the local level; there is justice only within the imminent logic of each language-game, but there is no overarching political justice by which to run the country. Any master principle of justice will, according to Lyotard, commit an injustice against those who do not share the language-game from which the overarching principle is derived.

But if there is no overarching principle, what is left for ethics and law? On what grounds can we decide how to act? It seems that the realm of law is precisely where we *need* overarching principles so that people can live peaceably. Without an overarching principle (a grand narrative for the political arrangement), what's to stop society from sliding into a war of all against all?

Lyotard offers a solution of sorts to this dilemma, first on the level of ethics and then on the level of law. On the level of ethics, he says that even though there is no overarching principle, we experience something like an imperative to do the right thing. We find ourselves as addressees of an obligation that has no sender: we are called upon to be ethical and to behave justly, yet we must remain ignorant of the source of this obligation. This obscure claim is analogized by Lyotard to the Judaic notion that God gives commands without revealing His exact nature; we must act while bracketing any doubts about the source of our obligation.[34] In other words, we experience an imperative "You Must," yet this imperative cannot be deduced from a descriptive claim and it cannot be grounded. We experience obligation, but it is ungrounded, for "it is proper to prescription to be left hanging in midair."[35] Lyotard sees this conception of obligation as a legacy from Kant and Levinas.[36] From Kant he borrows the notion that obligation is merely an Idea of Reason that cannot be traced to a source in the phenomenal world, and from Levinas he borrows the claim that one is called upon to do justice to the "other." Lyotard claims that this obligation is "contentless": it does not provide criteria or substantive grounds for our choices, but simply tells us that we must decide.[37] As such, we lack grounds for our decisions and must decide on a case-by-case basis. For example, at one point in *Just Gaming* Lyotard is asked whether it would be just to blow up an American computer that was programming the bombing of Hanoi. Lyotard says that it *would* be just to blow up the computer, but he refuses to give grounds for his decision:

> Who is right? It is up to everyone to decide. If you asked me why I am on that side, I think that I would answer that I do not have to answer the question "why?," and that this is on the order of . . . transcendence. That is, here I feel a prescription to oppose a given thing, and I think that it is a just one. This is where I feel that I am indeed playing the game of the just. . . . When I say "transcendence" it means: I do not know who is sending me the prescription in question.[38]

Strangely enough, Lyotard then appeals to the Kantian notion that the bombing of Hanoi is morally wrong because it "was doing something that prohibited that the whole of reasonable beings could continue to exist."[39] This appears very close to the Kantian claim that moral principles must be universalizable: "Act only on that maxim through which you can at the same time will that it should become a universal law."[40] Despite his reliance on a seemingly universal principle of justice, Lyotard continues to insist that no single principle should govern all the language-games, and that the games should remain autonomous. But this leads to a serious problem: if there is no principle of justice outside of the various language-games, then there would seem to be nothing unjust about one game overtaking another. For example, what is to stop the game of fascism from overtaking that of pacifism, and what grounds can we appeal to in our belief that the neo-Nazis are being unjust when they propose to deport all immigrants? If there is no metadiscourse of justice, how can Lyotard claim that each game should be left intact, or that the game of socialism is better than the game of fascism? It would seem that some sort of choice between games is necessary, that a metaprinciple is required for political action.

Lyotard's response to this dilemma is to argue that we should seek to preserve a plurality of differing conceptions of justice, each appropriate for a limited sphere:

> And the idea that I think we need today in order to make decisions in political matters cannot be the idea of the totality, or of the unity, of a [political] body. It can only be the idea of a multiplicity or of a diversity.

> Yes, there is a multiplicity of justices, each one of them defined in relation to the rules specific to each game.[41]

In order to ensure that each sphere remains intact, Lyotard further proposes that we adopt a universal rule of justice which operates as a referee, keeping the language-games separate so that no single conception of justice is hegemonic: "And then the justice of multiplicity: *it is assured, paradoxically, by a prescriptive of universal value.* It prescribes the singular justice of each game."[42] This is supposed to solve the question of how we can have a diversity of language-games without having any single game dominate the others.[43] But this universal prescription ("keep the games distinct") cannot be justified by Lyotard since he earlier denied that there is a metadiscourse that covers all the disparate language-games.[44] Lyotard recognizes the paradox, concluding *Just Gaming* (which takes the form of a dialogue) by laughing at his new, paradoxical role as "the great prescriber."[45]

Lyotard's conclusion, then, is that one should be tolerant of the various small narratives within our culture, and that one should resist the impulse to subsume all narratives under a single conception of justice. He clearly feels that the imposition of a master narrative results in a silencing of minorities, in much the same way that adopting a state-sponsored "History of the United States" from the perspective of propertied white males would perhaps silence the version of history offered by Native Americans. In order to be just, one must listen for the silencing of dissident voices[46] and must experiment with new moves in our existing language-games so that we "work at the limits of what the rules permit, in order to invent new moves."[47]

THE DIFFEREND

The Differend represents an updating and modification of Lyotard's earlier work, but certain factors remain constant. From *The Postmodern Condition* Lyotard has retained the notion that the postmodern political situation appears as a war between disparate language-games which advocate diverse and incommensurate political solutions such as market capitalism, socialism, and fascism. Again, there is no overlapping consensus (no collective criteria) by which one could deduce grounds for choosing between these language-games, since "heterogeneity makes consensus impossible." Lyotard affirms that postmodernity has given up on the modern quest for a neutral metalanguage and he reiterates the growing implausibility of grand schemes such as "liberation of the masses," "the forward march of history," or "the victory of the proletariat." Instead, one now finds a vast array of localized micronarratives which are not translatable into each other and which compete for political recognition. Within and between these games there is little rational dialogue but much "agonistics" (verbal jousting). From *Just Gaming* Lyotard has retained the idea that the differing conceptions of justice are heterogenous, and that the hegemony of one version over another will lead to a "silencing" of the party dominated by the controlling narrative.

In *The Differend* Lyotard has dropped his earlier references to language-games and now speaks in somewhat similar terms about "phrases" and "phrase regimens." He argues that the postmodern era appears as a vast system of incommensurate phrase regimens and genres. Just as he had argued in *Just Gaming* that each type of statement has its own logic, he now argues that each type of statement belongs to a unique phrase regimen.[48] Lyotard also introduces the term "differend" to denote the remainder or leftover produced by the incommensurability of phrases and phrase systems. The term implies a conflict, an imperfect matching between phrase systems, where one system is not translatable into the other. The differend is produced in the clash between two conflicting systems of justice, where the subordinate individual (the person being judged) does not share the basic tenets of the system under which he or she is judged.

Lyotard also points out that there is a danger which consists in denying a forum and a language to a person in order to explain how he or she has been harmed. For example, the wrong perpetrated against blacks in America does not consist merely in the fact that the government reneged on a promise to them ("three acres and a mule"); a deeper source of harm was that for centuries they lacked standing as a free people to bring actions for the cruelties inflicted upon them by the dominant Southern culture. It is not simply that they were violated *under* the law but that they were victimized by the *absence* of a forum in which they could speak. In such cases, the justice system excludes the individual from having a voice that can be heard on terms which the system will understand. Lyotard describes the differend in precisely this way:

> I would like to call a *differend* the case where the plaintiff is divested of the means to argue and becomes for that reason a victim.

> [A] differend would be a case of conflict, between (at least) two parties, that cannot be equitably resolved for lack of a rule of judgment applicable to both arguments.[49]

Lyotard distinguishes the differend from "damages," which can be *proven* to the satisfaction of the dominant system of justice and which are therefore reparable in a "litigation" under the law. A person who suffers a wrong that cannot be proven under the present system is a true victim, and his or her claim constitutes a differend lying outside the system of justice. The differend is silent since it cannot be recognized; it does not get a voice or a hearing under the existing system because the plaintiff lacks standing. As a result, the differend is reduced to a kind of mute silence because it cannot be understood by those who caused the differend to exist in the first place.[50] This analysis can lead to what some have termed "the ethics of the differend," which seeks to identify and give voice to the experience of incommensurability.[51]

Lyotard's examples of those who suffer the fate of the differend include Jews (because their reports about the Nazi gas chambers cannot be heard under the "logic" of neo-Nazi holocaust deniers), wage laborers (because their demand for nonalienating labor cannot be heard under a capitalist system in which labor is a commodity), and indigenous peoples (because their harms cannot be recognized by the justice system of their oppressors). An excellent example of the differend would be the fate of Native Americans who were denied standing to sue in colonial courts for the encroachment by colonists on their land.[52] Since the Native Americans were deprived (by law) of the right to sue, they suffered a harm that was beyond repair under the existing justice system; indeed, they were silenced because they never received a hearing on the merits of their case. The key point for Lyotard is that oppression is insidious and subtle: more often than not, one doesn't beat one's opponent through an argument inside a particular forum so much as deny him or her a forum in the first place. An example of this can be found in the fact that our current system of justice allows for equal access to the courts, but poor people are often incapable of getting a hearing in court because they lack the appropriate resources; as a result, their voices go unheard.

In a familiar move, Lyotard reiterates the claim that different speech-acts constitute different phrase systems; they are also heterogenous, such that they constitute different "universes."[53] Thus, the universe of prescriptives is separate from the universe of descriptives, and so on. According to Lyotard, "There are a number of phrase regimens: reasoning, knowing, describing, recounting, questioning, showing, ordering, etc. Phrases from heterogeneous regimens cannot be translated from one into the other."[54] When one genre or phrase system is mapped over another, the incommensurability produces a differend, a remainder, an injustice, or a wrong that cannot be communicated or translated into the universe of the phrase regime or genre which is responsible for causing the differend.

Turning to law and ethics, Lyotard thinks that legal and moral standards are associated with prescriptive and normative utterances of the type "you should do X" or "X is the right thing to do." According to Lyotard, we cannot do without prescriptives, but we can never ground them in descriptive statements, as we are wont to do, for example, when the preliminary statement "You must obey the law" is grounded in "because the law is authorized by God and the general will." For Lyotard prescriptives cannot be tied to an ontology, to a description of human nature or history: "I believe that one of the properties of paganism [postmodernism] is to leave prescriptions hanging, that is, they are not derived from an ontology. This seems essential to me."[55] This means that positions in law, ethics, and politics must be left hanging, ungrounded, lacking in justification; the differing positions must battle it out in an "agonistics" against other positions.

It is difficult to see how this approach can avoid lapsing into relativism, the view that there is no legitimate basis for choosing one political arrangement over another. Indeed, Lyotard says that there is no politics of reason and admits that "we do not have a rule for justice."[56] All the same, Lyotard argues that his approach is not nihilistic since he does provide at least one principle of justice, namely, that the disparate games should be kept separate: "The Idea of justice will consist in preserving the purity of each game."[57] The problem for Lyotard, of course, is finding a way to prove that this prescriptive claim is binding after having previously decried universal principles as terroristic.

Part of the solution to this paradox can be found in Lyotard's reliance on the notion of reflective judgment set forth in Kant's *Critique of Judgment*, especially his notion of the "sublime" as something which escapes categorization.[58] Because Lyotard's reliance on the *Critique of Judgment* is pervasive yet somewhat difficult to grasp, one should take the time to understand how Kant's work in aesthetics informs Lyotard's ideas on justice. After all, Lyotard has referred to himself as a Kantian "of the third Critique."[59]

Summarizing greatly, Kant distinguishes two types of judgments: determinate and reflective. Determinate judgment takes place when a particular representation is subsumed under a universal category in an act of cognition (this can occur in a *theoretical* judgment that a particular event had a particular cause, as well as in a *moral* judgment that a given action falls within the purview of the universal moral law). In a determinate judgment, a law is applied to a particular case, resulting in a truth claim that can be verified.

In contrast, reflective judgment takes place when a particular representation seems to evade criteria and categories, thereby setting the mind into a free play of faculties, spinning the imagination and the understanding in an effort to bring order to the experience. Once the faculties are put into play in reflective judgment, the free play can result in either a harmony or disharmony of the faculties. If a harmony results, we experience the Beautiful, but if there is disharmony, we experience the Sublime. When we experience the Sublime, we have a feeling that cannot easily be put into words because the Sublime cannot be delimited by space and time (I cannot *prove* that a painting is sublime by pointing at it). Kant thinks that the feelings triggered in reflective judgment are subjective since they lack objective instantiation, but at they same time they can be held in common by a "community of sense," a sort of idealized community of people who can compare their judgments with each other in a disinterested fashion. This means that matters of taste cannot be exhaustively formulated by a determinative standard (I cannot *prove* that a painting is beautiful), but one can still discuss aesthetics while lacking objective criteria (i.e., I might convince you to change your opinion of a painting).

All of this seems quite removed from the world of law and politics (some would say too removed),[60] but Lyotard thinks that we can use this approach as a model for how we might make judgments without objective criteria. It also provides a way of understanding how something fleeting (in Kant's case the Sublime; in Lyotard's the differend) could be felt so strongly yet resist encapsulation in words. As Lyotard writes, "In the differend, something 'asks' to be put into phrases, and suffers from the wrong of not being able to be put into phrases right away. . . . This state includes silence, which is a negative phrase, but it also calls upon phrases which are in principle possible. This state is signalled by what one ordinarily calls a feeling: 'One cannot find the words, etc.' "[61] Just as we search for an elusive formulation of the Sublime, we must be vigilant to ensure that marginalized groups are provided the means to give voice to their silent oppression.

Using this Kantian approach, Lyotard argues that discussions of justice evoke reflective judgments which cannot be placed within rigid categories. The desire to derive the just from the true (as in Plato) or from majority rule (as in Rousseau) is a misguided attempt to make an indeterminate judgment appear to have a determinate standard. According to Bill Readings, "The just judgment leaves the question of what justice might be open to discussion; it does not allow justice to become a determinate concept."[62] Lyotard's fear is that the adoption of a single, rigid conception of justice will become terroristic by ruling out all other versions, stifling new "moves" and experiments. Instead of grounding politics in claims of truth and reason, we should think of politics as a process of questioning our existing language-games and experimenting with new moves. In this way we "activate the differences [and] wage a war on totality."[63]

Problems with Lyotard's Account of Law and Justice

THE EMPTINESS OF LYOTARD'S NOTION OF JUSTICE

The first point I would like to raise is simply that Lyotard says too little about the structure of the just state. He spends a lot of time talking about justice, and he is aware that in a multicultural society there are different social groups with differing conceptions of justice who must somehow all get along. But ultimately he has not said very much about the principles and policies he thinks should be adopted as a framework for the just state, nor does he propose a procedural process (like Rawls' "original position" or Habermas' "ideal speech situation") which can be used to reach agreement on these principles. Lyotard argues that we must keep language-games distinct and autonomous, and he provides a universal prescription to ensure that this happens, but beyond that he seems to be curiously silent on substantive issues.

One will get a clearer idea of why he comes up short on a specific conception of justice by examining the extent to which he rules out various possible approaches. As we have seen, Lyotard denies that a given society can employ an overarching principle of justice, and he argues that every attempt at legitimation will fail. He thinks that, practically speaking, we must enact laws and make judicial decisions, but we have no criteria for such decisions. Furthermore, every decision will create a differend, a remainder lurking "outside" the system as an injustice. Finally, we cannot follow a model or plan for the just state (Plato), and we cannot rely on consensus to reach an agreement on the laws that will govern us (Rousseau).

Given this set of constraints, it is very difficult to see how a lawmaker or judge could ever perform his or her work, since every move is bound to create unjust differends and every decision must be made without criteria. It is hard to see how this could lead to an endorsement of *any* public arrangement, whether it be capitalism or communism, fascism or anarchism. Some reviewers have pointed out that Lyotard's failure to specify which political views are preferable leads him into a sort of inactivity or quietism that results in conservatism.[64] Even if Lyotard believes that we must have a "politics of opinion" instead of a "politics of reason," he would do well to present his own opinion and to prove, to the best of his ability, why others ought to share it.

It might be argued that Lyotard's notion of the differend can serve as an argument in favor of a limited form of government (perhaps a "minimal state" or "night watchman state") on the grounds that we should set up a political system which produces the *fewest* differends, a sort of "politics of least harm."[65] This is a charitable—and attractive—reading of Lyotard because it seems to entail limited governmental intrusion into private affairs, permitting the disparate language-games to flourish in the private sphere without being stifled by a hegemonic grand narrative.

The problem with this reading of Lyotard, as I have shown, is that one cannot find any support for the overarching principle which serves to keep the language-games distinct, given Lyotard's insistence (in *Just Gaming*) that one cannot have a metadiscourse of justice. But even if one tentatively accepts Lyotard's universalist prescription, there are problems with the consequences of recognizing the equal validity of a multiplicity of justices. It is easy to see how Lyotard's approach would let a thousand flowers bloom, but some of these are *dangerous*. If we are concerned to give a full platform to all marginalized groups, then we must be sensitive to hate groups like the Ku Klux Klan and the National Socialists, not to mention the Religious Right. It seems that most reviewers of Lyotard's work are content to suppose that when he says we should "activate the differences," he is arguing that we should give a voice to marginalized groups like gays, people of color, socialists, and so forth. But Lyotard's approach would also require giving a voice to hate groups which perhaps *should* be silenced by public opinion. What I am saying is simply that Lyotard's notion of the differend cuts both ways: it maximizes diversity, but in so doing it activates and legitimizes some groups who deserve to remain marginalized. Lyotard's heart is in the right place in wanting to effectuate a truly multicultural society that values diversity, but he does not realize that his approach actually empowers dangerous and reactionary groups.

I think one can best understand Lyotard's position if one views it as a humanitarian effort to avoid *all* the pitfalls of traditional political theory, but he does this only at the expense of failing to offer a program himself. Lyotard has a keen ear for the way in which minorities and marginalized groups have been oppressed and silenced, and his rejection of traditional concepts (e.g., neutrality, consensus, and legitimation) stems from his realization that great atrocities have been committed in their name. More than other contemporary thinkers, Lyotard correctly concludes that our current way of life is becoming harder to rationalize. Politicians talk about legitimate government, but people feel that the government is a joke. Lawyers speak of justice, yet the country is torn apart by race and class divisions. We plunder third world nations in order to "liberate" them, and we harm indigenous peoples and deprive them of their right to seek redress. Finally, we talk about consensus, but nobody really believes that we actually give ourselves laws; instead we feel that laws are imposed on us from above. Lyotard is correct in his diagnosis that we have begun to doubt the grand narratives that guided us in the past. Given this state, Lyotard is justifiably concerned about avoiding a simpleminded endorsement of our current system or a simplistic gloss on democracy and consensus as a cure-all. The problem, though, is that Lyotard is so afraid of offering up a particular set of principles of justice (for fear that any specific agenda will marginalize particular groups) that he comes up with no specific program at all. He never says which economic arrangement is just (though he variously criticizes capitalism and communism), nor does he specify the proper bounds of the criminal law (as do liberals like Mill, Feinberg, and Dworkin). Given his fear of consensus and his critique of autonomy, it is not clear whether Lyotard *can* even endorse democracy except to say that it makes sense according to one language-game but perhaps not according to others. In effect, he has backed himself into a theoretical corner such that no vision of the just state can be endorsed.

THE PARADOX OF JUDGING WITHOUT CRITERIA

A second problem involves Lyotard's notion that we must make ethical judgments without criteria, a position he purports to find in Aristotle's ethics and Kant's aesthetic theory. The philosophical sources which Lyotard cites for this claim do not seem to support his position. To begin with, Lyotard's reading of Aristotle is at odds with Aristotle's warning, in the *Politics,* that the just state must follow the *rule* of law: "Therefore he who bids the law rule may be deemed to bid God and Reason alone rule, but he who bids man rule adds an element of the beast; for desire is a wild beast, and passion perverts the mind of rulers, even when they are the best of men. The law is reason unaffected by desire."[66] Aristotle held that a judge's decision must be based on the criterion that it leads to the good life, which serves as the telos, or guiding principle, of ethical judgment and political legislation. The role of the legislator, then, is to inculcate virtuous habits, and this is the criterion for a good law: "For legislators make the citizens good by forming habits in them, and this is the wish of every legislator; and those who do not effect it miss their mark, *and it is in this that a good constitution differs from a bad one.*"[67] Lyotard's claim that we lack criteria is derived, in part, from Aristotle's claim that judgment is a habit or practice *(phronesis)* that proceeds on a case-by-case basis. It is true that Aristotle says that ethical reasoning cannot attain the same level of exactitude as mathematics because "fine and just actions . . . exhibit much variety and fluctuation," so in ethics we must be content to merely "indicate the truth roughly and in outline."[68] In other words, we can't have inflexible rules of morality which apply to every situation, but we can have general rules of thumb. The ultimate message is that rules for ethical and political decisions will be somewhat inexact, but this hardly supports the idea that we have *no* criteria.

Aristotle goes on to say that certain precepts of justice are natural laws, that is, laws which "exist everywhere [and have] the same force and do not exist by people thinking this or that."[69] This means that certain types of actions are just no matter where they take place. Given this, it is a mistake to suppose that Aristotle advocated the formulation of judgments without criteria. Aristotle said only that the just man does not possess perfect criteria in every case. In most ethical judgments, the goal of the virtuous man is to seek the mean, and this is itself a clear criterion in matters of ethics and justice: "Hence it is evident that in seeking for justice men seek for the mean or neutral, *for the law is the mean.*"[70] This hardly rules out the use of criteria per se, as Lyotard implies.

Apart from the fact that Aristotle never said that men must judge without criteria, one can dismiss Lyotard's claim as prima facie absurd. After all, what would it be like to make a choice without criteria, as Lyotard implies when he says that we make decisions "without the least criteria"?[71] The only way to satisfy this approach would be to choose arbitrarily, at random, without any sort of reasoning at all. Certainly this cannot be what Lyotard advocates. For these reasons Lyotard's claim that we must judge without criteria remains oblique and puzzling.

A similar distortion of traditional sources takes place in Lyotard's reading of Kant. By relying too heavily on the *Critique of Judgment* and ignoring Kant's writings on law and justice, Lyotard makes the claim that Kant eschewed determinate rules for judgments.[72] This may be true as for matters involving aesthetics (i.e., for judgments about the Beautiful and the Sublime), but in matters of justice Kant provided detailed, strict rules. Whatever Kant may have said about the Sublime in his aesthetic writings, he obviously never felt that we lacked criteria for decisions in law and politics, and he gave very specific determinations on such matters as the death penalty, the right of inheritance, private property, voting rights, the right to rebel, and marriage.[73] Kant even said that the idea of a hypothetical "original contract" could be used as a criterion (Kant's term!) for whether a law is just: "Specifically, it [the original contract] obligates every legislator to formulate his laws in such a way that they could have sprung from the unified will of an entire people. . . . For that is the *criterion* of every public law's conformity with right."[74] Kant calls the original contract an "idea of reason" which serves as an *"infallible standard."*[75] He also says that practical reason must "judg[e] according to concepts of Right."[76] It is thus somewhat odd that Lyotard relies on Kant for the notion that justice requires the presentation of the unrepresentable, and that there can be no formula for the just state. In fact, Kant himself thought otherwise and—*contra* Lyotard—held that the just state should be founded on the general (unified) will of the people and must take the form of a republic.[77] Kant did not think these requirements were subjective, nor did he view them as one language-game among others. On the contrary, he felt they were demanded by freedom and reason: "The concept of an external right in general derives entirely from the concept of freedom."[78]

Kant may have allowed that aesthetic judgments about the Sublime were based on subjective feelings that lacked determinate criteria, and Lyotard is within his rights in using Kant's aesthetic theory as a heuristic model to suggest how moral decisions might be made without objective criteria, but Kant himself never relied solely on this approach in matters of ethics and politics. It is thus a distortion of Kant's position to imply that he denied the necessity of criteria in political issues.

Finally, one can also see a distortion at work in Lyotard's appropriation of Wittgenstein's notion of language-games. Wittgenstein used the term "language-game" to designate primitive scenarios which illustrate that language has uses other than the simple naming of objects: "I shall in the future again and again draw your attention to what I shall call language-games. These are ways of using signs simpler than those in which we use the signs of highly complicated everyday language. . . . The study of language-games is the study of primitive forms of language or primitive languages."[79] Lyotard picks up on Wittgenstein's terminology but misses his main point, namely, that language-games in the real world are tied to customs and traditions: "I shall also call the whole, consisting of language *and the actions into which it is woven,* the 'language-game.'"[80] Language-games rest upon forms of life: "And to imagine a language means to imagine a form of life."[81] In other words, language-games do not need to be justified rationally—indeed, they *cannot* be justified or legitimated as a matter of logic: "What we have rather to do is to *accept* the everyday language-game, and to note *false* accounts of the matter *as* false. The primitive language-game which children are taught needs no justification; *attempts at justification need to be rejected.*"[82] Notice how Lyotard misses Wittgenstein's point. Wittgenstein is saying that language-games simply *are;* they do not need justification, because they are forms of life, customs, and habits. But Lyotard proceeds to ignore Wittgenstein's advice ("attempts at justification must be rejected") by asking how we can ground or justify the political/legal language-game of our culture (say, by asking how we can go from a descriptive phrase to a prescriptive claim).

Lyotard correctly sees that in Western culture there is a language-game in which laws are justified by a movement from descriptive to prescriptive claims: we move from "Man is endowed with inalienable rights" to "We should have a liberal democracy." Lyotard focuses on the fact that prescriptive statements are "ungrounded" in that they cannot be deduced from descriptives, but he ignores Wittgenstein's point that language games are not "grounded" in the first place. As long as prescriptive statements are customarily and habitually derived from descriptive statements in practice, they are as grounded as they need to be, regardless of whether they can or cannot be logically derived from descriptive statements.

THE ALLEGED GULF BETWEEN "IS" AND "OUGHT"

Lyotard's misreading of Wittgenstein is related to his claim that we cannot derive a prescriptive claim from a descriptive claim (i.e., that we cannot go from an "is" to an "ought"). In *Just Gaming* Lyotard traces this claim to Aristotle's *On Interpretation,* but a more likely source is David Hume's *A Treatise of Human Nature,* where Hume argued that it is impossible to logically derive an "ought" from an "is."[83] Hume's view was silently adopted by the majority of philosophers for quite some time until it came under serious attack by John Searle in 1964.[84] A flurry of critical responses to Searle's position were offered by some notable philosophers, and the issue has been controversial ever since. Unfortunately, Lyotard overlooks or ignores the vast literature on this point, thereby missing Searle's important argument, which (if true) forces a rethinking of Lyotard's claim that different speech-acts occupy different "universes."[85]

Searle's point against Hume was that different phrases are linked together indissociably in "institutional facts," such that a specific descriptive phrase will automatically entail a prescriptive phrase based upon collective habits, customs, and shared usage of terms. For example, if I say that "Jones borrowed five thousand dollars from Smith," then (all other things being equal) one can derive "Jones ought to repay Smith." This derivation (or implication) is based on the social institution of promise-keeping, which is firmly entrenched in our society, such that the term "promise" implies that if you borrow money, you ought to pay it back. If Searle is correct, descriptive and prescriptive phrases are linked through social institutions, so there is nothing wrong about going from one type of claim to another; in fact, it is perfectly normal and acceptable to do so.

Searle thinks that philosophers have erred by searching for a purely logical reason for how one type of statement can lead to another. That is, philosophers ask themselves how it is logically possible that a statement of promise can give rise to a statement about obligation. Philosophers like Hume and Lyotard are correct in claiming that one cannot *deduce* obligation from promising, and they therefore claim that there is no way to link the phrases. This error is caused by looking in the wrong place for a connection between the phrases. The phrases are linked by custom, not by logical inference; promising is simply the type of human institution that creates obligations. As Searle explains, "some philosophers ask, 'How can a promise create an obligation?' A similar question would be, 'How can a touchdown create six points?' And as they stand both questions can only be answered by stating a rule of the form 'X counts as Y.' "[86] I think that Searle has touched on something important here, and his analysis helps clarify the problem with Lyotard's supposition that the various phrase regimes occupy separate "universes" (whatever that means). In fact, the reverse seems to be the case: various phrase regimes are mutually necessary components of any language. For example, the question "Did you go to the ball game?" makes sense only if we assume that there are descriptive phrases such as "We went to the ball game," performative phrases such as "We hereby go to the ball game," as well as imperatives such as "Go to the ball game!" To say that these phrases occupy different universes seems strange, and I can find no support for this thesis in the field of linguistics or philosophy of language. In fact, structural linguists have created formulas which describe the way in which one type of phrase can be quickly translated into another, which indicates that the phrases are intimately related.

It seems that both Lyotard and Searle follow Wittgenstein's notion that our lives are permeated with disparate language-games which rely upon a mix of declarative and performative statements, yet Searle (following Wittgenstein) is not bothered by this mixture, whereas Lyotard feels that a mixture of different phrase regimes leads to an aporia of legitimation. It is hard to see what is wrong with mixing phrase regimens, so long as this is our custom. If we legitimate our government through a mixture of declarative and prescriptive phrases (as in the French Declaration of the Rights of Man and Citizen or the American Declaration of Independence), then so be it; this mode of legitimation is an acceptable "move," given our practices and our tradition, and it is not somehow invalidated because one type of speech-act is fused with another. If

Lyotard is correct in assuming that all governments falsely seek legitimation in an illegitimate move from descriptive to prescriptive statements, then it strictly follows that all governments are equally unfounded. But Lyotard can't hold this view since it implies that the American government is no more legitimate than that of the Third Reich. This conclusion should warn us that something is amiss in Lyotard's argument.

In a difficult series of passages in *The Differend,* Lyotard argues that the French Declaration is flawed because it purports to derive its legitimacy on the basis of two distinct sources: the ahistorical rights of men in general and the historical events in France at the time of the Declaration. Lyotard says that this move from a universalist to a historical discourse creates an "insoluble differend."[87] But this seems to be an overly dramatic conclusion. Consider the following scenario: a battered woman finally leaves her abusive husband and says, "What he did to me violated my human rights as well as our wedding vows." This is a perfectly acceptable, legitimate claim easily understood by virtually all people. This type of statement *works:* it gets its point across and it is legitimate. But on Lyotard's analysis there is a confusion of genres here because a universal appeal (to human rights) is combined with a historical appeal (to a contract between the parties). Yet this mixture does not seem to have the slightest effect on whether the statement is legitimate or not. Similarly, a mixture of discourses or genres in the French Declaration does not result in a problem of legitimacy. Indeed, many important rituals and documents contain heterogenous references without this mixture lessening their legitimacy. For example, a Catholic marriage ceremony is a binding contract despite the heterogenous appeals to religious foundations ("holy matrimony") and secular foundations ("By the powers vested in me by the State of Illinois, I now pronounce you man and wife"). All of this switching of genres takes place without calling into question the legitimacy of the wedding or the legal effect of the marriage.

If I am correct, political legitimacy and illegitimacy are not a function of linguistics or rhetoric but rather of context and custom. Lyotard is correct in stating that the French Declaration mixes genres, but he is incorrect in assuming that this has any effect whatsoever on the legitimacy of that document. The legitimacy of the Declaration or, for that matter, any form of government, is based on the events surrounding its creation and not on the linguistic structure of its founding documents.

OVERZEALOUS FEAR OF CONSENSUS

It is difficult to make sense of Lyotard's claim that consensus is "terroristic." After all, consensus must take place on some level in order for society to function; there must be some baseline agreement on language, customs, traditions, and so on. It is difficult to understand how this is terroristic. In fact, the opposite seems more accurate: if we lacked consensus, we would have no social order and no way to prevent terrorist acts.

Lyotard's point may be more subtle. Perhaps he is saying that we cannot achieve a *perfect* consensus, so every attempt at consensus has the result of excluding or marginalizing certain groups who disagree with the prevailing order. But if this is his point, then he is not saying anything very extraordinary; I know of no one who supposes that we can reach a *perfect* consensus in a pluralistic society; there will always be what Tocqueville called the "tyranny of the majority." However, we can certainly all consent to a democratic system in which we agree to disagree, that is, where we can agree that differences should be tolerated. This type of overlapping consensus (an agreement to hear each other out) seems absolutely essential for any civilized society. Furthermore, it would seem that Lyotard agrees that certain types of consensus are healthy, such as the consensus among migrant workers that they are being exploited by farm owners, or the consensus among South Africans that a free election should be held. He is right to worry about cases in which the views of a majority are imposed on an unwilling minority, thereby silencing and marginalizing the minority. But this is hardly a problem of consensus per se but rather of how to avoid a consensus which is intolerant of those who do not consent. Given this, it is difficult to see why Lyotard claims that "majority does not mean large number but great fear."[88]

PROBLEMS WITH THE CLAIM OF INCOMMENSURABILITY

A further problem relates to Lyotard's notion of the differend, which might be explored in connection with Donald Davidson's work on conceptual schemes and translation.[89] Put bluntly, I am not convinced that Lyotard's examples of differends involve cases of true incommensurability. Lyotard wants to claim that the differend is such that it cannot be translated into the terms of the dominant genre. But if this were true, then it must (by definition) be impossible to identify the differend as a differend. Take the example of the differend created by Western imperialists when they colonize third world countries and dig up ancient burial grounds. If the natives can somehow make their claim known to the imperialists, then it seems that we don't have a case of incommensurability between language-games but rather a disagreement over fundamental values. The imperialists can understand the natives' claim even if they don't find it convincing.

Lyotard's examples of differends don't seem to involve cases of incommensurate conceptual schemes so much as cases where the parties disagree (which is something quite different). Take Lyotard's example of wage laborers. They cannot reproach the capitalists at the bargaining table for turning labor into a commodity, but must instead bargain on the *assumption* that labor is a commodity. It seems perfectly clear that the wage laborers are capable of making their claim known to the capitalists in terms that the capitalists can understand (e.g., by reading them passages from Marx's works or by describing how a socialist society would operate). The capitalists may disagree, but there is no sense in saying that the laborers are completely denied a voice. The parties have different beliefs and different political power, but I don't see what is gained by claiming that they have incommensurate belief systems, given that they are able to negotiate with each other. I fail to see how anything constructive can come of the notion that phrase regimens constitute "separate universes." Indeed, Lyotard's claim might have the perverse effect of blocking the lines of communication between competing interests on the ground that genuine communication is impossible.

THE QUESTIONABLE RELIANCE ON KANT

I now come to the most problematic aspect of Lyotard's work, namely, his reliance on the Kantian idea of obligation as something beyond the empirical world. As I have shown, Lyotard's retreat to Kant involves him in a contradiction: he says that there is no metadiscourse of justice but then turns around and announces a universal prescription requiring that language-games be kept distinct. What I find most troubling about this position (apart from its inconsistency) is that it involves a kind of messianic claim that one is called to "be just." Lyotard says that this imperative "has no addressor," that is, its source must be "left hanging." This is all very mystical, especially for a person who argues that the self is a "narrative construction." If this is so, then why isn't morality a narrative construction as well? Why does morality have to issue from a higher authority?

It strikes me that Lyotard fails to see that ethical and political positions are tied to traditions, customs, and shared narratives: normative positions are not derived from some nameless, faceless, anonymous "addressor." For all his talk about how people are constructed in narratives, Lyotard fails to take the obvious step of grounding *our* ethics and *our* law in *our* shared narratives and traditions. As a result, his work retains Kant's transcendentalism while failing to follow the latter's lead in specifying principles on justice and law. Strangely, Lyotard devotes hundreds of pages to discussions of justice and law, but he never actually discloses the arrangement he thinks is most defensible. There is a lot of verbal gymnastics about ideas of reason, linguistic incommensurability, and multiple notions of justice, but in the final analysis Lyotard comes up somewhat empty. The reason for this, as I have suggested, is that Lyotard has tried so hard to avoid the problems of traditional approaches to justice (Platonic, Kantian, majoritarian, autonomy-based, communist) that he is left without a platform from which to speak.

The Lessons of Lyotard's Work

If I am correct, Lyotard's work leads to a single (unsupportable) principle of justice, namely, that we must keep language-games pure and distinct. This is too slender a reed on which to build a vision for the legal system and the just state. But while Lyotard does not construct a vision of a just set of laws, his work is useful as a "check" on our existing approach to justice and law.

Lyotard is at his best when describing the subtle ways in which people have been marginalized and silenced. He makes the excellent point that marginalized groups are not only at a disadvantage when they seek redress from within the legal system but, in many cases, are excluded from this system altogether. He also correctly notes that we cannot expect to hear the voices of the oppressed unless we take steps to give these people the means to make their voices heard. As far as legal scholarship goes, this could lead to some radical approaches. For example, Lyotard's notion of small narratives might lead to an examination of the criminal justice system from the point of view of defendants as a way of complementing the usual perspective of prosecutors and defense lawyers. Furthermore, Lyotard would have us approach legal history from viewpoints other than those of the dominant white male, which might give expression to the ways in which women and minorities have been denied access to the legal system. Finally, Lyotard would have us question the way in which the structural foundation of the current legal system gives rise to differends (e.g., by *assuming* the legitimacy of private property, commoditized labor, negative rights). In all these areas Lyotard's work can lead to an "activation of the differences" and a "war on totality."[90] This can and should result in a serious questioning of our current system of justice as well as a rethinking of what passes for acceptable legal scholarship. Lyotard's work takes us in interesting directions, forcing a decentering of the dominant perspective in legal theory, such that we will be more likely to incorporate different points of view on the law than the standard views offered by judges and lawyers. In addition, Lyotard's focus on the importance of narratives provides support for recent legal movements such as Critical Race Theory, Legal Storytelling, and Law and Literature. Yet in the final analysis, Lyotard frustrates us with his agnosticism toward specific solutions in politics and law. He captures a certain "feeling" or "condition" of postmodernity, but he fails to give us a workable postmodern justice, especially when it comes to hard cases.

7 &❧ Rorty's Postmodern Antifoundationalism

From Postmodernism to Antifoundationalism

In the first chapter I presented the postmodern position that the self is an effect of language and tradition and not what Foucault has called a "founding subject" or Cartesian *cogito*.[1] This point is perhaps best expressed in Althusser's statement that the subject has become "de-centered."[2] This means that there is no innate faculty of reason or morality that will "out" itself, and no Cartesian ego that somehow predates its immersion into a particular language and culture. In extreme versions of this thesis, as in the work of Jacques Lacan, the claim is that one must "oppose any philosophy directly issuing from the *cogito*."[3] The central idea behind these seemingly cryptic messages is that the self is always situated in medias res, embedded in (and constituted by) a specific language, history, and tradition. This stance is sometimes termed "antihumanism" because it does not proceed by trying to locate a core of humanity that exists within each of us; on the contrary, it holds that we differ radically in that our contingencies "go all the way down."

Richard Rorty is an influential American philosopher who purports to set forth an ethical and political theory which fully respects the contingency of the individual and his or her culture. Although he once referred to his position as "postmodern" (and he is often treated by others as a postmodernist), Rorty now favors the labels "antifoundationalist" or "pragmatist." For Rorty antifoundationalists and pragmatists understand that contingency is inevitable. For this reason they hold that ethical and legal theory must be based upon principles and practices imminent within a particular culture but which cannot pretend to be based on anything deeper. Indeed, the antifoundationalists hold that we must look closely at our traditions and customs in order to tease out a notion of justice and legality which already exists (more of less explicitly or implicitly) within our traditions. The point here is simply that all attempts to find a transcultural, ahistorical account of justice and morality have failed. It might be possible that a future philosopher will formulate such a neutral conception (e.g., someone might locate morality *as such*), but the failure of this project to

date gives us strong inductive reason to suspect that the entire project of finding universal rules of morality is ill-conceived. This starting point, namely, the
failure of the grand search for objectivity in morality and politics, is not exclusive to Rorty. For example, it can also be found in Alasdair MacIntyre's claim
that every notion of justice is always embedded within a given culture, which
casts doubt on the search for justice itself: "Morality which is no particular society's morality is to be found nowhere. There was the-morality-of-fourth-cen-
tury-Athens, there were the-moralities-of-thirteenth-century-Western-Europe,
there are numerous such moralities, but where ever was or is *morality as such*?"[4]
A similar point is made by Michael Walzer: "Justice is relative to social meanings. . . . A given society is just if its substantive life is lived in a certain way—
that is, in a way that is faithful to the shared understanding of the members."[5]
Like these thinkers, Rorty argues that we should give up the search for "rationality as such" since every conception of rationality is already within a tradition: "I do not have much use for notions like 'objective value' and 'objective
truth.' I think that the so-called 'postmodernists' are right in most of their crit-
icisms of traditional philosophical talk about 'Reason' "[6] The loss of objectivity means that philosophy (including ethical and legal theory) will necessarily
be ethnocentric: "*We* must start from where *we* are."[7]

Rorty has published only three essays to date which deal specifically with
legal theory,[8] yet his work has been discussed in hundreds of law-review articles and is having a serious effect on legal studies. Although he does not profess to offer a legal theory as such, his writings on the law have received special
attention from such luminaries as Richard Posner, Ronald Dworkin, and Stanley Fish.[9] In this chapter I want to formulate a Rortian perspective on the law
despite the absence of a central text on such matters by Rorty himself. I will
argue that Rorty's writings on ethico-political issues can be brought together
with his short papers on the law to generate a coherent, if flawed, approach to
legal theory. I will begin by examining Rorty's views on ethical and political
issues and will demonstrate how Rorty's views on these matters support his
pragmatist approach to the law. I will conclude by pointing out the problems
with a Rortian approach to legal theory.

Rorty's Antifoundational Pragmatism
(on Ethics / Politics / Law)

Rorty's articles on legal theory presuppose a familiarity with his work on ethics
and politics. I will therefore begin by taking a closer look at his work in those
areas before turning to his papers on law. I will first examine some of Rorty's

earliest writings (1983–87) and will then discuss his influential book *Contingency, Irony, and Solidarity* (1989).

RORTY ON ETHICS AND POLITICS

A useful point of departure is Rorty's controversial 1983 essay "Postmodern Bourgeois Liberalism," which presents much of Rorty's mature position in an early, abbreviated form.[10] In this essay Rorty identifies two competing groups of thinkers in contemporary ethical theory: Kantians and Hegelians. The Kantians attempt to ground their ethical and political positions by referring to ahistorical notions such as human dignity, natural rights, and humanity as an end-in-itself. The Kantians draw a sharp line between matters of justice, which issue from the categorical imperative, and matters of prudence, which involve hypothetical imperatives. Kantians sometimes appear to be appealing to a moral law which might hold for a "supercommunity" of all people (what Kant called a "kingdom of ends") where membership is based on humanity as such. Kantian theory is deeply universal.

The Hegelians, in contrast, argue that morality is not universal but local. They tend to see "humanity" as a biological classification that is relatively useless when fashioning a moral theory. Hegelians seek to derive moral and political principles from the contingent traditions of a specific community, eschewing the demand for a deeper grounding in something *essentially* and *ahistorically* human (such as autonomy or freedom). Hegelians think that the Kantian concepts of freedom and autonomy are useful ways of summarizing our local commitments, but they cannot be used as justifications or foundations for political arrangements, which have no ahistorical grounding. For example, for a Hegelian, Kant's categorical imperative is a useful metaphor for describing an ethical belief that happens to be widely held by twentieth-century Americans and Europeans, but it does not go below the surface of our contingent communities to express some universal layer of humanity or rationality.

It is clear that Western democratic traditions (such as fundamental rights to liberty and property, a free press, an independent judiciary, and due process) have traditionally been defended on some variant of the Kantian approach, such as an appeal to natural rights or innate human dignity. These Kantian notions have served as a buttress or foundation for some of our most cherished political institutions. For this reason many Kantians believe that the removal of these supports will lead to the collapse of democracy. According to Rorty, "Kantian criticism of the tradition that runs from Hegel through Marx and Nietzsche . . . rests on a prediction that such [democratic] practices and institutions will not survive the removal of the traditional Kantian buttresses, buttresses which include an account of 'rationality' and 'morality' as transcultural and ahistorical."[11] Rorty, however, denies that Kantian foundations are necessary to support the institutions and practices of Western democracy. This means that democracy is freestanding in that it cannot be justified based on "objective" foundations.[12] Rorty thinks that the Hegelian approach is a more promising method of defending our cherished institutions and practices because it avoids the untenable Kantian claims about ahistorical human attributes. Here is how Rorty defines a suitably nonmetaphysical Hegelian approach for the late twentieth century: "I shall call the Hegelian attempt to defend the institutions and practices of the rich North Atlantic democracies without using such [Kantian] buttresses 'postmodern bourgeois liberalism.'"[13] Each element of this formulation ("postmodern," "bourgeois," "liberalism") merits careful analysis.[14]

Rorty explicitly follows Lyotard's use of the term "postmodern" to designate "distrust of metanarratives," including such metanarratives as "absolute spirit," "victory of the proletariat," the "march of history," or "natural law." Rorty uses the term "bourgeois" to indicate that Hegelians are willing to recognize Marx's claim that many of our democratic institutions and practices are possible only under specific historical conditions, such as advanced capitalism, with its division of labor and private ownership of property. The term "liberalism" indicates that Rorty affirms traditional liberal values (democracy, freedom, equality, due process) without making the standard appeal to Kantian foundations.

Rorty goes on to say that the Kantians have erred in thinking that the moral self is a sort of substrate lying below the surface of contingent beliefs and interests. For Rorty people are simply the sum total of their interests, views, and talents, "with nothing behind it—no substrate beneath the attributes."[15] Morality, then, is entirely a function of the contingent beliefs and institutions we happen to share with others: "I would argue that the moral force of such loyalties and convictions consists *wholly* in this fact [of contingency], and nothing else has *any* moral force. There is no 'ground' for such loyalties and convictions save the fact that the beliefs and desires and emotions which buttress them overlap those of lots of other members of the group with which we identify for purpose of moral or political deliberations. . . ."[16] Rorty affirms Wilfrid Sellars' claim that morality is a matter of "we-intentions": morality is a set of claims about the type of things that "we" North Americans do and don't do: it is not about what humans, qua humans, should do or should not do.

If Rorty is correct, ethical and political theory should not attempt to find deep-structure principles which ground a vision of the just state. We cannot look to Locke's "state of nature," Jefferson's "natural laws," or Kant's "end-in-itself." Instead, our vision of the just state must come from within our existing self-conception as late-twentieth-century North Americans. This means that moral discourse should move away from general ethical principles and toward Wittgensteinian "reminders for a particular purpose," which Rorty sees as "anecdotes about the past effects of various practices and predictions about what will happen if, or unless, some of these are altered."[17] In effect, Rorty calls for piecemeal social engineering within the framework of welfare-state liberalism.

The view set forth in "Postmodern Bourgeois Liberalism" was affirmed in a subsequent provocative essay entitled "The Priority of Democracy to Philosophy."[18] The title of this essay was meant as a check against the pretensions of philosophers who assume that democracy requires a philosophical grounding. For Rorty the reverse is more accurate: a flourishing democracy makes it possible for philosophers to articulate the benefits of democracy; it is the practice (or custom) of democracy which is foundational to the philosophical articulation. In other words, we cannot start at ground zero by considering humanity as such and then work our way toward a justification of democracy; rather, we must begin with a commitment to democracy and then work our way toward an articulation of it. One of Rorty's goals is to defend John Rawls' recent claim (set forth in his work subsequent to *A Theory of Justice*) that his account of the Original Position is merely a heuristic device for describing how members of Western democracies already conceptualize their duties to others. As Rawls explains: "What justifies a conception of justice is not its being true to an order antecedent to and given to us, but its congruence with our deeper understanding of ourselves and our aspirations, and our realization that, given our history and the traditions embedded in our public life, it is the most reasonable doctrine for us."[19] Rorty approves the notion that liberal democracy does not need a philosophical *justification* but only a philosophical *articulation*. Put differently, we cannot achieve objectivity in politics (i.e., we cannot prove that democracy is really better than fascism in some deep sense that would convince all skeptics), but we can achieve solidarity to the extent that within our shared democratic practices (within our "ethnos") we share a common language and framework for discussing our utopian visions.

Rorty's view is admittedly ethnocentric because it is skeptical about our ability to transcend (let alone justify) the contingent practices which happen to be in place at the moment.[20] However, Rorty is not ethnocentric in the narrow sense in which a colonialist might claim that his way of life is objectively better than the lives of people in second and third world countries. Rorty tends to see ethnocentrism as "an inescapable condition—roughly synonymous with 'human finitude.'"[21] This means that we can justify our practices only from within a community of those who already share our practices and history. For example, an African bushman will have few constructive political suggestions for us, not because he is "backward" or "primitive" but because he does not

share our tradition and history. Although Rorty thinks we should try to understand our own culture from the perspective of foreign cultures in order to see
if they have any suggestions for improvement, in the final analysis their views
are only helpful to the extent that they can be meshed with our own self-understanding: "We cannot leap outside our Western social democratic skins when
we encounter another culture, and we should not try."[22]

Rorty puts a pragmatist spin on this ethnocentrism, arguing that we can justify our existing and future practices only by looking at their results:

> So the pragmatist admits that he has no ahistorical standpoint from which to
> endorse the habits of modern democracies he wishes to praise. . . . The prag-
> matists' justification of toleration, free inquiry, and the quest for undistorted
> communication can only take the form of a comparison between societies
> which exemplify these habits and those which do not, leading up to the sug-
> gestion that nobody who has experienced both would prefer the latter.[23]

This means that any justification of our practices will be circular: we judge our
practices by our preferences, and our preferences have been shaped by our
practices. For example, we should retain the right to trial by jury because it
leads to good results and captures part of who we are as late-twentieth-century
Americans, yet this indentity has itself been shaped by the existence of a right
to trial by jury. There is no way to justify our existing identity other than to
say it is the one we are stuck with; there is no way to step outside of ourselves
to ascertain if we are "rational" or "just" in some transcultural sense. Following this line of reasoning, Rorty claims that the welfare state is supportable
because it eliminates suffering and accurately captures who "we" are at this
time, but it cannot be justified on the grounds that it is "true to human nature,"
"more rational than other arrangements," or "more in accord with the categorical imperative."

Rorty thinks that moral progress is possible only from *within* our traditions,
not from some God's-eye perspective. That is, we can find better solutions to
social problems and more humane political arrangements without making the
claim that these arrangements are better in a transcendent sense. This means
that our political options for the future are somewhat limited because any viable
option must comport with how we presently see ourselves as members of
wealthy North American democracies. If we must start from where "we" are,
then it is unlikely that we will favor revolutionary change in either political
direction. According to Rorty, neither the radical Left (the Marxists) nor the
radical Right (the conservatives) have provided us with a workable picture of
an alternative society that retains the institutions we find worthwhile under our
current arrangement of welfare-state liberalism. The Marxist proposals have

proven unworkable in Russia and Eastern Europe, and the conservative proposals would take us back to a time before the welfare state, a period to which we do not wish to return. The only viable option, then, is a project of reforming the current system, which luckily provides an opportunity for self-criticism and reform through the free press, political debate, judicial activism, and so on.

After Rorty published these essays, many critics accused him of conservatism and quietism on the grounds that his self-confessed "ethnocentrism" effectively ruled out any radical approaches in politics, especially socialism or communism. Rorty responded to his critics in a 1987 essay entitled "Thugs and Theorists," which laid down a fairly specific political platform, namely, a left-leaning democratic socialism which reflects Rorty's doubts about the programs offered by the extreme left and right wings of the political spectrum.[24] The left-wing radicals (Marxists) fail to see that communism has been a failure in two respects: centralized economic planning has crippled growth, and communist regimes are undemocratic and harsh on human rights. Accordingly, Rorty finds unworkable the Left's call for revolution and nationalization of the means of production. On the other hand, right-wing politicians in America are continually trying to erode the essential welfare-state reforms that have softened the effects of free-market capitalism. Rorty therefore finds fault with both the left and right wing's visions for a better future. He tries to walk a fine line between these two poles by calling for a left-leaning arrangement: "Nobody so far has invented an economic setup that satisfactorily balances decency and efficiency, but at the moment the most hopeful alternative seems to be governmentally controlled capitalism plus welfare-statism (Holland, Sweden, Ireland). There is nothing sacred about either the free market or about central planning; the proper balance between the two is a matter of experimental tinkering."[25] This means that "we" social democrats (Rorty includes himself, Rawls, Habermas, and Charles Taylor in what might be called a "royal 'we'") must find the right balance between leftist reform and free-market capitalism. It is clear from this essay that Rorty is a classic liberal in his embrace of the notion that the government should not interfere with lifestyle decisions yet may engage in redistribution of income through taxation and social programs. This places Rorty's political position solidly to the left of center but certainly to the right of full-blown socialism.

Rorty's early essays set forth an ethico-political position that was modified somewhat in his 1989 study *Contingency, Irony, and Solidarity*. Because this book is divided into three sections (dealing with contingency, irony, and solidarity, respectively), I will treat each of these concepts separately and then link them together with Rorty's insistence on a split between public and private spheres.

Rorty's discussion of contingency is divided into three essays which point out, respectively, that language, selfhood, and community are "contingent," the product of historical accidents. That is, each of these might very well have been different if, for example, we had lost World War II or if we had not fought a civil war. With regard to language, Rorty says that it is a tool that is not necessarily linked with reality in the sense supposed by naive positivists. Borrowing heavily from Donald Davidson, Rorty argues that "meaning" and "truth" are a property of sentences, and sentences are human creations, tools for getting things done. This means that there is no "final vocabulary" which links up with "reality," no ultimate Truth to be discovered, but only a process of redescription in which we fashion increasingly useful metaphors. With regard to selfhood, Rorty follows Freud's notion that the self is a product of community and family and does not have a necessary or essential "sense of humanity," "inherent decency," or "faculty of Reason." The radical contingency of selfhood explains why people behave so chaotically, as exemplified by Nazi prison guards who killed Jews by day and spent their evenings at home with their families. This type of behavior casts doubt on the claim that there are distinctly uniform human faculties of "reason" and "sympathy" which exist below the surface of personality. Finally, with regard to community, the existing liberal community is contingent in that it has come about largely by accident and social experimentation. We should not suppose that our society is the culmination of reason, history, or truth (e.g., as it has been viewed by Francis Fukuyama).[26] For Rorty the contingency of community does not lessen the value of our traditions and practices since it is impossible for a community to be based on anything grander than contingent traditions and social experiments. Rorty quotes Joseph Schumpeter and Isiah Berlin to this effect:

> *Schumpeter:* To realize the relative validity of one's convictions and yet stand for them unflinchingly, is what distinguishes a civilized man from a barbarian.[27]

> *Berlin:* To demand more than this is perhaps a deep and incurable metaphysical need; but to allow it to determine one's practice is a symptom of an equally deep, and more dangerous, moral and political immaturity.[28]

The impact of these statements on Rorty cannot be overestimated, as can be seen from his own self-assessment: "The fundamental premise of this book is that a belief can still regulate action, can still be thought worth dying for, among people who are quite aware that this belief is caused by nothing deeper than contingent historical circumstance."[29] This means that we are "situated" to such a degree that we cannot step outside our culture to judge it according to some neutral moral framework, although, as was noted earlier, we can criticize our society from alternative perspectives.

Rorty's position has strong negative implications for philosophers and political theorists who believe they are working at a level below that of mere redescription and who insist they are fashioning a fundamental justification of democracy, free speech, and due process. For Rorty there is no way to begin one's inquiry with fundamental truths about rationality or freedom and then work one's way toward a justification of democracy and welfare-state liberalism. Theoretical constructions such as the "state of nature," the original position, and rational choosers in an efficient market are merely thought experiments (redescriptions) which have been offered to *articulate* a particular version of democracy, but they are not fundamental or essential to democracy itself. If Rorty is correct, genuine advancements in politics are rarely brought about by theory but rather through the creative use of language and imagination. It is for this reason that the cultural hero of his liberal utopia is the "strong poet" (the term is borrowed from Harold Bloom) who envisions a better future or warns us about the dangerous direction in which we are headed.[30]

Because our practices and institutions are contingent and subject to redescription, Rorty thinks we should have a strong sense of irony about the views we happen to hold at any given time. An ironist is a person who, among other things, has doubts about the finality of his or her current vocabulary. The ironist doubts that this vocabulary is any closer to the truth than alternative vocabularies but thinks that it helps articulate a vision of a better world. Most important, the ironist knows that any practice or institution can be made to look good or bad by redescription. For this reason, Rorty extols the virtue of the literary critic over the metaphysician because the latter vainly believes that he or she can *discover* something within human nature which can ground a political vision, while the literary critic (and the journalist) search for new ways to articulate the suffering of people we previously didn't care about: "We should be on the lookout for marginalized people—people whom we still instinctively think of as 'they' rather than 'us.'"[31]

One might better understand Rorty's emphasis on the importance of redescription by looking at the civil rights movement of the early sixties (an example suggested by Rorty himself). The legislative advances of the sixties (e.g., the Civil Rights Act of 1964 and the Voting Rights Act of 1965) did not come about because white people suddenly made a *metaphysical* discovery that blacks were equal to whites, or that blacks were rational beings or had value as ends-in-themselves. Rather, the speeches of Martin Luther King Jr. produced a redescription of a better world, a world in which his children could play with white children and go to white amusement parks without feeling inferior. This produced a change in our *description* of a better society; the liberal utopia had been redescribed to include black people alongside whites. The liberal ironist wants to make a similar move by remaining on the lookout for new and critical ways of describing our practices, in the hope of bringing about a change in these practices through redescription. A good example of this would be the work of George Orwell, whose negative utopian masterpiece *Nineteen Eighty-Four* (discussed at length by Rorty in *Contingency*) provides an excellent vision of the society we want to avoid.[32]

Turning from irony to solidarity, Rorty thinks that solidarity among people (or countries) does not come about when people recognize the existence of their common human nature. Rather, solidarity is created when people recognize a *contingent* connection with others: "[O]ur sense of solidarity is strongest when those with whom solidarity is expressed are thought of as 'one of us,' where 'us' means something smaller and more local than the human race."[33] Solidarity is not dependent on some neutral substrate common to all people; rather, it is based on people's upbringing and their ability to see themselves in others. Rorty illustrates this point by claiming that during World War II Jews had a better chance of escaping deportation to the death camps if they lived in Denmark than Belgium. This was not because the people of Belgium failed to recognize something inherently valuable about the Jews, nor was it because the Belgians lacked reason. Rather, the Belgians had a dangerously narrow sense of group solidarity: their sense of "we" was so narrow that it excluded the Jews. What protected the Jews in Denmark was the Danish sense of identification and solidarity with other ethnic groups. Rorty makes a similar point about the attitude of American liberals toward the plight of urban blacks; the liberal's desire to improve conditions in the ghettos is not so much motivated by the fact that urban blacks deserve better treatment as *humans* but rather as fellow *Americans*.[34]

Rorty's point is that solidarity has a contingent source in that it derives from a culture's ability to see outsiders as similar to "us": "Solidarity is not to be thought of as recognition of a core self, the human essence, in all human beings. Rather, it is thought of as the ability to see more and more traditional differences (of tribe, religion, race, customs, and the like) as unimportant when compared with similarities with respect to pain and humiliation—the ability to think of people wildly different from ourselves as included in the range of 'us.'"[35] The lesson of history is that moral progress seems to come about (or at least we are less dangerous) when we strive for an expanding sense of inclusion, a wide sense of the "we" which includes marginalized groups. The task of broadening the "we" is best accomplished by novelists and ethnographers because (moreso than philosophers) they sensitize us to the sufferings of others. This is why Rorty devotes two chapters of *Contingency* to Nabokov and Orwell: they portray the dangers of cruelty in the private (Nabokov) and the public (Orwell) spheres.

The fundamental basis of the liberal's sense of solidarity is the latter's willingness to acknowledge the pain and humiliation of others. Put differently, the liberal thinks that "cruelty is the worst thing we do" (Rorty borrows this phrase from Judith Shklar). In keeping with Rorty's antifoundationalism, there is no noncircular way to defend this conception of solidarity, no non–question-begging way to prove that cruelty is the worst thing we do. The best that we can say is that positive social changes have been brought about by broadening the sense of "we" from white European males to other groups (women, blacks, foreigners): "Solidarity is not discovered by reflection but created."[36] And literature has proven itself better than philosophy at creating solidarity.

Having discussed Rorty's notion of contingency, irony, and solidarity, I would like to address a fourth component which runs through *Contingency*, namely, the public–private split. Rorty argues that the public sphere (law, politics, economics) should be kept distinct from the private sphere (lifestyle, personal projects). The public sphere should be devoted to eliminating suffering and ensuring that each American has the means to actualize him- or herself in the private sphere. The private sphere should be devoted to self-actualization through work, hobbies, association with others, the arts, and so forth. Rorty's division of the public and private spheres borrows heavily from John Stuart Mill's "Harm Principle," which states that the sole legitimate ground for government interference with personal liberty is the prevention of harm to others: "Indeed, my hunch is that Western social and political thought may have had the last *conceptual* revolution it needs. J. S. Mill's suggestion that governments devote themselves to optimizing the balance between leaving people's private lives alone and preventing suffering seems to me pretty much the last word."[37] Rorty thinks that certain philosophers are relevant to the public sphere while others are relevant to the private sphere. Thinkers such as Marx, Rawls, and Habermas are useful in conceptualizing ways in which we can lessen suffering in the public sphere. Thinkers such as Derrida, Nietzsche, and Foucault are relevant to the private project of self-actualization: "*Privatize* the Nietzschean-Sartrean-Foucauldian attempt at authenticity and purity, in order to prevent yourself from slipping into a political attitude which will lead you to think that there is some social goal more important than avoiding cruelty."[38] Rorty sees the public sphere as an area for "conversation" in which the free exchange of ideas will lead to new proposals for ways to lessen suffering and bring about an enlargement of the leisure class so that everyone can exprience private self-actualization. The discussion within the public sphere aims at the construction of a "liberal utopia"; this is achieved not through theory but by creatively describing a better version of society." This is part of Rorty's "general turn against theory and toward narrative": "Instead of appealing from the transitory current appearances to the permanent reality, appeal to a still only dimly imagined future practice. Drop the appeal to neutral criteria, and the claim that something large like Nature or Reason or History or the Moral Law is on the side of the oppressed. Instead, just make invidious comparisons between the actual present and a possible, if inchoate, future."[39] This approach is referred to by Rorty as "pragmatism," although it might also be described as a shotgun wedding of utilitarianism, communitarianism, and antifoundationalism.

RORTY'S WORK ON THE LAW

My discussion of Rorty's ethical and political theory has been detailed and protracted for two reasons. First, Rorty has not written very much on law per se, so my construction of a "Rortian jurisprudence" relies heavily on his nonlegal works. Second, the few essays that Rorty has written on the law presume a familiarity with his earlier work, so there is no way to avoid an engagement with those texts.

Turning to the essays that deal specifically with law and legal theory, Rorty's most important comments on law are set forth in two law-review essays published in the early nineties. In these Rorty identifies himself repeatedly as a "pragmatist" and an "antifoundationalist." On my reading, *two* important jurisprudential positions are raised here: a critique of formalism and a pragmatic/experimental approach to legal matters.

In "The Banality of Pragmatism and the Poetry of Justice" Rorty admits that his brand of pragmatism is "banal" in that it does not offer a series of formulas for deciding cases, nor does it offer a legal theory in the strict sense of a theory about the nature of law or justice. Instead, pragmatism follows Holmes' truism that "the life of the law has not been logic: it has been experience."[40] Pragmatism stands opposed to Legal Formalism, especially the version espoused by Dean Langdell of Harvard Law School, who saw the law as a consistent set of first principles which could be applied straightaway to various fact scenarios.[41] Rorty points out that Langdell's notion of law as "science" has been thoroughly discredited; lawyers are now willing to consider more open-ended approaches to the law, incorporating critical perspectives from Marxism, literary theory, and feminism. Rorty sees this trend as evidence of a growing antiformalism that bespeaks an acceptance of pragmatism; he includes Richard Posner, Roberto Unger, and Ronald Dworkin within his very loose conception of "pragmatism."[42]

Rorty follows Dewey's belief that pragmatism favors social experimentation over theory: "[O]ne advantage of pragmatism is freedom from theory guilt. Another advantage is freedom from anxiety about one's scientificity. So I think it is in the spirit of Dewey to say that the test of the power and pertinence of a given social science is how it works when you try to apply it."[43] The basic idea is that lawyers and judges should be formulating new visions for the legal system and then putting these visions into practice. These visions do not have (nor do they need) philosophical support: "To put forth a vision is always one of Fitz-James Stephen's 'leaps in the dark.'" The visionary leap is a "romantic" move which tries to forge new legal paradigms through a creative, "poetic" act of imagination.

Rorty makes the interesting point that some of the best legal decisions of this century were aberrations and anomolies from a legal perspective because they circumvented settled areas of law. The Supreme Court decisions in *Brown v. Board of Education* and *Roe v. Wade* were the result of judicial activism in which the Court refused to defer to either preexisting case law or legislative solutions involving segregation and abortion. In both cases the Court could have followed racist or sexist precedents or passed the buck to state legislatures; instead it took a leap, creating a new social experiment by articulating a wider scope of fundamental rights. The justices could not have know in advance that they had made the right decision, but they created an experiment that turned out well, and we can't seriously countenance a return to the era before these decisions were made.

Rorty rejects the notion that cases like *Brown* and *Roe* involved the *discovery* by the Court of preexisting rights; these decisions are better understood as visionary experiments, leaps in the dark that seemed morally correct at the time and have proven their mettle as good decisions. There is no generalized legal theory which can show that these decisions are "right" and that others are wrong, just as there is no formula which can tell a judge how to make "right" decisions in the future. The best that a judge can do is to try to be a visionary, taking into account our shared traditions and aspirations. This means that judges will act in a way that is somewhat "unprincipled," but Rorty thinks that we have little to gain by imposing restrictive formulas which would tell judges how to decide cases. Rorty also says that there is no theoretically interesting way to prevent judges from making bad decisions, no overarching principles (such as those offered by Dworkin and others) which would ensure that the best decision is always reached. Only in the fantasies of legal philosophers can it be thought that the right theory will somehow magically lead to right answers in actual legal cases.[44]

Rorty thinks that we occasionally need visionary paradigm shifts to break up a chain of bad precedents which have become embedded as binding law. For example, consider the right to privacy which was first announced as a "penumbral" right in *Griswold v. Connecticut*.[45] Rorty would reject the notion that the Court discovered a preexisting right to privacy, a right that had been lying below the surface of the law, somehow embedded in the aura of the Constitution. Rather, he would see *Griswold* as a visionary effort to create a better world, where people are free from state interference with personal reproductive decisions. Rorty offers a similar antiformalist reading of other key cases: "I think of *Brown* as saying that, like it or not, black children are children too. I think of *Roe* as saying that, like it or not, women get to make hard decisions too, and of some hypothetical future reversal of *Bowers v. Hardwick* as saying that, like it or not, gays are grown ups too."[46] This antiformalist stance is continued in Rorty's 1992 article, "What Can You Expect from Anti-Foundationalist Philosophers?," which stresses Rorty's pragmatist perspective. Rorty sees the "good prophet" (in this case the good lawyer or the good judge) as someone who thinks of himself or herself as a person who has a good idea for solving a problem, much as an inventor creates a new and useful product. Possessing neither "legitimacy" nor "authority," the good prophet makes no claim that his or her proposal is backed by reason, autonomy, human nature, and so on. Focusing on a "utopian future," the good prophet measures the worth of his or her vision by its results, not by whether it seems philosophically grounded in conceptual niceties.[47]

A striking implication of this position is that "theory" (broadly construed as an activity divorced from praxis) is not very important in jurisprudence. There is no compelling way to create a formula which will prove the moral superiority of the decisions we favor and the moral bankruptcy of those we dislike. As Rorty has stated elsewhere, "There is no way to consolidate our enemies [or our heroes] in any interesting 'theoretical' way."[48] This means that legal philosophy of the sort practiced by Dworkin will not be of much use to the visionary judge because Dworkin prescribes a set of complicated rules for judges to use when searching for the "right" answer. For Rorty there can be no guarantees when deciding cases; one can only formulate a vision and then say, "Let's try it!"[49] Rorty thinks that positive change comes about by piecemeal tinkering in the real world: "The fantasy that a new set of philosophical ideas— a new contribution to the Aristotle–Wittgenstein sequence—can do quickly and wholesale what union organizers, journalistic exposés, activist lawyers, charismatic left candidates, and the like can do, at best, very slowly and at retail, seems to me the result of a failure of nerve."[50] In summary, Rorty doubts that one can create a legal theory that will solve our problems by telling judges how to behave; the best that one can do is to suggest a better vision of the future and to hope that the vision succeeds in practice.

What Would a Rortian Jurisprudence Look Like?

Combining the ideas expressed in Rorty's ethico-political writings with his work on law, one can begin to formulate a Rortian jurisprudence, as it were. Although the details must remain somewhat sketchy, one can say that he favors an antifoundational, pragmatic, experimental, and ironic approach to the law. Rorty never provides an answer to one of the key questions in legal theory: "How should judges decide cases?" The omission is deliberate, I think, because Rorty eschews formulas in favor of experimental tinkering. In a similar move, Rorty refuses to provide answers to questions about how much time one should devote to fighting injustice, how many innocent people one should allow to be tortured to save a greater number of innocents, or whether one should save a family member before helping a stranger in the event of a natural disaster: "Anybody who believes that there are well-grounded theoretical answers to this sort of question—algorithms for resolving moral dilemmas of this sort— is still, in his heart, a metaphysician. He believes in an order beyond time and change which both determines the point of human existence and establishes a hierarchy of responsibilities."[51] Rorty would probably say that there can be no specific method which tells a judge how to decide a case in advance; in effect, this will be a matter of judgment, vision, openness to new perspectives, and a willingness to engage in piecemeal social engineering.[52] Certainly judges must follow precedents, but there are cases in which the precedents would lead to injustice, as in *Dred Scott v. Sanford* or *Bowers v. Hardwick*, and there are also situations in which the precedents should be followed, as in the cases falling under *Roe v. Wade*. There can be no a priori workable formula for deciding when to ignore precedents and endorse a new social vision. Our best hope is that a judge will be compassionate and sensitive enough to know how to decide cases in an appropriate manner consistent with the tradition of great judges in America. Unlike most legal theorists, Rorty does not provide a theoretical stop- gap to prevent another *Dred Scott v. Sanford* or *Plessy v. Ferguson* by appealing, for example, to "natural law" or "law as integrity." From Rorty's perspective, it is a mistake to suppose that theory alone will provide such a stopgap: "[A]s a pragmatist, I do not believe that legal theory can do much to prevent another *Dred Scott* decision."[53] All that we can do is to ask that judges work toward a better society, yet this cannot be accomplished in a systematic manner by means of a jurisprudential formula.[54]

In place of providing some sort of formula for deciding cases, Rorty sees the primary role of the pragmatist as one who clears the "philosophical underbrush" which has grown up around legal philosophy.[55] That is, the pragmatist program is essentially *critical*; it does not embrace a totalizing end-state program, instead adopting an openness to social experimentation. For this reason Rorty agrees with Richard Posner (a recent convertee to pragmatism) that "judges will probably not find pragmatist philosophers—either old or new—useful."[56]

Richard Posner also claims that the new legal pragmatism espoused by Rorty harkens back to the pragmatist positions of Justices Oliver Wendell Holmes and Benjamin Cardozo, who both eschewed formal rules in favor of social engineering.[57] This seems correct; in addition I would accept Hilary Putnam's suggestion that the new (Rortian) pragmatism draws upon certain existentialist themes that can be found in the work of William James and Jean-Paul Sartre.[58] We can look to these thinkers to flesh out Rorty's approach to the law.

Holmes' pragmatism was evidenced by his critique of the legal formalism so popular in his day, as well as by his insistence on the importance of experience over formal logic: "The life of the law has not been logic: it has been experience."[59] A similar understanding comes through in Cardozo's work:

> My analysis of the judicial process comes down to this, and little more: logic, and history, and custom, and utility, and the accepted standards of right conduct, are the forces which singly or in combination shape the progress of the law. Which of these forces shall predominate must depend largely upon the comparative importance or value of the social interests that will thereby be promoted or impaired. . . . If you ask how he [the judge] is to know when one interest outweighs another, I can only answer that he must get his knowledge just as the legislator gets it, from experience and study and reflection; in brief, from life itself.[60]

Cardozo thought that hard cases presented genuine options which could not be systematically ranked through a formula or code for deciding cases. In the final analysis, Cardozo suggests, the judge must "gather his wits, pluck up his courage, go forward one way or the other" and pray that he has made the right choice.[61] Cardozo acknowledges that most cases will be resolved quite easily through the application of settled precedents, but occasionally there are cases which present an opportunity for major change in the law, and these cases provide an avenue for social engineering through the creative act of fashioning a new legal solution. These hard cases are not decided by looking at relations between concepts but by an ad-hoc mixture of logic, history, common sense, sociology, precedent, and personal prejudice.

With regard to the influence of James and Sartre, Rorty's notion that legal theory involves a "leap in the dark" harkens back to James' quotation from Fitz-James Stephen in "The Will to Believe":

> We stand on a mountain pass in the midst of swirling snow and blinding mist, through which we get glimpses now and then of paths which may be decep-

tive. If we stand still we shall be frozen to death. If we take the wrong road we shall be dashed to pieces. We do not certainly know whether there is any right one. What must we do? "Be strong and of a good courage." Act for the best, hope for the best, and take what comes.[62]

This does not mean that the pragmatist must take a wild, unprincipled leap in the dark when deciding difficult questions. Rather, the point concerns the *limits of theory*, which can only take a person so far, at which point there must be an educated guess as to the best option in light of background factors. A similar point is made by Sartre:

> We cannot decide *a priori* what there is to be done. I think that I pointed that out quite sufficiently when I mentioned the case of the student who came to see me, and who might have applied to all the ethical systems, Kantian or otherwise, without getting any sort of guidance. Never let it be said that this man . . . has made an arbitrary choice. Man makes himself. He isn't ready made at the start. In choosing his ethics, he makes himself, and force of circumstances is such that he cannot abstain from choosing one.[63]

A good judge will not act in "bad faith" by mechanically applying precedents, nor can he or she act as a freewheeling philosopher-king enforcing a private moral vision. There is no formula that the judge can use to decide cases; he or she must cope with the anxiety surrounding decisions and try to be a visionary.

I hope that this detour through Holmes, Cardozo, James, and Sartre has been useful in fleshing out the contours of a Rortian jurisprudence. As a final point, one must keep in mind Rorty's debt to Dewey and the importance of Deweyan social experimentation. When all of these factors are combined, the result is an antiformalist, antifoundationalist, pragmatic call for judges to act as piecemeal social engineers by exploring new visions for a better democratic society. This sounds liberating because it purports to release legal theory from the metaphysical baggage it has been carrying for so long. But is this approach workable in the final analysis?

What Is Objectionable About Rorty's Pragmatism?

I think that Rorty's theory is quite unobjectionable precisely because it is not a legal theory, in the strict sense, but rather a set of reminders for judges and legal theorists about the pitfalls and mistakes they should avoid. These reminders are *about* legal theory but they are not *within* legal theory: they are metatheoretical but not within the practice of legal theorizing. This means that his theory is somewhat empty in terms of its practical use to people who are trying to use legal theory to arrive at solutions to particular problems (e.g., abortion, affirmative action, flag burning). This point, however, is somewhat vitiated by the fact that Rorty concedes that pragmatism is "banal."

Rorty is quite right that we should not try to ground legal theory in ahistorical conceptions of human nature, utility, reason, or history. He is also correct that "we must start from where we are" in the sense that our endeavor to do justice will be based on the concepts of justice already embedded in our contingent institutions and practices. This is all good advice, but it does not provide grounds for changing the legal system in any coherent way; it leaves the language-games of the law intact. Rorty's "pragmatism" admits that there are no formulas for deciding legal cases, but he fails to offer even an amorphous game plan indicating how we should proceed, other than to suggest that we should be experimental and imaginative. The problem is that we need *grounds* for deciding hard cases, and it will not do to simply state that judges must experiment and hope for the best.

This problem can best be illustrated if one looks at specific cases, such as *Bowers v. Hardwick*, the Supreme Court case on sodomy which I discussed earlier. Rorty says that he is looking forward to a reversal of this decision, and he hopes that the reversal has the following message: "[L]ike it or not, gays are grown ups too." But it is hard to see how this message could serve as a guide for a legal determination of an actual court case that is reconsidering *Bowers*. I suppose that Rorty's point is that a good decision would recognize that gays, like others, have a right of autonomy, and this right is broad enough to encompass the liberty of the individual to engage in unpopular acts of consensual homosexual sex. But if this is Rorty's point, he has taken the path of least resistance. Instead of *showing* how "we" value autonomy to the extent that we should permit autonomous decisions like this, he merely asserts that this is the case. A more thorough approach would be to check our legal precedents for holdings that support this interpretation and then show how our precedents and shared values demand a reversal of *Bowers*. This task might be accomplished by pointing out that a strong respect for autonomy is implicit in the right to vote and the right to free speech (neither of which can be outweighed by majorty sentiment), such that in *Bowers* the defendant's right of autonomy should have outweighed the majority sentiment for criminalizing homosexuality.[64]

The problem here is that Rorty's pragmatism is an amorphous strategy for reaching specific decisions. Rorty's salute to bravery and experimentation fails to explain when we should bravely experiment and in what direction. For some reason Rorty tends to assume that Deweyan experimentation would require the adoption of left-leaning arrangements, but there is no reason to suppose that experimentation would exclude forays into conservatism or perhaps even fascism. And when one looks at the particular decisions that Rorty favors (*Brown*, *Roe*, a reversal of *Bowers*), one can see that they are linked not by experimentalism or pragmatism but by a concern with human autonomy and freedom. Each decision held that the right to autonomy outweighed popular sentiment that would have effectively limited it (through segregation, abortion laws, and criminal laws against homosexual sex). Rorty would have us believe that these decisions were unprincipled experiments, but this depiction does not do justice to the rationale behind these cases. The job for a legal theorist is to articulate the rationale or theory which drives these "good" decisions, not to throw up one's hands and say that there is simply no formula at work here.

One should pay attention to Rorty's claim that just political arrangements can be determined on an ad-hoc experimental basis by adopting novel arrangements and then seeing how well they work. For example, Rorty suggests that third world countries might experiment with absolute equality of income to see what effect it might have (though he recognizes that this arrangement is inconsistent with the values and traditions in America).[65] The problem with this suggestion is that it simply pushes back the key issue, which is the problem of determining when an arrangement "works." Experimentalism alone is of no use if one is deeply divided as to when a situation can be said to "work." Liberals may think that the welfare state "works," while conservatives feel the opposite, so what is needed is a theory which will convince one side to reconsider its position. The disagreement is precisely over what one means by "works," which implies that "workability" is not a decisive standard for political and legal arrangements. This problem also plagues Rorty's advocacy of "invidious comparison" as a way of choosing between the present system and its alternatives. He is certainly correct that few people would choose to live in a Nazi state or a pure communist society, but how are we to compare the current system with alternatives that are less extreme, such as socialism or a nightwatchmen state? Once again, mere comparison is not enough: we need grounds for saying that one arrangement is better than another, and it will not do to say that one "works" better.

Rorty is correct, I think, in his antifoundationalist notion that political and legal arrangements (and the justifications offered to support them) are inescapably contingent. Rorty is also correct in saying that contingency should provide us with a certain sense of irony about the values that we presently hold. Yet we might question whether there isn't something foundational lurking beneath Rorty's claim that solidarity should be the key to ethics, politics, and law. This idea that our efforts should be directed toward the elimination of suffering sounds rather like a utilitarian metanarrative which tells us that we have a duty to eliminate suffering and maximize utility. Where does this duty come from? Perhaps this duty is itself merely a contingent imperative, which is fine, but Rorty fails to show how this committment is central to our contingent institutions and practices. He has not shown that we (in the narrow sense of "we Americans") have been particularly dedicated to the elimination of suffering. Furthermore, it would seem that legal issues such as abortion and affirmative action are questions of principle (about desert, equality, neutrality) and *not* questions about the elimination of suffering.

These are just a few of the problems with Rorty's theory. In reaching my claim that his theory is not very helpful to legal theorists, I have specifically avoided passing judgment on Rorty's public/private split, nor have I focused on the obvious problems with formulating the "we" in a society that is split down the lines of race and class. These objections to Rorty have been raised elsewhere, so I won't dwell on them here except to say that they spell out important limitations for Rorty's theory.

Now, there is a very real sense in which Rorty's message of contingency is liberating. As Elizabeth Mensch reminds us, "The most corrosive message of legal history is the message of contingency. Routinely, the justificatory language of the law parades as the unquestionable embodiment of Reason and Universal Truth; yet even a brief romp through the history of American legal thought reveals how quickly the Obvious Logic of one period becomes superseded by the equally obvious, though contradictory, logic of subsequent orthodoxy."[66] But what follows from the insight that the categories of the legal system are contingent and fluid? I suspect that the lesson to be gleaned from this insight is that we ought to be ironic and fallibilistic about the legal doctrines we advocate. Granted, but at any given time we are unavoidably situated within a certain stage of this evolving system and we must design solutions to legal problems by using the categories currently operative in this system. The reminder about contingency is just that—a reminder—and therein lies its limited scope: it does not provide one solution or another in particular cases. I suspect that Ronald Dworkin is correct in his assessment that the pragmatist's tendency to see legal concepts as contextually relative does not affect the internal workings of legal practice: "But though contextualism provides a needed reminder to the complacent, it is essentially *external* to the argumentative and justificatory side of science, morality, and law. It cannot count as an argument against someone's scientific or moral or legal opinions that he would not have had these in other times and circumstances. If that were a sound skeptical argument, little would be left of our beliefs and convictions."[67] In other words, the message of contingency does not tell us how to handle legal disputes within the current legal scheme of rules and principles. For that we need a positive jurisprudence.

Why Rorty Stops Short of a Positive Jurisprudence

All of these problems should not—and do not—radically undermine Rorty's important central message that that there is no way to stand outside of our traditions to assess them from some sort of neutral Archimedian point. The legal system is itself merely a contingent tradition. Rorty is correct in assuming that we stand in medias res when doing legal theory, making our practice unavoidably ethnocentric and circular.

One might ask, Why support a legal system that cannot be philosophically grounded in basic truths about human nature, autonomy, or reason? Why give credence to the Declaration of Independence if one no longer believes in God or "natural law"? The antifoundationalist response to this question is to point out that such a grounding was a mistaken ideal in the first place, so there is no choice other than to adopt a circular, ethnocentric justification of our practices. This strategy can be understood as a "hermeneutic turn" of sorts, in which political theorists and lawyers turn away from universal first principles and toward the social meanings that are embedded in local practices and institutions.[68] Rorty takes the hermeneutic turn because he correctly sees that there can be no sense in identifying sources of law which are transcendental, but, having made this point, he fails to take the necessary step of painstakingly identifying the *contingent* sources of law which are appropriate for "us" as presently situated.

This is why I say that Rorty "stops short." He correctly sees that legal theory is a matter of coherence, not correspondence (i.e., the best legal decision in a court case is the one which is most faithful to the contingent traditions and principles held by our society), and he also realizes that these contingent traditions cannot themselves be tested against some objective standard. But, having made this point, Rorty should go on to explore our contingent traditions, to find out what they demand as a matter of justice. This is the path taken by John Rawls in *Political Liberalism* and it is also the path attempted by Ronald Dworkin in *Law's Empire* and Michael Walzer in *Spheres of Justice*. In contrast, Rorty's law review articles seem to take the position that there is very little interesting philosophical work to be done once we have eliminated the last vestiges of Platonism and metaphysics from legal theory: "I find it hard to see any interesting *philosophical* differences between Unger, Dworkin, and Posner; their differences strike me as entirely *political*."[69] Rorty is correct in concluding that these thinkers share a distrust of metaphysical first principles of law, but he fails to see that they are radically divided on the question of how courts should decide cases. Indeed, Posner has written extensively against some of Dworkin's main points, and vice versa.[70] If Rorty feels that the sole task of the philosophy of law is to remove transcendental foundations, then he is correct that these thinkers are similar. But the loss of metaphysical foundations is where philosophy of law must begin anew, teasing out a contingent notion of justice for our society. This second effort is indeed a philosophical matter, altough Rorty fails to recognize it as such.

Like the other postmodernists discussed in previous chapters, Rorty's take on legal theory is essentially *external*: his goal is to attack the foundational and metaphysical principles which have long plagued legal theory. He is correct that ethics and law can be grounded only in shifting, contingent traditions, and that the search for ahistorical criteria to ground political visions ("species being," "human reason," "utility") has been something of a failure. Like the other postmodernists, he stresses that legal theory is always situated, always embedded in power relations and discursive practices.

Although all of these are important points, they remain external to the business of legal theory. Once we weed out the Platonism from particular viewpoints, there remains a level of internal debate at which Rorty cannot help us. In the end, we must join those thinkers who are trying to interpret our contingent, local, fallible institutions and practices to determine if proposed laws and case decisions are in harmony with our collective moral committments. Rorty doesn't see anything *philosophical* going on at this internal level, but I would suggest that if philosophers such as Walzer and Dworkin are working at this level, then something philosophical is indeed going on. And it is at this internal level that additional work must be done once Rorty has made the important contribution of "clearing the philosphical underbrush" of legal theory.[71]

8 ❧ Conclusion: The Benefits and Drawbacks of Postmodern Legal Theory

Having completed a preliminary review of the key postmodern thinkers, it is now time to take stock of the accomplishments and drawbacks of postmodern legal theory as a collective movement. In keeping with my commitment to explore postmodern legal theory by presenting it in its most favorable light, in this chapter I will focus initially on the benefits to be derived from postmodernism. I will then criticize postmodern legal theory by returning to the two large-scale problems I raised in chapter 2, namely, the adoption of the external viewpoint and the extreme rejection of foundations. After considering these problems, I respond negatively to the major question raised at the beginning of this book: can postmodernism offer what I call a "positive jurisprudence"? Despite the lack of a positive jurisprudence, postmodernism *does* have something to offer legal theory by virtue of what I will refer to as "thinking the other of the law." In conclusion, I will attempt to delineate the circumstances under which postmodernism can make this contribution.

The Insights of Postmodern Legal Theory

There are four general categories of insights generated by postmodern legal theory: (1) the importance of genealogy and an awareness of contingency, (2) an understanding of incommensurability and marginalization, (3) the deconstruction of supposedly neutral doctrines, and (4) an awareness of language and discourse in the law. Collectively these insights establish a reasonable justification for my foray through the work of the enigmatic postmodern thinkers.

GENEALOGY AND THE AWARENESS OF CONTINGENCY

Several important ideas may be derived from Nietzsche's and Foucault's genealogical analyses of the law. Both thinkers point out that our existing conceptual scheme in the law (i.e., our legal categories of rights, crimes, causes of action, and property interests) is not some sort of changeless and static set of principles written into the fabric of the universe but is "contingent" in the sense that it could have been strikingly different had other power relations prevailed in the past. For example, Nietzsche shows that the present system of equal rights is not inevitable or natural (as Jefferson thought it was) but is a historical outgrowth of a "transvaluation" of values held prior to Christianity. Similarly, Foucault points out that our present system of punishment (in which imprisonment, normalization, and reeducation have replaced all other methods of dealing with criminals) is merely the latest in a series of experiments in methods of punishment; the present method may seem humane, yet it is largely ineffective and subtly dangerous. The effect of these genealogical and historical insights is that they counteract our tendency to reify the existing legal order and elevate it to the realm of necessity or "reasonableness," a process in which we come to view our existing arrangement as the only available option. This tendency toward reification can be seen in the incredulity encountered by radical thinkers who assert the existence of previously unrecognized rights, such as those of meaningful work or housing. Since these rights are beyond the widely accepted negative rights of liberty and due process, they appear "too much" or "impracticable" to those who are deeply embedded in the current legal framework.[1] The genealogical critique shows that the current system parades itself as "natural" but is no more natural than other arrangements.

One of the best ways to illustrate the power of the genealogical approach in legal philosophy is to look at the way in which it affects a different social practice, namely, psychiatry. Consider the analysis of madness put forth by Foucault in *Madness and Civilization*.[2] In that book Foucault pointed out that "madness" is in some sense a socially constructed malady. To be sure, certain people in any society can be classified as unquestionably insane under any possible definition of "sanity." But Foucault points out that throughout history there have been outsiders and dissidents who were classified as insane for, say, being unemployed, having a different sexual orientation, or not conforming to the particular social roles of their day. This means that people who were not insane in any deep sense were nevertheless classified as insane to serve various social purposes (e.g., getting the unemployed off the streets, filling the empty lepersaureums, mainstreaming those who appear different, teaching "hysterical" women their proper place in society).

One might rightly ask how Foucault's genealogical work in this area can be of use to psychiatrists. Foucault's investigation does not help in the day-to-day tasks these doctors face on the inside of their practice; Foucault does not make specific arguments about, say, whether manic-depressive illness has a physical or social cause, nor does he provide a general psychological framework for assessing the mental well-being of patients. He certainly does not offer a theory of the mind in the grand style of Freud or Jung. However, his work is important in a more oblique way because his genealogical point about the social construction of madness can act as a check or reminder against the blind application of psychiatric classifications that seem to be socially constructed. A psychiatrist who reads Foucault may be more likely to understand that a patient who is homosexual does not have a mental disorder for that reason, even though homosexuality has historically been treated as a mental illness to be "cured." Furthermore, Foucault's work teaches us that many psychological illnesses only *seem* to be a matter of individual pathology but are actually caused by society at large, as in the cases of anorexia and bulimia, which are certainly afflictions that affect particular individuals but also have a social component due to the unrealistic conceptions of female beauty which dominate our culture. As a historian, Foucault cannot change the practice of psychiatry on its own terms, but he can force a "relativizing" or critical posture toward the standard practice; the external, historical insight might affect the internal practice of psychiatry, if only by providing a measure of caution and an element of doubt about the practice as presently configured.

Just as Foucault's work on madness can act as a reminder that our psychiatric categories are fluid, so his (and Nietzsche's) work on law can remind us that *legal* categories are constructed through shifting power relations. Just as *Madness and Civilization* does not present a comprehensive theory of the mind, so Foucault's major work on the prison system, *Discipline and Punish,* does not present a *general* theory of criminality, though he does make the important point that our present system of incarceration actually breeds criminality and produces criminals under the guise of reforming them. Foucault's notion that criminality is socially constructed is driven home by the fact that most of the prisoners in federal prisons are serving time on drug charges. These "criminals" have merely engaged in consensual arrangements for the sale and purchase of drugs (not unlike other business transactions in a capitalist society), and they would not be considered "criminals" in other Western countries which have a more tolerant attitude toward consensual drug use. This insight does not force an immediate change from the inside of criminal law and practice (e.g., Foucault does not provide the blueprint for a new criminal code), but his work can force a rethinking of our present mode of classifying criminal behavior and treating criminality.

The genealogical analysis, then, is not useful if one is looking for a large-scale metatheory to provide a foundation for legal decisions from within the current arrangement. However, it has a more limited use as a way of countering our tendency to see the present arrangement as natural and unchangeable.

Growing up under a particular legal system, we find it difficult to conceive of a different way of structuring the law. As one Critical Legal Studies theorist put it, "The dominant system of values has been declared value-free; it then follows that all others suffer from bias and can be thoughtlessly dismissed."[3] By way of illustration, many people think that private property is inevitable, or that it would be absurd for there to be a constitutional right to shelter, just as they find it unthinkable that we might tolerate lifestyle experiments by, say, permitting gay marriages. Long ago Marx correctly pointed out that people tend to replicate the social order of which they are a part. As a result, they cannot see any "outside" to the current arrangement, such that every call for radical change seems unreasonable, reactive, an affront to common sense. The genealogical approach offered by Nietzsche and Foucault counters this tendency by showing that the current arrangement is no more "natural" than the order which it replaced. This does not provide a game plan for creating a new legal system, but it does give us a certain critical distance or irony toward our practices, thereby allowing for new approaches and ideas.

AWARENESS OF INCOMMENSURABILITY AND MARGINALIZATION

A second valuable insight of postmodern theory comes from Lyotard's notion that any legal system will give rise to "differends," that is, to claims which cannot be adjudicated for lack of a neutral arbiter.[4] I think that this point is related to Derrida's deconstructive claim that (in politics no less than literary interpretation) we must focus on the margins as well as the text (e.g., on what is *not* said).[5] Foucault echoes this point when he suggests that "to find out what our society means by sanity, perhaps we should investigate what is happening in the field of insanity. And what we mean by legality [by looking at] the field of illegality."[6] The postmodern message here is that legal systems (as *closed* systems) necessarily exclude certain people from receiving a hearing by virtue of the ground rules of the system. Certain claims are excluded from the discourse of rights which prevails in our legal system. As Lyotard shows, the marginalized discourse is silenced by the language-game of the presiding court. Typically, the claims which fall silent are those of the powerless, such as indigenous peoples, minorities, and women.[7]

Tellingly, there is a specific legal term for a grievance which cannot be recognized under the legal system, namely, "failure to state a claim." The Federal Rules of Civil Procedure which govern proceedings in federal cases (and which have been adopted in large mesure by state courts) provide that a case will be dismissed if the plaintiff fails to set forth facts sufficient to state a cause of action.[8] This determination is made by seeing whether the plaintiff has set forth the required elements of an established claim. For example, to state a claim for breach of contract, one must allege the existence of an offer, an acceptance, consideration, breach, and damages. Upon motion by the defendant, the court will refuse to "hear" any claim that does not satisfy the elements of an established "cause of action."

The problem which arises here has to do with the boundaries which are set on whether a claim is "legal" and can find recognition in a court of law. For example, a homeless man may rightly feel that any country which can send half a million soldiers to Iraq to fight in the Gulf War and can send astronauts to the moon should guarantee minimal housing to people who have tried to secure work but cannot find a job that guarantees a living wage. Despite the homeless man's sense that his country should provide him with housing, this feeling does not mean that the homeless man has a *right* to housing, that is, that he has a legal claim against the state for the provision of housing. A person may feel wronged and yet not be able to translate that feeling into a claim that can be stated in legal terms. The task of the legal theorist, then, is to articulate this experiential harm as a legal harm, as a damage which can be compensated within the legal system. This process brings something from outside the legal system (an external claim) to a position within the system (as an internal claim). The project here is to change the ground rules or boundaries by which the legal system operates, to work at the margins.

This transformation can be seen in the evolving doctrine of sexual harassment. Recall that women were once told that they must simply endure sexual harassment as the price for holding a job in a man's world. The rationale for the absence of legal protection against sexual harassment was that a law prohibiting harassment would be impossible to enforce due to the conflicting reports that would be given by the victim and the perpetrator, and thus the law would inevitably require an unwarranted judicial intrusion into private affairs between individual citizens. Because of this logic, women who suffered sexual harassment during the sixties and seventies lacked a voice that could be heard in the legal system; they were denied a legal forum to express their injury. The innovation of feminist legal scholars was to help formulate the harm which these women suffered in such a way that it could be recognized as a legal harm. As Catharine MacKinnon explains, "It became possible to do something about sexual harassment because some women took women's experience of violations seriously enough to design a law around it. . . . Sexual harassment, the legal claim—the idea that the law should see it the way its victims see it—is definitely a feminist invention."[9]

If Lyotard is correct in his notion that the legal system gives rise to differends, then some of our energy should be focused on behalf of Lyotard's admonition that we ought to be listening for the silence of differends which fail to state a claim under the current legal system. The most obvious cases that fall within this category are situations in which someone feels that a harm has been done but the legal system does not recognize the harm as something which ought to be remedied under the law. A good example of this would be the crime of spousal rape. Traditionally husbands could not be convicted of spousal rape on the theory that marriage constituted a consent to sexual activity of any kind, however willing or unwilling. Yet many women felt that they had been raped within the confines of marriage, notwithstanding the lack of legal recognition that an offense had been committed. Eventually the legal rule was changed to give a voice to this harm.[10]

There will certainly be cases where we have grave doubts about whether a perceived harm should be recognized under the legal system. A controversy is now raging over whether there should be a tort action or injunctive relief for group slander. That is, should minorities be compensated for the public transmission of epithets directed at their ethnicity? Should they be able to enjoin public speech which contains group slanders? There are two views on this issue. The liberal view holds that this harm must be endured as the price of free speech. In contrast, the view of certain believers in so-called Critical Race Theory is that the racial epithets are akin to a slap in the face and ought to be seen as a harm that requires compensation or, at the very least, should not be given the status of protected speech under the First Amendment. Minority groups are starting to challenge the prevailing legal rule that freedom of speech protects racial insults. For example, in 1996 a Polish-American group sued the National Broadcasting Company for allegedly airing anti-Polish material.[11] Certainly, there will be much debate on the question of whether this group should be allowed recovery under the law, and this may be a case in which there is a *felt* harm which cannot be translated into a claim that is recognized by the legal system.

Irrespective of the solution to that case, Lyotard's work reminds us that the legal system has historically rejected certain claims as inactionable, only to later recognize these very claims. Lyotard's point, I think, is that we ought to give a voice to people who presently feel harmed but are denied a means of expressing this harm: "To give the differend its due is to institute new addressees, new addressors, new significations, and new referents in order for the wrong to find expression and for the plaintiff to cease being a victim. . . . In the differend, something 'asks' to be put into phrases, and suffers from the wrong of not being able to be put into phrases right away."[12] Part of this project involves finding the right terms with which to express a harm that has been lying inchoate. One of most fearsome aspects of powerlessness is the lack of a voice, the absence of a language to express one's outrage. Empowerment results when a voice can be found and is given recognition by the legal system. Postmodern legal theory can be of special help in this project because it focuses (to a greater extent than Anglo-American legal theory) on seemingly external and marginal matters (i.e., on people and ideas which are outside the mainstream), and this orientation forces a rethinking of the boundary which separates the "legal" from that which is marginalized as "nonlegal." Postmodernism is especially useful in this regard because it would have us stand outside of our practices to examine the boundaries and parameters which presently constitute those practices.

DECONSTRUCTION OF SUPPOSEDLY NEUTRAL DOCTRINES

In the chapter on Derrida I argued that Derrida's philosophy of law puts forth a theory of justice which is foundational, and hence inconsistent with his earlier, more deconstructive writings. I still feel strongly that the method of deconstruction can be used to interrogate and question some key legal concepts. The goal here would be to use Derrida's method of reading texts, in which special attention is paid to the artificial status of binary and hierarchical structures that have been set up by an author. As I stated in chapter 5, deconstruction is concerned with breaking down or destroying the distinctions between part/whole, text/margin, inside/outside, public/private, and individual/collective. Typically, one side of these hierarchies is privileged at the expense of the other, and once the hierarchy is exposed as arbitrary or groundless, the text allegedly collapses in on itself and "deconstructs."[13]

As I mentioned earlier, it is somewhat surprising that this method of deconstruction was not used by Derrida in his lectures on jurisprudence, and that he chose to focus instead on deeper questions about the nature of justice and law. However, some legal thinkers have succeeded in using Derrida's method of deconstruction to examine specific doctrines in the law, and I think that this is an area where postmodernism can have a positive influence. For example, in an interesting article Clare Dalton has focused on what she calls the "ideology of contract law," which she uncovered in her deconstructive reading of the so-called palimony lawsuits of the eighties.[14] These lawsuits revolved around the question of whether a live-in girlfriend could recover alimony from her former lover even though the couple was unmarried (hence "*pal*imony"). I will not repeat Dalton's findings, but her close reading of these cases reveals that the courts were engaged in an ideological struggle as well as a struggle to find the correct legal solution to the question of whether these women should receive alimony. On a legalistic level, the courts spoke in jargon-laden terms about whether there was a contract between the parties analogous to a marriage contract, whether there was consideration for such a contract, whether the relationship was a private matter that was beyond the reach of the courts, and so on. All of these are important legal questions. However, on a more ideological level, the courts were exploring various frameworks for understanding the relationship between the female plaintiff and male defendant in these cases. Specifically, when close attention was paid to the language of the judicial opinions, the crux of these cases often revolved around whether women in these situations (i.e., living with a man for a long time) should be seen as an angelic quasi-wife or, alternatively, as a harlot who seduced the man into promising to take care of her forever. Dalton's deconstructive reading uncovers a hidden layer of what might be called "sexual reasoning" in which ideological notions of femininity are glossed over by legal terms such as "contract," "consideration," "public/private," and so on. By examining these decisions in greater detail, one can find hidden ideological forces at work in the judicial process; these forces can subsequently be brought to light where one can deal with them directly. The "deconstructive" project here is to identify a hidden tension at work in these cases, a value choice between different conceptions lurking below the level of purely legal analysis. I don't think that one can generalize from Dalton's work to claim that deconstruction is a guaranteed path for generating insights into controversial cases—many deconstructive readings lead nowhere and serve only to make cases more confusing—but it is a viable avenue for insight into the law.

A second method of reading legal texts in a deconstructive manner involves taking an important legal decision and showing how it rests upon an unstable and somewhat arbitrary balancing of competing interests and doctrines. This approach is popular in Critical Legal Studies, particularly in Duncan Kennedy's argument that most areas of private law (contracts, torts, property) are shot through with two contradictory impulses: an altruistic impulse which harbors a collectivist vision of society and an individualistic impulse which harbors an atomistic vision of society.[15] Some questions of contract or tort law (e.g., whether a tortfeasor should be liable for unforeseen damages) cannot be resolved apart from this struggle between the two competing worldviews. There is no preexisting *legal* solution to this type of problem which is not really a *political* solution masquerading as a supposedly correct legal solution, so the law deconstructs into opposing forces which cannot be ranked or reconciled. The law is not a set of neutral principles existing autonomously and distinct from political commitments but is itself a mirror of deep political conflicts. Judges, then, are political actors whether or not they choose to see themselves as such. In addition to making value judgments about which doctrines to apply, judges must choose whether to use bright-line rules ("a person over the age of eighteen can consent to a contract") versus amorphous standards ("consent must be determined on a case-by-case basis, such that a seventeen-year-old may be liable on a contract while a twenty-year-old may lack the capacity to consent"). This choice between rules and standards is also a political choice because a rules-based approach favors a formal society with clear rules of personal interaction, while a standards-based approach favors a more collectivist vision. I have argued elsewhere that legal doctrine may not be as indeterminate as Kennedy suggests,[16] but there is something important in his effort to identify the structural constraints and conflicting worldviews which permeate legal theory. Ever since the era of the Legal Realists (such as Jerome Frank and Karl Llewellyn), lawyers have been aware that legal outcomes are somewhat indeterminate and unpredictable; perhaps deconstruction can help to uncover the forces which drive this indeterminacy.

One reason that postmodernism can undertake a deconstructive reading of legal doctrine is that it assumes a fundamentally external perspective on the legal system. As I mentioned earlier, internal theory cannot adopt the deconstructive view that legal doctrine is hopelessly contradictory because the internal perspective privileges the viewpoint of the judge who must assume that the law is preexisting and clear. A useful aspect of postmodern legal philosophy is precisely its freedom from the institutional constraints that fetter judges' and lawyers' views of the law. Sometimes the most incisive view of the law is not available to those on the inside of the practice. In this regard, the radical perspectivism of postmodernism might prove useful in fostering new perspectives on the legal system (e.g., by seeing the system from the perspective of criminals, clients, or jurors).

THE SHAPING OF LEGAL DISCOURSE AND THE "UNSAYABLE"

A cardinal virtue of postmodernism is its sensitivity to language and its insistence that the individual is shaped by the discourses in which he or she is immersed. This claim reaches an extreme form in Lacan's notion that "language speaks the subject" and in Foucault's belief that the subject is nothing over and above the product of the prevailing discourses and disciplines. If one acknowledges that language and discourses shape the individual, one must pay very close attention to the ways in which language is controlled and manufactured. In the context of the legal system, this means that one must ask questions like, "Who has the right to set the parameters of legal discourse?" "Who sets the 'moves' of the legal system?" "Who decides what can be said and what must be left unsaid?" In *The Archaeology of Knowledge*[17] Foucault explains that social practices (such as law) are perpetuated by a special group of insiders authorized to speak and play specific roles within the practice. The social practice takes on a self-identity as the players learn a new language and a mode of behavior which separates them from the public at large. Within the practice of the law, the "players" are licensed professionals, law school graduates who have passed the bar exam and been admitted to the bar. Due to the high costs of an education through college and law school, it should come as no surprise that in our society these players have been drawn predominantly from a particular stratum (propertied, white, male), though this is changing. As part of their training, these players are provided with a stock set of concepts in which their arguments must be stated, and they are given certain stock roles to choose from (counselor, litigator, prosecutor). The law as a social and discursive practice has a very rigid set of boundaries which establish what can be said and what is beyond the sayable. The establishment of a private language (so-called legalese) helps to keep the majority of people alienated from the law, feeling almost as if the language of the law is a foreign tongue. Lawyers are restricted in what they can say and do by the rules of the discursive practice of the law, yet they customarily work *within* this practice and do not stand outside of it.

There is an additional element of restriction on what can be said or done within the practice of law due to the fact that law works by precedent; under the principle of *stare decisis,* past decisions control present decisions. This tradition ensures a perpetuation of past ways of thinking by keeping alive the language of the remote past (e.g., "fee simples," "easements by prescription," "springing remainders") and elevates this discourse to the level of a mystical code which can be understood only by the special chieftains of the law. Legal discourse is manufactured through a series of ground rules which more or less restrict what will be recognized as a *legal* argument and who can assert these arguments. To gauge the force of this situation, imagine what would happen if the language of the law was reformed so that ordinary citizens could assert their rights in a court of law through a simplified method of pleading and proof. The lack of a simplified system makes us question why the present system is too complex for ordinary citizens (let alone the poor and uneducated) to seek redress in a court of law.

Postmodernism makes us sensitive to the way in which power relations regulate the production of legal discourse and practice. Hence it should come as no surprise to learn that postmodernists are concerned with law schools and legal education because it is here that students pick up many of the attitudes and behaviors which they will be using in private practice.[18] As Duncan Kennedy explains, "Law schools are intensely political places despite the fact that the modern law school seems intellectually unpretentious, barren of theoretical ambition or practical vision of what social life might be. [Law school involves] ideological training for willing service in the hierarchies of the corporate welfare state."[19] Postmodernism, then, opens up legal studies to an analysis of the ways in which legal discourse is generated. This means that legal studies need not be restricted to looking at the substance of legal doctrine ("What are the formal elements of a contract?") but can also look at the way in which legal doctrine is shaped ("For whom is contract law necessary? Whom does it benefit?") This, I think, is where "legal studies" meets "cultural studies," where legal theory begins to theorize about itself as a cultural artifact. This is also the point at which legal studies intersects with anthropology, semiotics, Marxism, and other external approaches to the law.

One might pause here to ask what it is about these insights that is particularly *postmodern*. Why must we look to postmodernism to generate these insights? Can't they be found in the work of more mainstream thinkers as well? For example, the Nietzschean point about revolutions in the legal system can be found in Harold Berman's book *Law and Revolution* and, more generally, in Thomas Kuhn's book *The Structure of Scientific Revolutions*. Foucault's points about the social construction of legal categories can be found in such mainstream texts on the evolution of American law as Lawrence Friedman's *History of American Law*. And Derrida's deconstructive readings of case decisions are really quite similar to standard ideology critiques offered by Marxists and feminists. So what is the genuinely postmodern insight that makes it vitally important to read all of these postmodern thinkers?

The honest response to this question, I think, is to admit that the postmodern insights *can* be found in the works of other thinkers, and that there is nothing absolutely necessary about reading the postmodernists to get these points. Having said this, I would add that there is at least one major reason to read them: the postmodernists are influencing many areas besides law, such as literary theory, feminism, sociology, art, and, of course, philosophy. By reading the postmodernists, one lays the foundation for further work in other areas of the humanities. Apart from this, I can offer no special reason that one ought to read the works of these thinkers if one is interested solely in legal theory. Then, again, it is difficult to convince a skeptic that he or she should read *anything;* there is no way to conclusively prove that a person should (or must) be familiar with certain texts. I have tried to articulate the benefits of postmodern legal theory, and beyond this there is nothing more I can say by way of convincing someone that this work is important and interesting.

Two Big Problems: Externality and Lingering Foundationalism

Having set forth what I see as the benefits of postmodern theory, I would now like to turn to what I see as the limitations of postmodern legal theory. I will be recapitulating the problems discussed in chapter 2: the external perspective taken by postmodernism, as well as its radical distrust of foundations.

EXTERNALITY

At the beginning of this book I dealt at length with the notion that postmodern legal theory tends to offer an *external* critique of the legal system because it refuses to adopt the language-games and terminology used (often unreflectively) by officials of the legal system. I pointed out that this perspective differs greatly from the internal viewpoint adopted by mainstream Anglo-American jurisprudence, especially in the influential work of H. L. A. Hart and Ronald Dworkin. I now want to focus a little more closely on the problems resulting from the adoption of an external point of view.

As Americans—and especially as legal theorists—we have a need for both an internal and an external perspective on the law. Every day we read in the newspaper about legal controversies that are being fought in our courts, and we know that these controversies will be settled under the law as it has been construed by our highest courts. No matter which side of the controversy we personally favor, we know that the bottom line will come down to the law, which means that we must ask ourselves the *internally* oriented question, "What is the law on this topic?" We ask that question because we know on some level that the case will be decided from the internal perspective of the judge. Thus, if the case deals with an affirmative action program, we have to ask whether such a program is constitutional in light of the Fourteenth Amendment; if the case deals with abortion, we must ask if the fetus constitutes a "person" under the law and whether the mother's right to liberty or privacy encompasses the right to an abortion. The courts are charged by law with looking at legal doctrine from an internal perspective, and we expect them to do so. Indeed, the existence of an internal perspective is what allows for the rule of law, stability, predictability, and due process for litigants. These are values which are central to our way of life. Nobody, then, can rationally suggest that lawyers and judges should abandon the internal perspective on the law, because the abandonment of this perspective might destroy the practice of law altogether. To grasp this last point, consider how the game of chess would be destroyed if the players took a purely external attitude toward the game—for instance, by sitting around the chessboard discussing the social significance of chess. Like chess, the legal system is a game that must be played from the inside, and the events at this internal level determine the outcome of the game. Therefore, to focus exclusively on the outside or the social context or the history of a social practice (such as the legal system) is to miss the internal side of the practice. If we read a judicial opinion solely from a historical perspective or if we read an opinion as a symptom of bourgeois illusions then we miss what Dworkin calls the internal, argumentative aspect of the law.[20]

On the other hand, legal controversies do not occur in a vacuum, and the law (unlike chess) is not a system of rules divorced from the larger social context. We are a society divided by race and class, with the result that legal doctrine is itself shaped by fundamental unspoken assumptions and biases in favor of certain arrangements (private property, competition, wage-labor, negative rights) and against others (positive rights, collective ownership, altruism). The law can harbor ideological distortions and it can contain rules which are downright absurd and counterintuitive. Therefore, it is often necessary to see the legal system from the outside, to get a glimpse of the law from the critical perspective which judges usually avoid in their official capacity as judges. For example, in *Brown v. Board of Education* the Supreme Court looked to empirical sociological studies to reach the conclusion that the legal notion of "separate but equal" did not conform to the experiences of African-Americans, who felt separate and *un*equal.[21] Only through a similar process of stepping outside the legal system can we determine if the concepts used within the system are "off" or "skewed."

A stunning metaphor for the internal and external perspectives was offered a few years ago by Richard Delgado, a law professor who specializes in Critical Race Theory.[22] Delgado published a series of fictional conversations with a minority law student, one of which dealt with the law school curriculum, specifically with its focus on business matters at the expense of social issues such as homelessness and poverty. The student said that the law faculty (and many of the students) were living in a bubble which they mistook for the real world. Those on the outside (which is where the minority student placed himself) can see the curvature of the bubble, thereby revealing its contours and limitations. Those on the inside see something entirely different because they mistakenly think that there is nothing outside the bubble. The image is striking and, I think, an appropriate way to describe the legal system. To understand the law in a complete sense, we must be able to assume both an internal and external perspective in the hope that each will complement the other so that a complete picture will emerge.

In this book, I have demonstrated that postmodern legal theory takes place at a level of thought far removed from the language-games in which laws are enacted and cases decided. Postmodern theory questions the foundational concepts of the legal edifice with the intended goal of destabilizing or criticizing the entire system (or at least of questioning an entire area of law, such as property law or criminal law). Paradoxically, this strategy often fails completely because the critique is so external to the practice of law that it leaves the internal workings of the legal apparatus untouched. As Wittgenstein similarly remarked about philosophy, the questioning of foundations from an external perspective "leaves everything as it is."[23] In other words, the practice is approached from such a critical distance that it is left unchanged. One can agree with the postmodernists that legal theory is becoming incredulous toward metanarratives, that the foundational metaphysical principles are crumbling. But this claim can't change the inner workings of the legal system until the insight is couched in the internal terms of that system.

Similarly, an external critique of the law does little to disrupt the decisions of legislators and judges for the simple reason that these legal actors are already operating (and must operate) within a different language-game from the one used in the external critique. For example, the postmodern critique of the autonomous "self" or *cogito,* as a purely theoretical matter, cannot directly influence the legal doctrines (say, in the criminal law), which are built upon the notion of a free *cogito,* unless it enters into the language-game of the law and challenges doctrines based on the *cogito*—for example, by showing that the legal notion of *mens rea* (the mental state which causes a criminal act) presupposes a naive view of the self as fully transparent and self-present. The grand critique of foundations is of little practical help unless it can be translated into the language-game of the law. To illustrate this point in an extreme form, consider how absurd it would be for a postmodernist to appear in a courthouse in order to argue that election results should be thrown out on the basis of Lyotard's claim that "consensus is totalitarian." In this case and others, the external perspective is simply too far removed from the actual workings of the legal system to effect any genuine change in that system. This means that the postmodernists should not be content to state their positions at the level of external generalities but must try to bring their analysis down to the level at which decisions are made, which requires a translation from the external to the internal perspective. Although this translation can be done—indeed, *should* be done—most of the postmodern thinkers discussed in this book have failed to take this necessary step.

The problem of taking an extremely external perspective is not, of course, particular to postmodernism. This perspective is found quite often in Critical Legal Studies, as can be seen from a leading advocate's summary of some tenets of that movement:

> Judges are often the unknowing objects, as well as among the staunchest supporters, of the myth of legal reasoning. Decisions are predicated upon a complex mixture of social, political, institutional, experiential, and personal

factors; however, they are expressed and justified, and largely perceived by judges themselves, in term of "facts" that have been objectively determined and "law" that has been objectively and rationally "found" and "applied." Social and political judgments about the substance, parties, and context of a case guide [a judge's] choices even when they are not the explicit or conscious basis of decision.[24]

The argument here is that judges are really influenced by political and personal factors (external forces) and not by the demands of the law (internal forces); in any event, the legal precedents are so malleable that they can be construed to support any legal position which the judge happens to hold as an external matter. This type of claim holds that the internal rationales offered by judges and lawyers to explain their actions are completely delusory. In Marxist terms, the judges and lawyers have a "false consciousness" which prevents them from understanding the true sources of their decisions.

The problem with this line of thinking is that it totally dismisses the first-person accounts of the judges and lawyers who struggle to discover the internal, legal solution to cases in light of the rules, principles, and policies in the law. There is something important going on at this internal level, and this activity should not be defined away or simply dismissed. The implausibility of an extremely external point of view can be found in David Kairys' statement that "there is no legal reasoning in the sense of a legal methodology or process for reaching particular, correct results."[25] Kairys' approach overlooks the fact that there *is* a unique method of legal reasoning used by lawyers and judges every day, and they feel that this method of reasoning constrains their decisions. Furthermore, if Kairys really believed that there is no such thing as a correct legal solution to a problem, he would be in the position of holding that there is nothing wrong with any judicial decision because, after all, there is no right or wrong decision, legally speaking. This radical skepticism cannot give rise to any platform for changing the legal system, let alone the left-leaning platform advocated by Critical Legal Studies. The problem here is that the external critics want to have it both ways: they want to say that the courts err by ruling in favor of big business and the wealthy and also that legal reasoning is indeterminate and a sham, that there is no rule of law. These claims are inconsistent. A more reasonable approach is to acknowledge that the legal system possesses a coherent decision-making process for solving legal disputes, but that this process must be interrogated from a critical, external perspective.

Perhaps this is why some CLS thinkers hold that legal theory must adopt both an internal and external perspective. As Duncan Kennedy explains, "What is needed is to think about law in a way that will enable one to enter into it, *to criticize it without utterly rejecting it,* and to manipulate it without self-abandonment to *their* system of thinking and doing."[26] Kennedy recognizes that radically external legal theory cannot give rise to a positive jurisprudence because it completely reduces law to politics and fails to see any internal logic in the actions of judges and lawyers. The message of radical external theory (of the type offered by Nietzsche, Foucault, or Kairys) is that the *entire* legal process is ideological. This, in turn, leads to a kind of nihilism or quietism in which one has so utterly rejected the legal system that there are no possible grounds for improving it from the inside.

The point here is that a purely negative or critical posture is not very useful in legal theory. Thus, when Catharine MacKinnon announces that "the state is male,"[27] there is no way to generate a jurisprudence out of such claims because they are purely external and critical; they do not build anything, yet, paradoxically, they rest on a hidden and unproven claim that gender neutrality is a good thing in the first place. This is typical of the trouble which awaits when legal theory is too external: it wallows in criticism while hinting at but not articulating a preferable internal legal practice.

Certainly, there is something to fear from the opposite extreme, which occurs when a legal theory is exclusively *internal* to the point where it discounts all external insights. The postmodern thinkers' distrust of the internal perspective in legal theory is a result of their belief that much liberal theory fails to achieve any critical distance from the concepts which the players in the legal system happen to be using. This seems to be the case when theorists (especially legal philosophers such as Hart and Dworkin) use the same terminology as lawyers and judges, sticking so closely to the participants' language-game that there seems to be no distance between what theorists and lawyers are doing. In such cases it seems that the legal philosophers are acting as Monday-morning quarterbacks and are merely mimicking judges, without ever asking why they analyze the social phenomenon of law by assuming the perspective of an appellate judge. Thus, we find much liberal theorizing about whether the Supreme Court made the right decision in this or that case, yet rarely is there a questioning of the system as a whole, that is, the framework of rights, private property, wage-labor, and so on. The tendency of legal theory to occupy the same universe as legal practice makes the postmodernists worry that liberal theory has collapsed onto the practice of law, such that theorists cannot stand outside the legal system and critique it in any serious way. Richard Posner has suggested that the prevalence of the internal perspective is probably the result of the way in which the law is taught in law schools, which immerse students in legal decisions from the judge's perspective but neglect sociological (external) approaches: "[T]he study of law is begun *in medias res,* and here I add that this procedure forestalls the emergence of a critical, an external, perspective. It presents law as something not to be questioned, as something that has always existed and in approximately its contemporary form. Within a few months of entering law school the student has lost the external perspective."[28] The problem with being mired in the internal perspective is that this perspective tends to cut off possibilities for advancement and radical shifts in the law. From an internal perspective on the law, for example, it is difficult to justify the abolition of inheritance or the existence of a right to shelter because there is no precedent for these within the legal system. The external critic who wants to promote these types of radical reforms in the law will face the nearly impossible task of proving that these reforms are necessitated from within the framework of the existing system, perhaps as a function of our commitment to equality or liberty.[29] There is indeed a sort of conservatism within the internal perspective, if only because it gives great weight to the demands of past precedents (Dworkin refers to this weight as "gravitational force"), which tends to rule out new approaches. The conservative effect of this gravitational force is encapsulated in Dworkin's claim that a good judge must conform his decisions to the prevailing ethos of the law:

> Judges should enforce only political convictions that they believe, in good faith, can figure in a coherent general interpretation of the legal and political culture of the community. . . . A judge who accepts this constraint, and whose own convictions are Marxist or anarchist or taken from some eccentric religious tradition, cannot impose these convictions on the community under the title of law, however noble or enlightened he believes them to be because they cannot provide the coherent general interpretation he needs.[30]

Dworkin is, by and large, correct that judges are institutionally constrained to enforce the law as written, such that they can be a Marxist or anarchist only "in private," whereas they have to be liberals in public. It is easy to see why a judge must adopt this internal perspective, but it is harder to justify when adopted by a legal philosopher, especially if he or she hopes to achieve some critical distance from the object of study. One of the central lessons of postmodernism is that the internal perspective has an amorphous boundary, so those (like Dworkin and Hart) who profess to adopt a purely internal perspective are nevertheless influenced by "external" factors such as class, race, and gender, such that the decision-making process on the inside is infected with external affairs to such a degree that one can no longer insist on an impermeable internal/external distinction. However, those on the inside continue to claim that law has a distinctly autonomous character (and a unique set of internal constraints) which keeps it from dissolving into external affairs.

I have tried to demonstrate that many of the important postmodern thinkers are externalists who discount the internal perspective and thereby cut themselves off from the important task of arguing about decisions in particular cases or fashioning a program for legal reform within the current system. I have also tried to point out that internalists blind themselves to external insights and therefore operate in what seems to be a sort of self-perpetuating vacuum. What we seek, I think, is either an external theory that is not afraid to step into legal practice and debate legal doctrine from the inside and/or an internalist view which can expand at crucial moments to take an external perspective on the language-games and practices at work within the law. This combined approach, offered neither by traditional postmodern theory nor by mainstream Anglo-American legal theory, may perhaps be forged by those who can somehow negotiate or mediate between these two approaches.[31]

LINGERING FOUNDATIONALISM

As I demonstrated in chapter 2, postmodern legal theory begins with a critique of the foundational concepts of classical legal theory (e.g., the autonomous legal subject, consensus, natural law, God). When the postmodern critique of these foundations turns into a full-blown rejection, a vacuum is created which makes it look like postmodernism will slide into relativism and nihilism because it lacks any basis upon which to ground a vision of a just political order. Given this possibility, there is a perceived need to offer substitute foundations to replace those swept away with the classical theories of the modern period. This results in a second movement in which there is a search for new foundations. Unfortunately, the search for new foundations has not resulted in anything sufficiently robust to merit the title of a "positive jurisprudence." The Nietzschean will to power, the Derridean notion of justice as a call to the other, Lyotard's heterogeneity of discourses, Foucault's aesthetics of the self: each of these is offered somewhat sheepishly by postmodernists as potential new foundations for revising the political and legal system, but, as I have shown, they are too weak to provide the richness we seek in a workable program of legal reform. In every case, the philosopher's critical movement ("negative jurisprudence") was so sweeping that no basis for political action remained upon which to build something positive.

This assessment extends to every philosopher discussed in this book, with the possible exception of Rorty. In each case the philosopher undertakes a critical movement so powerful that it nullifies any later attempt by the same philosopher to justify a position in law or politics. For example, Derrida's early deconstructive works are so critical that they "deconstruct" Derrida's later notion of justice. That is, in order to expound a theory of justice, Derrida lapses into the sort of metaphysical claims he found problematic in other thinkers. The same applies to Lyotard. He argues that political theories based on consensus and universal rules are "terroristic," yet his own version of justice lapses into the very sort of universalizing claims he found problematic in other thinkers. Finally, Nietzsche warned against the reliance on foundations, but ultimately used the will to power as a sort of foundation upon which to ground his view of the law. In each case the first, critical attack on foundations destroys or undercuts the second, system-building movement. My point is simply that postmodern legal theory purports to remove us from foundational thinking in matters of law and politics, but its attempt to do this has been something of a failure because in each case there is a retreat to foundations of a new but unworkable sort. Perhaps some type of foundation is necessary to launch a legal theory in the first place. Rorty, I think, is the one postmodern thinker who recognizes that our existing institutions and practices provide all the foundation we need to ground an ethico-political legal theory.

This points up a troubling aspect of much postmodern theory, namely, its tendency to hold that our *entire* way of life is suspect, that things are rotten to the core. For example, it is possible to read Nietzsche as saying that most of our legal system should be rejected as a type of slave morality. One could read Foucault as saying that the entire legal apparatus may be a rationalization for the exercise of power relations. Similarly, one could read Derrida as saying that much of the legal system is based on logocentric fictions, and Lyotard seems to be saying that the consensus which supports our traditions is a bogus or manufactured consent. It is difficult to see how any political or legal theory (apart from, say, anarchism) could follow from such an attitude of distrust toward our practices and traditions. Hilary Putnam has summarized this point: "Many thinkers have fallen into Nietzsche's error of telling us that they had a 'better' morality than the entire tradition; in each case they only produced a monstrosity, for all they could do was arbitrarily wrench certain values out of their context while ignoring others. We can only hope to produce a more rational conception of rationality or a better conception of morality if we operate from *within* our tradition."[32] It seems that Rorty is the only postmodernist who correctly sees that there can be no foundation other than our contingent institutions and practices, and that these will have to do. It is certainly important to question our traditions, but there is no sense in escaping them altogether, for that would leave us nowhere. Rorty alone understands that the contingent traditions and practices of our society are foundation enough upon which to build a positive jurisprudence, which is odd since they all stress that the self is radically situated.

As I mentioned in chapter 2, Anglo-American theorists such as Dworkin and Rawls are no longer advocating a foundational liberalism based on conceptions of innate human nature, natural law, or some primordial social contract. Instead, they see the foundation for legal theory as being supplied by the contingently held aspirations and overlapping values of members of our society. For these thinkers, political and legal theory is an attempt to articulate values which we already hold, not an attempt to find eternal values which can steer us to justice in some absolute, objective sense. One can illustrate the move away from modern foundations with an example offered by Dworkin to prove that legal theory does not require objective, eternal, rock-solid foundations:

> Suppose I say that slavery is wrong [according to the local traditions in our culture]. I pause, and then add a second group of statements: I say that slavery is *"really"* or *"objectively"* wrong, that this is not just a matter of opinion, that it would be true even if I (and everybody else) thought otherwise, that it gives the "right answer" to the question of whether slavery is wrong, that the contrary answer is not just different but mistaken. What is the relation between my original opinion that slavery is wrong and these various "objective" judgments I added to it?[33]

For the modernist, the second statement (viz. slavery is *objectively* wrong) is thought necessary to ground the first statement (viz. slavery is *locally* wrong). What I have tried to demonstrate is that the postmodernists are critical of foundational attempts by "modern" thinkers to make the deep-structure type of statement previously discussed, but they end up offering foundations of their own which, like the modernists they reject, often appeal to a level below that of our contingent traditions. Rorty is the only postmodernist who recognizes that we cannot descend to this level, and perhaps it is for this reason that he stresses that we cannot derive an ethical or political theory from Nietzsche, Foucault, Lyotard, or Derrida.[34]

If I am correct, the important task for legal philosophy is to theorize without transcendental foundations, aiming only at making the legal system the best it can be by bringing it into line with our intracultural aspirations and standards, while striving to incorporate insights from alternative traditions and perspectives. The implausibility of the postmodern agenda is that it wants to simultaneously reject the traditional metaphysical foundations while also claiming that our contingent traditions cannot serve as the basis of a program for political and legal change. This move can be made only at a high cost: once we reject both transcendental values and contingent values, there are no viable options left for a positive jurisprudence other than a vague and implausible sort of anarchism or nihilism.

All this fuss over foundations is something of a red herring. In the final analysis, metaphysical foundations of the type once offered by Hobbes, Smith, Locke, and Aquinas are not necessary, and the most sophisticated versions of political and legal theory have already shed these foundations. The postmodern critique of *metaphysical* foundations arrives somewhat late in the day, and the postmodern critique of *contingent* foundations is overly pessimistic because it eliminates the only foundations which remain when we have shed the metaphysical foundations. When these two critiques are combined, there is no foundation remaining upon which to build a viable postmodern jurisprudence.

The Use of Postmodern Theory in Thinking the Other of the Law

Earlier in this chapter I discussed the Nietzschean and Foucauldian point that legal systems (and legal philosophy) pass through paradigm shifts in which the central elements of the law (contract, tort, property, liberty) change their meaning. One can understand the legal system as it presently exists as a conceptual framework for resolving disputes. At any given time these concepts are relatively stable, with the result that there will be a sort of map, scheme, or gestalt of the law. If this is correct, one might expect to find some theorists working from within a paradigm of mainstream scholarship, while others will be working at the margins of the current system. In what follows I want to stress the importance of those thinkers who occupy the margins, who push the law in new directions, especially since postmodernists tend to be working at the margins more than mainstream thinkers.

One of the purposes of any conceptual scheme is to make sense of the world, to unify experience and bring order out of what William James once called "a booming, buzzing confusion." The basic categories of the law function as a conceptual scheme which allows us to solve interpersonal disputes in a systematic way. For example, consider a dispute between landowners over an apple tree that has its roots on one person's property but drops unwanted apples, which spoil the grass, on another person's property. A question might arise as to whether the owner of the "servient" estate can force his neighbor to cut down the tree in its entirety (assuming that the tree cannot be trimmed to prevent apples from falling on the servient estate). Disputes such as these fall within the basic categories of property law, so there is an existing framework according to which one can assess the rights and remedies of the parties (e.g., in terms of "fee simples," "easements by prescription," "nuisance," "encroachments," and "quiet enjoyment"). This framework may be relatively stable or unstable for different reasons (e.g., the area of law may be in a state of crisis, there may be a "majority" and "minority" rule, proposals may be in the works for changing the law). Yet the very existence of the legal framework provides a starting point for approaching the dispute, and the existence of a settled rule of law allows for stability and predictablity in the ordinary course of events.

Yet notice that there is always something that is "other" or "outside" these legal categories. In the example of the property dispute over the apple tree, notice that one views the dispute between landowners from the assumption that property should be held privately and not collectively. This assumption is itself not in play in the dispute precisely because it is an *assumption* of property law. This shows that legal categories at any time will be determinate enough to assume certain arrangements as permissible while ruling out others as impermissible. As I mentioned earlier, perhaps there is a role to be played by postmodernism in thinking about what is "other" or "outside" the existing law.

To see the relationship between what is inside and outside the parameters of the law, recall that for much of our legal history women were outside the legal system. Although it now seems ludicrous, there was once a time when women couldn't vote, serve on juries, hold title to property, or practice law.[35] In fact, the Supreme Court upheld the refusal by the state of Illinois to grant a license to a female law graduate, stating: "Man is, or should be, woman's protector and defender. The natural and proper timidity and delicacy which belongs to the female sex evidently unfits it for many of the occupations of civil life. . . . The paramount destiny and mission of women are to fulfil the noble and benign offices of wife and mother."[36] This sounds absurd to us today, as it should, but we must remember that this was written over 120 years ago, when a different mindset prevailed. It is all too simplistic to assert that the Supreme Court was merely stupid or ignorant of women's obvious equality with men. Given the thinking at the time, women were other: a nonmale, nonlegal subject. Somehow they eventually won equal standing in the eyes of the legal system.[37]

The other to the legal system is not merely composed of *people* who have been denied a voice (women, Native Americans, blacks); it is also composed of doctrines or ways of thinking which stand outside the accepted practice of the legal system at any given time. To use an obvious example, it was once inconceivable that our legal system would countenance federal or state regulation of the workplace. This is why legislation limiting working hours for bakery employees was struck down by the Supreme Court as unconstitutional in the famous 1905 decision in *Lochner v. New York*. Yet by the forties there was a slew of cases upholding government intervention in the workplace to prevent industrial accidents and employee overwork.

The most recent example of what is other to contemporary legal philosophy arose in the controversy surrounding Lani Guinier's failed appointment to the civil rights division of the attorney general's office. The controversy over Guinier surrounded her claim (published mainly in law-review articles) that the traditional principle of majority rule has had an adverse impact on minorities.[38] Guinier's proposals for alternative voting schemes to ensure minority representation were seen as an attack on democracy itself, and she was roundly criticized by conservatives—as well as some liberals—for challenging the one man/one vote orthodoxy. Yet it should be pointed out, with some irony, that alternative voting schemes (such as cumulative voting) have long been used in corporations to ensure adequate representation of minority directors; indeed, alternative voting schemes were given consideration by the founding fathers. The Lani Guinier episode illustrates the opposition people will muster in refusing to consider new approaches to the law.

Changes in the law can be instigated by those who are willing to think the other of the legal system, those who practice what Thomas Kuhn has called "revolutionary science" by swimming against the tide of "normal science."[39] There is a sense in which the great judges were able to effectuate silent revolutions in the law which amounted to gestalt switches, and there is no disputing that such revolutions ("paradigm shifts") fuel the progress of the law. As a result, we value those who have risked their reputations by pushing the parameters of the law, and our most esteemed judges, legislators, and scholars are those who could break with the past. Because of its external perspective and its rejection of foundations, postmodern theory is free of traditional approaches to such an extent that it will be quite helpful in this task of thinking the other of the law. One could even argue that the legal system advances principally through decisions and events which are extralegal.[40] That is, many of the great decisions of the past have a freewheeling element about them, as if the judges have gone beyond the boundaries previously laid down for them. For example, consider the famous case of *Marbury v. Madison* (1803),[41] which established judicial review in America. There was little genuine precedent for the process of judicial review, and no other country on earth allowed a judicial branch to declare legislative acts void. In one fell swoop Justice Marshall effected a movement that would transform the judicial branch from the weakest to arguably the strongest branch of government. Consider also the Supreme Court's 1965 decision in *Griswold v. Connecticut*, which was the first case to declare the existence of a right to privacy.[42] The court argued that a "zone of privacy" existed within a penumbra carved out by several amendments, and this zone was infringed by a Connecticut statute which criminalized the distribution of materials designed to prevent pregnancy. The majority opinion in *Griswold* spoke of the right of privacy as something that was "older than the Bill of Rights." In a strong dissent which took an internal perspective, Justice

Stewart said, "I can find no such general right of privacy in the Bill of Rights, in any other part of the Constitution, or in any case ever before decided by this Court." The decision in *Griswold* is still controversial today, and such notable thinkers as Robert Bork have argued that the Court made a fundamental error by recognizing a right that was nowhere mentioned in the Constitution.[43] Yet *Griswold* is now an accepted part of our constitutional heritage, serving as the cornerstone of *Roe v. Wade*, not to mention the powerful dissent in *Bowers v. Hardwick*. Although the rationale in *Griswold* had little or no textual support in the Constitution or the case law, it nevertheless exerted a powerful legacy. *Griswold* would seem to support Justice Cardozo's claim that judging is not merely a process of finding the law but *creating* it as well.[44] Sometimes we create the law by finding new sources from *outside* the rationales and doctrines which have heretofore ruled the law.

Here is where one finally discovers the chief point of utility for postmodern legal theory: it opens up the range of conversation in legal theory by holding out a perspective that is other, that negates the system. The importance of "negative thinking" was stated succinctly by Herbert Marcuse: "[It] frees thought from its enslavement by the established universe of discourse and behavior, elucidates the negativity of the Establishment (its positive aspects are abundantly publicized anyway) and projects its alternatives."[45] This, I think, is the spirit in which postmodern legal theory should be viewed: it offers a critique from "outside," a critique that purports to negate the established universe of legal thought. This is a worthwhile project, even if we must ultimately conclude that the negative jurisprudence offered by postmodern legal theory cannot be wedded to a larger vision for a positive jurisprudence.

Notes

1. To avoid unnecessary confusion, I will not accentuate the subtle (but very real) differences between postmodernism and poststructuralism but will encompass both movements within the former term. This means that certain thinkers who are more appropriately thought of as poststructuralists (such as Barthes, Derrida, and Foucault) will be labeled as postmodernists in this study. This slight misuse of terminology should not cause any problems since nothing in my analysis hinges on the distinction between postmodernism and poststructuralism. For a more detailed discussion of these classifications, see Madan Sarup, *An Introductory Guide to Post-Structuralism and Post-modernism* (Athens: University of Georgia Press, 1989), and Douglas Kellner and Stephen Best, *Postmodern Theory* (New York: Guilford Press, 1991).

2. A useful list of postmodern thinkers and writers is found in Ihab Hassen, *The Postmodern Turn* (Columbus: Ohio State University Press, 1987), 84–96.

3. Gary Minda, *Postmodern Legal Movements* (New York: New York University Press, 1995).

4. Costas Douzinas and Ronnie Warrington, *Postmodern Jurisprudence* (New York: Routledge, 1991).

5. Mary Joe Frug, *Postmodern Legal Feminism* (New York: Routledge, 1992).

6. *Postmodernism and Law: A Symposium*, 62 U. COLO. L. REV. 439 (1991). See also *Postmodernism and Law*, ed. Dennis Patterson (Aldershot, Eng.: Dartmouth, 1994).

7. *Deconstruction and the Possibility of Justice*, 11 CARDOZO L. REV. 919–1726 (1989), and subsequent articles.

8. See Alan Hunt, *Foucault's Expulsion of Law: Towards a Retrieval*, 17 LAW AND SOCIAL INQUIRY 1 (1992), and subsequent articles.

9. See Lynn Baker, *Just Do It: Pragmatism and Social Change*, 78 VA. L. REV. 697 (1992), and subsequent articles.

10. See Jacques Derrida, *For the Love of Lacan*, 16 CARDOZO L. REV. 699 (1995), and subsequent articles.

11. Francis J. Mootz III, *Is the Rule of Law Possible in a Postmodern World?* 68 WASH-INGTON L. REV. 249, 250 (1993).

12. Indeed, textbooks on jurisprudence now include a section on postmodernism. For example, see *Jurisprudence: Contemporary Readings, Problems, and Narratives*, ed. Robert Hayman Jr. and Nancy Levit (St. Paul, Minn.: West, 1995), 507–75. It is surprising that postmodern theory is now regularly discussed in mainstream texts from

established presses. See, e.g., Dennis Patterson's *Law and Truth* (New York: Oxford University Press, 1996), especially chapter 8, "Postmodern Jurisprudence," and Richard Posner's *Overcoming Law* (Cambridge, Mass.: Harvard University Press, 1995), especially the chapter entitled "Postmodern Medieval Iceland."

13. For example, the postmodern influence is notable in such important books as Patricia Williams' *The Alchemy of Race and Rights* (Cambridge, Mass.: Harvard University Press, 1991), where she characterizes her book as being about "floating signifiers" and the social construction of race and gender.

14. A recent LEXIS–NEXIS search revealed that Lyotard, Nietzsche, Derrida, Foucault, and Rorty have each been mentioned in well over two hundred articles published in American law journals.

15. See, e.g., Honi F. Haber, *Beyond Postmodern Politics* (New York: Routledge, 1994), and Linda Hutcheon, *The Politics of Postmodernism* (New York: Routledge, 1989).

16. I have in mind Drucilla Cornell's *Philosophy of the Limit* (New York: Routledge, 1992), and Gillian Rose's *Dialectic of Nihilism: Post-Structuralism and Law* (Oxford: Basil Blackwell, 1984), both of which are interesting books that remain largely inaccessible to analytic philosophers. Another noteworthy book which has received some attention but is difficult for mainstream thinkers to follow is *Post-Modern Law*, ed. Anthony Carty (Edinburgh: Edinburgh University Press, 1990).

17. One explanation for the lack of dialogue is that the followers of the various postmodern thinkers tend to be fiercely loyal. My own experience—as someone who is intrigued by postmodernism while also being critical of it—is that writers sympathetic to Derrida and Lyotard tend to disparage any work which is critical of these thinkers no matter how well argued the critique happens to be. In particular, as John Searle has observed, Derrida's supporters often seem to employ the dubious tactic of asserting that anyone who is critical of Derrida has misread him! See John Searle's essays "The World Turned Upside Down," *New York Review of Books*, October 27, 1983, and "Reply to Mackey," *New York Review of Books*, February 2, 1984, both rpt. in *Working Through Derrida*, ed. Gary Madison (Evanston, Ill.: Northwestern University Press, 1993), 170–88.

18. For example, Dennis Patterson's interesting and otherwise engaging book *Law and Truth* (New York: Oxford University Press, 1996) has a chapter devoted to postmodern jurisprudence yet fails to discuss Nietzsche, Derrida, Lyotard, or Foucault.

19. In the context of legal theory, Ronald Dworkin has stated the principle of charity in a useful way: "Roughly, constructive interpretation is a matter of imposing purpose on an object or practice in order to make of it the best possible example of the form or genre to which it is taken to belong." See his *Law's Empire* (Cambridge, Mass.: Harvard University Press, 1986), 52.

20. It is worth noting that some postmodern thinkers might reject my entire project as a misguided attempt to subject postmodern legal theory to the foundational criteria of analytic jurisprudence. The fear is that I will wrongly chastise postmodernism for failing to offer the standard features of an analytic approach to the law (viz. a focus on doctrinal argument, formal logic, and normative prescription) when it was never the purpose of postmodern theory to offer these features in the first place.

While I agree that postmodern legal theory might justifiably be analyzed under criteria somewhat different from those used to critique analytic theory, I hesitate to completely exempt postmodern theory from a rigorous analytic critique. If postmodern theory is to be truly compelling, it must embody features which appeal to the full range of thinkers, including those in the analytic tradition. To think otherwise is to segregate analytic and postmodern philosophy into separate schools of thought, to deny the possibility of translation from one genre to the other. It strikes me that a fair amount of postmodern theory is devoted to a critique of the Anglo-American approach (exemplified by Hart and Dworkin) for its insensitivity to postmodern insights, so I see nothing wrong in undertaking the same project from the opposite perspective. I will ultimately be arguing that the best approach in legal theory is one which combines elements of both traditions, allowing them to mediate one another.

1: UNDERSTANDING POSTMODERNISM GENERALLY

1. Quoted in Jerome Frank, *Law and the Modern Mind* (Gloucester, Mass.: Peter Smith, 1970), 59–60.

2. On the rise of pastiche and schizophrenia, see Fredric Jameson, "Postmodernism and Consumer Society," in *The Anti-Aesthetic: Essays in Postmodern Culture*, ed. Hal Foster (Seattle, Wash.: Bay Press, 1983).

3. Jean-François Lyotard, *The Postmodern Condition: A Report on Knowledge*, trans. Geoff Bennington and Brian Massumi (Minneapolis: University of Minnesota Press, 1984).

4. See, e.g., Honi F. Haber, *Beyond Postmodern Politics* (New York: Routledge, 1994); Linda Hutcheon, *The Politics of Postmodernism* (New York: Routledge, 1989); Alan Hunt, *The Big Fear: Law Confronts Postmodernism*, 35 MCGILL L. J. 508 (1990).

5. Jacques Derrida, *The Truth in Painting*, trans. Geoff Bennington and Ian McLeod (Chicago: University of Chicago Press, 1987).

6. Michel Foucault, *This Is Not a Pipe*, trans. James Harkness (Berkeley, Calif.: University of California Press, 1983).

7. Jean-François Lyotard, *Toward the Postmodern*, ed. Robert Harvey and Mark Roberts (Atlantic Highlands, N.J.: Humanities Press International, 1993).

8. Richard Rorty, *Contingency, Irony, and Solidarity* (Cambridge: Cambridge University Press, 1989).

9. The following discussion characterizes modernism in broad strokes as a movement which employs metaphysical or epistemic foundations. While this criterion encompasses most of the philosophers of the modern era (e.g., Hobbes, Locke, and Kant), there are a few modern philosophers who do not fit neatly into this taxonomy. For example, Mill can be considered a type of foundationalist in that he purported to justify ethical and legal positions in terms of general utility; on the other hand, he did not possess a rigid view of human nature and recognized that political judgments can vary from one culture to the next. Similarly, Marx's early work relied heavily on a metaphysically laden conception of the free laborer who recognized himself in his products, while his later works purported to be scientific and devoid of metaphysical

speculation. Because of these difficulties of classification, I will be using the term "modernism" to denote a family resemblance among a group of diverse theorists who in some way relied upon ontological or epistemic foundations and who justified their conceptions of justice with reference to nonempirical, deep-structure notions of the self, reason, or nature.

10. See especially Max Horkheimer and Theodor Adorno, *Dialectic of Enlightenment*, trans. John Cumming (1947; rpt. New York: Continuum, 1991).

11. Immanuel Kant, "An Answer to the Question: What Is Enlightenment?" in *Perpetual Peace and Other Essays*, (Indianapolis, Ind.: Hackett, 1983), 41.

12. Robert Hollinger, introduction to *Hermeneutics and Praxis*, ed. Robert Hollinger (Notre Dame, Ind.: University of Notre Dame Press, 1985), x.

13. The method of grounding political and legal positions in metaphysical assumptions about human nature, reason, or history has increasingly seemed less plausible to Anglo-American political theorists such as John Rawls, Michael Walzer, and Ronald Dworkin, who argue that political and legal philosophy must be based on values which are held imminently within a particular culture and not on sweeping claims about human nature as such. The movement away from foundations is documented by Georgia Warnke in *Justice and Interpretation* (Cambridge, Mass.: MIT Press, 1992), which focuses on the "hermeneutic turn" of such thinkers as Walzer, Rawls, Dworkin, and Habermas.

14. Lyotard, *The Postmodern Condition*, xxiii–xxiv.

15. Michel Foucault, "The Subject and Power," in *Michel Foucault: Beyond Structuralism and Hermeneutics*, by Hubert Dreyfus and Paul Rabinow (Chicago: University of Chicago Press, 1982), 210. Foucault points out that racism and fascism were presented as "rational" solutions to political dilemmas, so we must be suspicious of claims that are based on reason: "This [racism and fascism] was, of course, an irrationality, but an irrationality that was at the same time, after all, a certain type of rationality." Michel Foucault "Space, Knowledge, and Power" in *The Foucault Reader*, ed. Paul Rabinow and trans. Christian Hubert (New York: Pantheon, 1984), 249.

16. On this point see Horkheimer and Adorno, *Dialectic*.

17. Immanuel Kant, *Critique of Pure Reason*, trans. Norman Kemp Smith (New York: St. Martin's, 1965), sec. Axi–xii, p. 9.

18. René Descartes, *Meditations on First Philosophy*, trans. Donald Cress (Indianapolis: Hackett, 1979), 35.

19. John Locke, *The Second Treatise of Government*, sec. 6: "On the State of Nature," in *What Is Justice?* ed. Robert Solomon and Mark Murphy (Oxford: Oxford University Press, 1990), 94.

20. Foucault, "Space, Knowledge, and Power," 249.

21. Horkheimer and Adorno, *Dialectic*, 3, xi. It is worth mentioning that despite being cited as an inspiration for the postmodernists, Horkheimer and Adorno nevertheless still believed in the value of a type of reason, albeit not in the Kantian sense.

22. Jean-François Lyotard (with Jean-Loup Thébaud), *Just Gaming*, trans. Wlad Godzich (Minneapolis: University of Minnesota Press, 1985), 82.

23. Rorty, *Contingency, Irony, and Solidarity*, 32–33.

24. Descartes, *Meditations on First Philosophy*, 49.

25. Immanuel Kant, *Groundwork of the Metaphysic of Morals*, trans H. J. Paton (New York: Harper & Row, 1964), 96.

26. John Rawls, *A Theory of Justice* (Cambridge, Mass.: Belknap Press of Harvard University Press, 1971), 560. Rawls' more recent work backs off from the position that the self is somehow lurking below contingent personality features. Rawls now insists that the choosers in the original position were never decontextualized and unencumbered.

27. Quoted in Madan Sarup, *An Introductory Guide to Post-Structuralism and Postmodernism* (Athens: University of Georgia Press, 1989), 1.

28. Richard Rorty, "Postmodern Bourgeois Liberalism," in *Hermeneutics and Praxis*, 217.

29. Louis Althusser, "Freud and Lacan," *Lenin and Philosophy*, trans. Ben Brewster (New York: Monthly Review Press, 1971), 218–19 (emphasis added).

30. Michel Foucault, *The Order of Things: An Archaeology of the Human Sciences* (New York: Vintage, 1994), 387.

31. René Descartes, *Rules for the Direction of Mind*, vol. 1 of *The Philosophical Works of Descartes*, ed. and trans. Elizabeth Haldane and G. R. T. Ross (Cambridge: Cambridge University Press, 1931), 5–22.

32. Betrand Russell, *The Problems of Philosophy* (New York: Oxford University Press, 1980), 128–30.

33. Friedrich Nietzsche, *Beyond Good and Evil* (New York: Vintage, 1989), sec. 35, p. 47.

34. Richard Rorty, "Introduction: Pragmatism and Philosophy," *Consequences of Pragmatism* (Minneapolis: University of Minnesota Press, 1982), xiii–xiv.

35. Jacques Derrida, "Differance," *Margins of Philosophy*, trans. Alan Bass (Chicago: University of Chicago Press, 1982), 6, 11.

36. Michel Foucault, "Truth and Power," in *Power/Knowledge: Selected Interviews and Other Writings, 1972–77*, trans. Colin Gordon et al. and ed. Colin Gordon (New York: Pantheon, 1980), 133.

37. Thomas Jefferson, Declaration of Independence, in *What Is Justice?*, 149.

38. Martin Luther King Jr., "Letter from Birmingham Jail," in *Philosophical Problems in the Law*, ed. David Adams (Belmont, Calif.: Wadsworth, 1992), 60.

39. Nietzsche, *Beyond Good and Evil*, sec. 16, p. 23.

40. Michel Foucault, "Human Nature: Justice Versus Power" (debate with Noam Chomsky), in *Reflexive Water: The Basic Concerns of Mankind*, ed. Fons Elders (London: Souvenir Press, 1974), 187.

41. Antonio Gramsci, *Selections from the Prison Notebooks*, trans. and ed. Quinton Hoare and Geoffrey Nowell Smith (New York: International Publishers, 1971), 325–26.

42. Judge Iredall's famous opinion in *Calder v. Bull*, 3 U.S. 386 (1798) is summarized in John Ely, *Democracy and Distrust* (Cambridge, Mass.: Harvard University Press, 1980), 1.

43. Edwin Meese III, "Our Constitution's Design: The Implications for Its Interpretation," 70 MARQUETTE L. REV. 381, 383 (1987) (emphasis added).

44. E. D. Hirsch Jr., "In Defense of the Author," in *Art and Its Significance*, ed. Stephen David Ross (Albany: SUNY Press, 1994), 336.

45. Roland Barthes, "The Death of the Author," *Image-Music-Text*, trans. Stephen Heath (New York: Hill & Wang, 1977), 146–47.

46. Michel Foucault, "What Is an Author?," in *The Foucault Reader*, 118–19.

47. Jacques Derrida, "Structure, Sign and Play in the Discourse of the Human Sciences," *Writing and Difference*, trans. Alan Bass (Chicago: University of Chicago Press, 1978), 280.

48. G. W. F. Hegel, *Lectures on the Philosophy of History*, quoted in Peter Singer, *Hegel* (New York: Oxford University Press, 1983), 11.

49. Karl Marx, Preface to "A Contribution to a Critique of Political Economy," in *The Marx–Engels Reader*, ed. Robert Tucker (New York: Norton, 1978), 5.

50. Francis Fukuyama, *The End of History and the Last Man* (New York: Free Press, 1992), ix, 199–200.

51. Friedrich Nietzsche, *The Anti-Christ*, #4, in *The Complete Works of Friedrich Nietzsche*, trans. R. J. Hollingdale (Middlesex, Eng.: Penguin Books, 1968), 116.

52. Jean-François Lyotard, *The Differend: Phrases in Dispute*, trans. Georges Van Den Abbeele (Minneapolis: University of Minnesota Press, 1988), 179.

53. Michel Foucault, "Nietzsche, Genealogy, History," in *The Foucault Reader*, 85.

54. A useful summary of the main tenets of postmodernism can be found in Peter Schanck, *Understanding Postmodern Thought and Its Implications for Statutory Construction*, 65 S. CAL. L. REV. 2505, 2508 (1992).

55. Rorty, *Contingency, Irony, and Solidarity*, 73.

56. Derrida, "Structure, Sign, and Play," 280–81.

57. Mark Tushnet, "The Politics of Constitutional Law," in *The Politics of Law*, ed. David Kairys (New York: Pantheon, 1990), 232.

58. See Friedrich Nietzsche, *On the Genealogy of Morals*, trans. Walter Kaufmann (New York: Vintage, 1989), book 2; and Michel Foucault, *Discipline and Punish: The Birth of the Prison*, trans. Alan Sheridan (New York: Vintage, 1979).

59. For more on the notion of the self in postmodern political theory, see Haber, *Beyond Postmodern Politics*, 4–5.

2: THE ORIENTATION OF POSTMODERN LEGAL THEORY

1. H. L. A. Hart, *The Concept of Law* (Oxford: Oxford University Press, 1961), 55, 86–87, 96.

2. Ronald Dworkin, *A Matter of Principle* (Cambridge, Mass.: Harvard University Press, 1985), 167–77; *Law's Empire* (Cambridge, Mass.: Harvard University Press, 1986), 12–15.

3. Peter Winch, *The Idea of a Social Science and Its Relation to Philosophy* (London: Routledge, 1958).

4. Ibid., 89.

5. See, for example, *Understanding and Social Inquiry*, ed. Fred Dallmayr and Thomas McCarthy (Notre Dame, Ind.: University of Notre Dame Press, 1977), 77–80.

6. This is not to imply that internally oriented scholars remain hopelessly mired in the internal perspective all the time. In fact, internal thinkers often make use of external information in the course of resolving internal questions. For example, when addressing the legal issue of sexual harassment, an internally oriented thinker may look to empirical data about the prevalence of sexual harassment or to historical studies which examine the history of sexual harassment. Typically, the internal theorist steps outside the internal perspective only momentarily in an effort to gain ammunition when he or she returns to the doctrinal arguments being waged inside the practice.

7. This point is stressed by Alan Hunt: "There is one important and very visible difference between liberal and critical theory: critical theory employs the concept 'ideology,' a concept systematically absent from liberal theory. . . . [W]hat the concept 'ideology' provides is precisely a way of problematizing the attitudes, beliefs and values of legal actors." "The Critique of Law: What Is 'Critical' About Critical Legal Theory?," in *Critical Legal Studies*, ed. Alan Hunt and Peter Fitzpatrick (Oxford: Basil Blackwell, 1987), 12.

8. See the cases discussed under "Burglary," 13 AM. JUR. 2d, sec. 10, pp. 326–27 (1964).

9. This attitude toward the law is expressed in the *Communist Manifesto:* "But don't wrangle with us so long as you apply, to our intended abolition of bourgeois property, the standard of your bourgeois notions of freedom, culture, law, etc. Your very ideas are but the outgrowth of the conditions of your bourgeois production . . . , just as your jurisprudence is but the will of your class made into a law for all." Quoted in *The Marx-Engels Reader,* ed. Robert Tucker (New York: Norton, 1978), 487.

10. Alternative external approaches could also be brought to bear on this case. For example, one might cite statistics on the prevalence of burglary cases in urban areas, the social background of the burglary defendants, and the relationship between criminal law and capitalism.

11. One must remember that even Nazi law can be seen as a coherent system of rules if viewed internally, yet it was morally repugnant when viewed externally. In this connection, recall Hart's insistence that the Nazi legal system was classifiable as a bona fide legal system; see his *Positivism and the Separation of Law and Morals,* 71 HARVARD L. REV. 593 (1958). Hart's position was subjected to a heated critique by Lon Fuller, who argued that Nazi law lacked sufficient "inner morality" to earn the status of bona fide law; see his *Positivism and Fidelity to Law—A Reply to Professor Hart,* 71 HARVARD L. REV. 630 (1958).

12. This opinion is categorically stated in Jeffrie Murphy and Jules Coleman, *Philosophy of Law*, rev. ed. (Boulder, Colo.: Westview, 1990), 26.

13. John Austin, *The Province of Jurisprudence Determined* (1832), rpt. in *Philosophy of Law*, 5th ed., ed. Joel Feinberg and Hyman Gross (Belmont, Calif.: Wadsworth, 1995), 31–42. Austin defined a sovereign as a person or set of persons who are habitually obeyed by a majority of the population but who are not themselves in the habit of obeying a higher authority.

14. St. Thomas Aquinas, "The Essence of Law," in *Introduction to St. Thomas Aquinas*, ed. Anton Pegis (New York: Random House, 1948), 649.

15. Quoted in H. L. A. Hart, *Positivism and the Separation of Law and Morals*, 71 HARVARD L. REV. 593 (1958).

16. Hart, *The Concept of Law*, 80; the phrase also appears in Hart's "Positivism and the Separation of Law and Morals."

17. Ibid., 55

18. Ibid., 88.

19. By way of example, Hart cites a law prohibiting vehicles in public parks: there is a core meaning to the term "vehicle" which includes cars and motorcycles, yet there are borderline cases such as toy motorcars. Ibid., 126.

20. Ronald Dworkin, *The Model of Rules*, 35 U. OF CHICAGO L. REV. 14 (1967).

21. Ronald Dworkin, *Taking Rights Seriously* (Cambridge, Mass.: Harvard University Press, 1977), 66–67.

22. Notice, of course, that Hercules (who is, after all, a judge and not a sociologist or revolutionary) has an *institutional duty* to view the settled law as a coherent doctrine, unlike nonjudges and nonlawyers, who, from their third-person, nonparticipatory perspective, are free to see the law as chaotic, contradictory, and irrational. One wonders why Dworkin insists on taking the internal view, given that (as an academic) he has no institutional duty to do so.

23. Dworkin, *Law's Empire*, 13–14.

24. Ibid., 14.

25. Ibid. (emphasis added).

26. Hunt, "The Critique of Law," 10 (emphasis added).

27. See, e.g., Jeffrey Segal and Harold Spaeth, *The Supreme Court and the Attitudinal Model* (Cambridge: Cambridge University Press, 1993), 62–65.

28. Dworkin does provide a critique of some themes in Critical Legal Studies; see *Law's Empire*, 271–75.

29. See, e.g., Nietzche's *Beyond Good and Evil*, trans. Walter Kaufmann (New York: Vintage, 1989), sec. 219, pp. 147–48; idem, *On the Genealogy of Morals*, trans. Walter Kaufmann (New York: Vintage, 1989), third essay, sec. 25, p. 154.

30. Michel Foucault, "On Popular Justice: A Discussion with Maoists," in *Power/Knowledge: Selected Interviews and Other Writings, 1972–77*, ed. Colin Gordon and trans. Colin Gordon et al. (New York: Pantheon, 1980), 1–36.

31. See the account presented in *The Foucault Reader*, ed. Paul Rabinow (New York: Pantheon, 1984), 3–7.

32. Foucault's statement first appeared in "Va-t-on extrader Klaus Croissant?" *Le Nouvel Observateur*, November 14, 1977, and is quoted in James Miller, *The Passions of Michel Foucault* (New York: Anchor, 1993), 297–98.

33. See "L'Affaire Derrida Pits Theorist Who Founded Deconstruction Against Editor of Book on Heidegger's Role in Nazi Era," *Chronicle of Higher Education*, February 17, 1993, A8.

34. The book was originally published by Columbia University Press, but publication was halted after the initial print run; a subsequent edition was published by MIT Press. For an account of the entire affair, see Thomas Sheehan, "A Normal Nazi," *New York Review of Books*, January 14, 1993, 30.

35. Quoted in "L'Affaire Derrida," A8.

36. Wolin's description of the affair is set forth in the preface to *The Heidegger Controversy* (Cambridge, Mass.: MIT Press, 1993), ix–x.

37. *The Critical Lawyers' Handbook*, ed. Ian Grigg-Spall and Paddy Ireland (London: Pluto Press, 1992).

38. This phrase is found in Engels' *Socialism: Utopian and Scientific* and is quoted in Christine Sypnowich, *The Concept of Socialist Law* (Oxford: Oxford University Press, 1990), 1.

39. Kim Economides and Ole Hansen, "Critical Legal Practice: Beyond Abstract Radicalism," in *The Critical Lawyers' Handbook*, 143.

40. Jacques Derrida, *Of Grammatology*, trans. Gayatri Spivak (Baltimore, Md.: Johns Hopkins University Press, 1976), 158.

41. See E. Allan Farnsworth, *Contracts* (Boston: Little, Brown, 1982), sec. 7.2.

42. Declaration of Independence of the United States of America (1776), United States Code Service, Art. I–III, "Documents Antedating the Constitution" (San Francisco: Bancroft-Whitney, 1986), 1–2.

43. Immanuel Kant, "On the Proverb That May Be True in Theory But Is of No Practical Use," in *Perpetual Peace and Other Essays*, trans. Ted Humphreys (Indianapolis, Ind.: Hackett, 1983), 77–78.

44. Hegel claimed, "For the history of the world is nothing but the development of the idea of freedom." In other words, history has an inner logic as it moves through determinate stages. See *The Philosophy of Hegel*, ed. and trans. Carl Friedrich (New York: Modern Library, 1954), 157. Marx's notion of the inexorable progress toward communism runs through much of his work but is most succinctly stated in his letter to Joseph Weydemeyer, reprinted as "Class Struggle and the Mode of Production," in *The Marx-Engels Reader*, 220.

I should note that Hegel and Marx's status as modernists is somewhat cloudy. Anticipating postmodernism, Hegel claimed that the philosophy of law cannot rely on ahistorical notions but will instead reflect the society from which it emerges: "Whatever happens, every individual is a child of his time; so philosophy, too, is its own time apprehended in thoughts. It is just as absurd to fancy that a philosophy can transcend its contemporary world as it is to fancy that an individual can overleap his own age." G. W. F. Hegel, *The Philosophy of Right*, trans. T. M. Knox, in *What Is Justice?* ed.

Robert Solomon and Mark Murphy (New York: Oxford University Press, 1990), 180. Marx's early work was characterized by quasimetaphysical notions like "species being," yet his later work was intentionally derisive of metaphysics in favor of a "scientific" model.

45. According to Mill, "the ideally best form of government . . . is attended with the greatest amount of beneficial consequences." *Considerations on Representative Government*, in *The Philosophy of John Stuart Mill*, ed. Marshall Cohen (New York: Modern Library, 1961), 408–9.

46. See Elyse R. Rosenblum, *The Irony of Norplant*, 1992 TEXAS J. OF WOMEN AND THE LAW 275 (1992), citing *People v. Johnson*, Case No. 29390, Tulane County, Calif., Superior Court, June 2, 1991, and *State v. Knighton*, Case No. 601619, Harris County, Tex., 262nd District Court, October 5, 1991.

47. The fundamental right to procreate is an implied right that was announced in *Skinner v. Oklahoma*, 316 U.S. 535 (1942) and affirmed in *Griswold v. Connecticut*, 381 U.S. 479 (1965).

48. See Catherine Albiston, *The Social Meaning of The Norplant Condition: Constitutional Considerations of Race, Class, and Gender*, 9 BERKELEY WOMEN'S LAW JOURNAL 9 (1994), who argues that the imposition of Norplant as a condition of parole infringes on "personhood and autonomy rights" and is an affront to "human dignity."

49. John Rawls, *A Theory of Justice* (Cambridge, Mass.: Harvard University Press, 1971). Rawls' view has become much less foundational as expressed in such later works as "Justice as Fairness: Political not Metaphysical," *Philosophy and Public Affairs* 14 (1985): 223–51. See also Alan Gewirth, "The Basis and Content of Human Rights," in *Human Rights: Essays on Justification and Applications* (Chicago: University of Chicago Press, 1982).

50. Francis Fukuyama, *The End of History and the Last Man* (New York: Free Press, 1992).

51. Karl Marx, *Economic and Philosophical Manuscripts of 1844*, ed. Dirk Struik and trans. Martin Milligan (New York: International Publishers, 1964).

52. According to Kant, "No one will doubt that the pure doctrine of Right needs metaphysical first principles." *The Metaphysics of Morals*, Part I: *The Doctrine of Right*. Part II: *The Doctrine of Virtue*, trans. Mary Gregor (Cambridge: Cambridge University Press, 1991), pt. II, 124–25, 181.

53. Jean-François Lyotard, *The Postmodern Condition: A Report on Knowledge*, trans. Geoff Bennington and Brian Massumi (Minneapolis: University of Minnesota Press, 1984), xxiv.

54. Ibid., xxiv–xxv.

55. See Dworkin's discussion of slavery in *Law's Empire*, 80–81, and in *A Matter of Principle*, 172–73.

56. *Symposium: The Critique of Normativity*, 139 U. PA. L. REV. 801 (1991); see especially Pierre Schlag, *Normative and Nowhere to Go*, 43 STAN. L. REV. 167 (1990).

57. This argument is put forth most clearly by Pierre Schlag in *Normativity and the Politics of Form*, 139 U. PA. L. REV. 810 (1991).

58. According to Pierre Schlag, "It is these very normative questions that allow legal academics to continue to address (rather lamely) bureaucratic power structures as if they were rational, morally competent, individual humanist subjects. [Normative theory depicts legal actors] as self-directing individual humanist subjects at once rational, morally competent, and in control of their own ships, the Hercules of their own empires, the authors of their own texts. It isn't so." *The Politics of Form,* 139 U. PA. L. REV. 805 (1991). See also Pierre Schlag, *The Problem of the Subject,* 69 TEX. L. REV. 1627 (1991).

59. 478 U.S. 186 (1986).

60. 60 U.S. (19 How.) 393 (1857).

61. Richard Delgado (always an interesting thinker) has suggested that it might be theoretically possible to denude legal theory of all normative conceptions to the point where the field of legal studies "becomes a branch of hematology" (i.e., becomes concerned with facts instead of values). *Norms and Normal Science: Towards a Critique of Normativity in Legal Thought,* 139 U. PA. L. REV. 933, 959 (1991). But, as Dworkin has pointed out, law is a unique social practice because it is fundamentally and inescapably argumentative and normative (*Law's Empire,* 13). To follow Delgado's suggestion would be to adopt a methodology which misses one of the very features which makes law what it is.

62. Jürgen Habermas, *The Philosophical Discourse of Modernity,* trans. Frederick Lawrence (Cambridge, Mass.: MIT Press, 1987), 83.

3: NIETZSCHE'S THEORY OF LAW

1. Prominent work on Nietzsche during the past decade includes: Richard Weisberg, *Text into Theory: A Literary Approach to the Constitution,* 20 GA. L. REV. 936 (1989) and *The Failure of the Word* (New Haven: Yale University Press, 1984); Phillipe Nonet, *What Is Positive Law?,* 100 YALE L. J. 667 (1990); Peter Berkowitz, *On the Laws Governing Free Spirits and Philosophers of the Future: A Response to Nonet,* 100 YALE L. J. 710 (1990); Gerald Frug, *Argument as Character,* 40 STAN. L. REV. 869 (1988); and Gillian Rose, *Dialectic of Nihilism: Post-Structuralism and Law* (Oxford: Basil Blackwell, 1984). A recent LEXIS–NEXIS search on Nietzsche reveals that nearly three hundred law review articles have discussed or cited Nietzsche in the last ten years.

2. The four-hundred-page index to *The Complete Works of Friedrich Nietzsche* indicates that the topic of law is addressed only eleven times throughout the complete works. See *Index to the Complete Works of Friedrich Nietzsche,* comp. Robert Guppy (New York: Russell & Russell, 1964), 160. Even more telling is the fact that these few references to law are scattered throughout various works, indicating that Nietzsche did not provide a sustained analysis of law in a single text. Given Nietzsche's meager output, his thoughts on law cannot be fruitfully compared to the classic works of analytic jurisprudence, such as John Austin's *Province of Jurisprudence Determined* in *Lectures on Jurisprudence* (London: John Murray, 1873), H. L. A. Hart's *Concept of Law* (Oxford:

Oxford, 1961), Lon Fuller's *Morality of Law* (New Haven: Yale University Press, 1964), and Ronald Dworkin's *Law's Empire* (Cambridge, Mass.: Harvard University Press, 1986). In this chapter, however, I take the position that a Nietzschean theory of law can be formulated despite the fact that Nietzsche did not present a totalizing, systematic analysis of law.

3. I use the term "legal nihilism" to designate the position that there is no basis for asserting the moral superiority of one law over another, that disagreements about law are merely disguised political disagreements; and that there can be no right (or even 'better') answers to legal questions. For a further discussion of legal nihilism, see Rose, *Dialectic of Nihilism;* Brian Leiter, *Intellectual Voyeurism in Legal Scholarship,* 4 YALE J. OF LAW AND HUMANITIES 79 (1992); and Joseph Singer, *The Player and the Cards,* 94 YALE L. J. 1 (1984). The notion that Nietzsche rejects basic human rights can be found in Andre Mineau, "Human Rights and Nietzsche," *History of European Ideas* 11 (1989): 877–82.

4. See *The New Nietzsche,* ed. David Allison (Cambridge, Mass.: MIT Press, 1985); *The Fate of the New Nietzsche,* ed. Keith Ansell-Pearson and Howard Caygill (Aldershot, Eng.: Avery Publications, 1993), 1–10.

5. Jacques Derrida's debt to Nietzsche is acknowledged in his *Spurs: Nietzsche's Styles,* trans. Barbara Harlow (Chicago: University of Chicago Press, 1979). For a discussion of Nietzsche's influence on deconstruction and poststructuralism generally, see Madan Sarup, *An Introductory Guide to Post-Structuralism and Postmodernism* (Athens, Ga.: University of Georgia Press, 1993), 45–47; and *Nietzsche as Postmodernist,* ed. Clayton Koelb (Albany: SUNY Press, 1990). One of Derrida's Anglo-American expositors gave the following description of Nietzsche's influence: "More than any other philosopher in the Western tradition, Nietzsche pressed up against the limits of language and thought which Derrida attempts to define. He anticipates the style and strategy of Derrida's writings to a point where the two often seem engaged in a kind of uncanny reciprocal exchange." Christopher Norris, *Deconstruction: Theory and Practice* (London: Methuen, 1982), 57.

6. See Stephan A. Erickson, "Nietzsche and Post-Modernity," *Philosophy Today* 34 (1990): 175–79.

7. For the notion that Nietzsche might be read as a pragmatist, see Richard Rorty, *Essays on Heidegger and Others* (Cambridge: Cambridge University Press, 1991), 2–5, and *What Can You Expect from Anti-Foundationalist Philosophers? A Reply to Lynn Baker,* 78 VA. L. REV. 719 (1992). See also Maudamarie Clark, *Nietzsche on Truth and Philosophy* (Cambridge: Cambridge University Press, 1990), 2–3 (citing various authors who have interpreted Nietzsche as a pragmatist). For a discussion of legal pragmatism, see, e.g., *Symposium on the Renaissance of Pragmatism in American Legal Thought,* 63 SO. CAL. L. REV 1569 (1990), especially Richard Posner's *What Has Pragmatism to Offer Law?,* at 1653.

8. For the relation between critical legal studies and legal nihilism, see Peter Goodrich, *Law and Modernity,* 49 MODERN L. REV. 545 (1986); and Ted Finman, *CLS, Professionalism, and Academic Freedom: Exploring the Tributaries of Carrington's River,* 35 J. OF LEGAL EDUCATION 180 (1985).

9. What follows is a chronological listing of works by Nietzsche that bear more or less directly on law or legal issues. *Human, All Too Human [HAH]*, trans. R. J. Hollingdale (Cambridge: Cambridge University Press, 1986): vol. 1, #s92, 459; vol. 2, part 1, #9; part 2, #26. *Daybreak*, trans. R. J. Hollingdale (Cambridge: Cambridge University Press, 1982): #s14, 20–21, 68, 112. *The Gay Science [GS]*, trans. Walter Kaufman (New York: Vintage, 1974): book 1, #43; book 2, #59; book 3, #s109, 117; book 4, #291. *Thus Spoke Zarathustra [TSZ]*, trans. Walter Kaufman (New York: Penguin, 1966) part 3, #12. *Beyond Good and Evil [BGE]*, trans. Walter Kaufman (1966; rpt. New York: Vintage, 1989): #s164, 188. *On the Genealogy of Morals [GM]*, trans. Walter Kaufman (1967; rpt. New York: Vintage, 1989): essay 2, #s5–12. *Twilight of the Idols [TI]*, trans. R. J. Hollingdale (New York: Penguin, 1968): #s45, 48. *The Anti-Christ [AC]*, trans. R. J. Hollingdale (Middlesex, Eng.: Penguin, 1968): #57. *The Will to Power [WP]*, trans. R. J. Hollingdale and Walter Kaufman, ed. Walter Kaufman (New York: Vintage, 1968): #s204, 279, 629–32, 889, 957. When these few sections are measured against the sum total of Nietzsche's prodigious output, it is apparent that he did not devote a great deal of time to the question of law.

10. See Raymond Belliotti, *Justifying Law* (Philadelphia: Temple University Press, 1992), especially chapter 1: "The Immanent Moral Order and Law's Objectivity: Natural Law." For a summary of some of the basic tenets of natural law theory, see Jeffrie Murphy and Jules Coleman, *Philosophy of Law*, rev. ed. (San Francisco: Westview, 1990), 11–15.

11. This proposition was most clearly expressed in St. Augustine's dictum that "a law that is not just is not a law." St. Augustine, *On Free Choice of the Will*, trans. Anna Benjamin and L. H. Hackstaff, book 1, chap. 5, #s33–34 (Indianapolis, Ind.: Bobbs-Merrill, 1964), 11. Augustine's pronouncement was picked up by St. Thomas Aquinas, who paraphrased it thus: "A law that is unjust would seem to be no law at all." See his *Summa Theologica*, partially reprinted in *Philosophy of Law*, 4th ed., ed. Joel Feinberg and Hyman Gross (Belmont, Calif.: Wadsworth, 1991), 24.

12. Aristotle, *Nicomachean Ethics*, #5.7.1134b, and *Rhetoric*, 1.13.1373b, in *The Complete Works of Aristotle*, ed. Jonathan Barnes (Princeton, N.J.: Princeton University Press, 1984). For a more detailed discussion, see Yves Simon, *The Tradition of Natural Law* (New York: Fordham University Press, 1965), 131–32.

13. Cicero, *De republica*, partially reprinted in Robert M. Wilkin, "Cicero and the Law of Nature," in *Origins of the Natural Law Tradition*, ed. Arthur Harding (Dallas, Tex.: Southern Methodist University Press, 1954), 23–24.

14. The Christian version of natural law theory, which reached fruition in the works of Aquinas, was a mélange of Platonic, Aristotelian, and biblical sources. See Josef Fuchs, *Natural Law* (New York: Sheed & Ward, 1965). For a compendium of biblical law, see *The Law in the Scriptures*, ed. Edward White (Holmes Beach, Fla.: Wm W. Gaunt, 1990).

15. St. Thomas Aquinas, *Summa Theologica* (questions 90–108), in *The Basic Writings of Saint Thomas Aquinas*, trans. R. J. Henle and ed. Anton Pegis (New York: Random House, 1945). For a more detailed treatment, see the introduction by R. J. Henle

to St. Thomas Aquinas, *The Treatise on Law*, ed. R. J. Henle (Notre Dame, Ind.: University of Notre Dame Press, 1993).

16. Aquinas, *The Treatise on Law*, 63.

17. Aquinas, *Summa Theologica*, Ia(2ae)(95)(2), in *Philosophy of Law* at 24. For more on this point, see Passerin d'Entreves, *Natural Law* (London: Mayflower Press, 1951), 42–44.

18. Of course, the perennial problem of natural law theory is that there are difficulties in determining the exact tenets of the natural law; there seems to be no way to resolve a disagreement about whether a given law is in accord with the natural law. In fact, it seems that natural law could provide the grounds for justifying slavery or oppression on the theory that such oppression is in accordance with natural law. As Alf Ross explains, "Is it nature's bidding that men shall be as brothers, or is it nature's law that the strong shall rule over the weak, and that therefore slavery and class oppression are part of God's meaning for the world? Both propositions have been asserted with the same support and the same 'right.' . . . Like a harlot, natural law is at the disposal of everyone. The ideology does not exist that cannot be defended by an appeal to the law of nature." *On Law and Justice* (Berkeley: University of California Press, 1974), 259–61.

19. See *BGE*, #38, p. 49; *HAH*, #463, p. 169.

20. In *On the Genealogy of Morals* Nietzsche writes: "I think that the sentimentalism which would have [the state] begin with a 'contract' has been disposed of. He who can command, he who is by nature 'master,' he who is violent in act and bearing—what has he to do with contracts!" (*GM*, 2, #17, p. 86). For more on Nietzsche's rejection of the social contract model and his relationship to Rousseau generally, see Keith Ansell-Pearson, *Nietzsche Contra Rousseau: A Study of Nietzsche's Moral and Political Thought* (Cambridge: Cambridge University Press, 1991), 146–48.

21. For an explanation of how the concept of natural law gave birth to that of natural rights, see d'Entreves, *Natural Law*, who writes that "on the eve of the American and French revolutions, the theory of natural law had been turned into a theory of natural rights" (p. 60). Henle writes in his introduction to Aquinas' *Treatise on Law*: "Today natural law theorists accept the modern rights language and have no difficulty in deriving human rights from their foundations in St. Thomas and in other earlier natural law theorists" (p. 93). For more on the transformation of natural law into natural rights, see John Finnis, *Natural Law and Natural Rights* (Oxford: Clarendon Press, 1980), 198–210.

22. Declaration of Independence of the United States of America, July 4, 1776. My discussion of natural rights in the American context is indebted to Louis Henkin, *The Age of Rights* (New York: Columbia University Press, 1990).

23. Murphy and Coleman, *Philosophy of Law*, 13–15.

24. *WP*, #632, p. 336.

25. *GS*, book 3, #109, p. 168.

26. *BGE*, #22, p. 30.

27. *BGE*, #21, p. 29.

28. *HAH,* vol. 2, #9, p. 216.

29. *GS,* book 5, #374, p. 356.

30. *WP,* #552, p. 298.

31. *BGE,* #22, p. 30.

32. *BGE,* #9, p. 15.

33. *BGE,* #38, p. 49.

34. *BGE,* #6, p. 13.

35. *BGE,* #5, p. 12.

36. *GS,* book 4, #335, p. 266.

37. *Daybreak,* #108.

38. A similar point was made by Jeremy Bentham in his review of the French Declaration of the Rights of Man and of Citizens: "We know what it is for men to live without government—no government, consequently, no rights. . . . [A] reason exists for wishing that there were such things as rights. But reasons for wishing there were such things as rights, are not rights;—a reason for wishing that a certain right were established, is not that right—want is not supply—hunger is not bread." "Anarchical Fallacies," in *Human Rights,* ed. A. I. Melden (Belmont, Calif.: Wadsworth, 1970), 31–32.

39. For more on this point, see Keith Ansell-Pearson, "The Significance of Michel Foucault's Reading of Nietzsche," *Nietzsche-Studien* 20 (1991), 267–83.

40. *GM,* essay 1, #13, p. 45.

41. *BGE,* #21, p. 29.

42. *BGE,* #5, pp. 12–13.

43. "On Truth and Lies in a Nonmoral Sense" ["OTL"], in *Philosophy and Truth,* trans. and ed. Daniel Breazeale (Atlantic Highlands, N.J.: Humanities Press International, 1979). Of course, one must be careful not to rely too heavily upon Nietzsche's unpublished work, including his early essays (some of which are compiled in *Philosophy and Truth*), as well as the compilation posthumously assembled and published under the title *The Will to Power.*

44. "OTL," 81.

45. *GS,* book 3, #110, p. 171.

46. *HAH,* vol. 1, #11, p. 16.

47. *GS,* book 3, #121, p. 177.

48. A Nietzschean critique of rights talk is set against Leo Strauss' theory of natural rights in Thomas Haskell's article "The Curious Persistence of Rights Talk in the 'Age of Interpretation,'" *Journal of American History* 74 (1987): 984–1012. For an excellent introduction to rights talk as well as a discussion of Haskell's article, see Neal Milner, *The Denigration of Rights and the Persistence of Rights Talk: A Cultural Portrait,* 14 LAW AND SOCIETY REV. 631 (1989).

49. Mary Ann Glendon, *Rights Talk* (New York: Free Press, 1991), xi.

50. *GS,* book 3, #108, p. 167.

51. *GS,* book 5, #374, p. 336.

52. *TSZ,* part 3, chap. 12, #25, p. 212.

53. *GM,* essay 2, #17, p. 86.

54. *Daybreak*, #112, pp. 66–67.

55. *HAH*, vol. 1, #92, p. 49.

56. HAH, vol. 1, #45, pp. 36–37.

57. *GM*, essay 2, #11, p. 76.

58. *GM*, essay 2, #11, p. 75.

59. *GS*, book 4, #335, p. 264.

60. E.g., see the variation on "natural law" offered by Hart in *The Concept of Law*, 188–89 ("minimal content" natural law as right to survival); see also Fuller, *The Morality of Law* (natural law as a demand of procedural process, not as a canon of substantive law).

61. Many commentators have been too quick to assume that the will to power implies the release of pure power in any form, including violence. Consider Joan Williams' claim that "Nietzsche argued that once God was dead, morality comes tumbling after, leaving only the raw exercise of power." *Rorty, Radicalism, Romanticism*, 1992 WISC. L. REV. 131, 132 (1992). I think that this is a misreading of Nietzsche's use of the term "power." While there are passages in which Nietzsche seems to speak of the will to power in terms of *raw* power, his refined view is that "power" involves self-mastery, discipline, and self-overcoming. According to Keith Ansell-Pearson, "For Nietzsche 'power' exists as potentiality, so that in the term 'will to power' the word 'power' denotes not simply a fixed and unchangeable entity, like force or strength, but an 'accomplishment' of the will overcoming or overpowering itself." *An Introduction to Nietzsche as Political Thinker* (Cambridge: Cambridge University Press, 1994), 46.

62. The secondary literature often fails to distinguish between the weak and strong versions of nihilism. For example, consider the definition offered by Peter Goodrich: "Nihilism in the context of legal studies means loss of faith in the community of legal doctrine and refusal to . . . believe in the foundational myths of legal doctrine." *Law and Modernity*, 49 MODERN L. REV. 545, 553 (1986). I think that this definition covers only nihilism in the weak sense, i.e., nihilism as the loss of foundations. In this weak sense, which equates nihilism with nonfoundationalism, Nietzsche is a nihilist, but so are Rorty, Dewey, and Dworkin (which shows that the term is not meaningfully applied). Full-blown nihilism means something more than the loss of foundations: it holds that there can be no justifiable basis for choosing one law over another and no basis for saying that one decision is better or worse than another. This is nihilism in the true, or strong, sense—and it is thus *not* a position held by Nietzsche.

63. *GM*, essay 3, #27, p. 161.

64. Nietzsche, "Notes on *Thus Spake Zarathustra*," in *Complete Works of Friedrich Nietzsche*, 263.

65. For more on this approach, see Margaret McDonald, "Natural Rights," in *Human Rights*, 53–54.

66. *GS*, book 4, #335, p. 266.

67. *GS*, book 3, #270, p. 219.

68. *GM*, essay 3, #27, p. 161.

69. Singer, "The Player and the Cards," 66–67.

70. 478 U.S. 186 (1986).

71. 347 U.S. 483 (1954).

72. See, e.g., *AC* #57; BGE, #257.

73. Richard Rorty, *Contingency, Irony, and Solidarity* (Cambridge: Cambridge University Press, 1989), 54, 65.

74. Andre Mineau, "Human Rights and Nietzsche," 880. This view is also put forth by Ted Sadler, "The Postmodern Politicization of Nietzsche," in *Nietzsche, Feminism, and Political Theory*, ed. Paul Patton (New York: Routledge, 1993), 225–43. Sadler argues that the only political theory consistent with Nietzsche's writings is an apolitical longing for an aristocratic society based on rank ordering. This view is largely confirmed by J. P. Stern, *A Study of Nietzsche* (Cambridge: Cambridge University Press, 1979), 122–25; and Ofelia Schutte, *Beyond Nihilism: Nietzsche Without Masks* (Chicago: University of Chicago Press, 1984), esp. chapter 4: "Nietzsche's Politics." For a discussion of whether Nietzsche was antipolitical or apolitical, see Peter Bergmann, *Nietzsche, the Last Antipolitical German* (Bloomington: Indiana University Press, 1987), 1–8.

75. Even if one grants that Nietzsche rejects *innate* rights, one can still debate whether Nietzsche would allow the use of a rights hypothesis on other grounds, namely, as a life-preserving fiction. As Mineau has observed, what Nietzsche finds objectionable is not so much the notion of rights as the notion of a "rights founding principle." A Nietzschean can still justify rights as a provisional hypothesis—without also holding a position of rights foundationalism—by allowing the provisional rights to be overridden under limited circumstances.

76. *WP,* #470, p. 262

77. *WP,* #600, p. 326.

78. *GM,* essay 3, #27, p. 161.

79. For a similar conclusion, see Keith Ansell-Pearson, *Nietzsche Contra Rousseau,* 102 (rejecting the notion that Nietzsche is offering a "new natural law" based upon the will to power).

80. *WP,* #354, p. 195.

81. *WP,* #854, p. 457.

82. *BGE,* #257, p. 201.

83. *EH,* #5, p. 267.

84. *WTP,* #753, p. 397.

85. *TSZ,* part 1, #11, p. 51.

86. *AC,* #57, p. 179.

87. E.g., Ted Sadler ("The Postmodern Politicalization of Nietzsche") argues that Nietzsche's repeated insistence on a rank order of individuals rules out the possibility of a Nietzschean justification for pluralism. Ofelia Schutte is equally skeptical: "Nietzsche erroneously believed that the overcoming of nihilism required the crushing of democracy and of all movements inspired by the French Revolution: death of liberty, equality and fraternity for all." *Beyond Nihilism,* 161.

88. For a similar approach to Nietzsche's more outrageous passages on political matters, see Mark Warren, *Nietzsche and Political Thought* (Cambridge, Mass.: MIT Press, 1988). Warren argues that Nietzsche's outlandish political comments were weighed down by a series of false assumptions; therefore such comments must be discounted in order to formulate a coherent Nietzschean politics based upon the more philosophical works. In other words, Nietzsche himself failed to follow through on the political implications of his own philosophy. I adopt the same methodological approach in my formulation of a Nietzschean jurisprudence and feel that it is necessary to overlook some of Nietzsche's specific comments in order to obtain a coherent approach to law. Not everyone agrees with this approach, and it is easy to see why: the selective approach to Nietzsche may have a distorting effect. The dangers of this approach are summarized by Ofelia Schutte: "The weeding out of the least attractive elements in Nietzsche's work amounts to self-deceit or censorship, and, in any case, this practice keeps us from understanding the whole of Nietzsche's vision." *Beyond Nihilism,* 186.

89. Ludwig Wittgenstein, *Philosophical Investigations,* trans. G. E. M. Anscombe (New York: Macmillan, 1958), sec. 127, p. 50e.

4: FOUCAULT ON LAW

1. Foucault is often seen as a critic of the "Enlightenment Project," continuing the critique put forth by Max Horkheimer and Theodor Adorno in *Dialectic of Enlightenment,* trans. John Cumming (1947; rpt. New York: Continuum, 1991). See Stephen Best and Douglas Kellner, *Postmodern Theory* (New York: Guilford Press, 1991), especially chapter 2: "Foucault and the Critique of Modernity." Orwell and Huxley have also been interpreted as critics of the Enlightenment; see Sheldon Wolin, "Counter-Enlightenment: Orwell's 1984" in *Reflections on America, 1984: An Orwell Symposium,* ed. Robert Mulvihill (Athens, Ga.: University of Georgia Press, 1986), 98–114.

2. See Laura Engelstein, "Combined Underdevelopment: Discipline and the Law in Imperial and Soviet Russia," *American Historical Review* 98 (1993): 338–53. Engelstein argues that since Foucault makes empirical claims about the emergence of a disciplinary society from a premodern society of coercive law, his claims should be tested against the actual evolution of the legal systems in various countries. Engelstein tests Foucault's account by asking whether it can predict and explain the changes in the legal system in nineteenth- and twentieth-century Russia. She concludes that Foucault's account is incorrect because it does not accurately predict the way in which law and discipline developed in Russia. The responses to Engelstein's article raise the important issue of whether Foucault's work should be judged primarily as a strict historical account or, alternatively, as a form of social criticism not dependent on historical validation. See the following two articles in the same issue of the *American Historical Review:* Rudy Koshar, "Foucault and Social History: Comments on 'Combined Underdevelopment,' " 354–63, and Jan Goldstein, "Framing Discipline with Law: Problems and Promises of the Liberal State," 364–75.

3. See Annie Bunting, *Feminism, Foucault, and Law as Power/Knowledge*, 30 AL-BERTA L. REV. 829 (1992). See also Carol Smart, "The Influence of Foucault," *Feminism and the Power of Law* (New York: Routledge, 1989), 6–14.

4. See Bob Fine, *Democracy and the Rule of Law: Liberal Ideals and Marxist Critique* (London: Pluto Press, 1985), 189–202. For an excellent reading of Foucault's writings on law, see Alan Hunt, *Foucault's Expulsion of Law: Toward a Retrieval*, 17 LAW AND SOCIAL INQUIRY 1 (1992) (Hunt's article is followed by several commentaries and a reply), as well as Alan Hunt and Gary Wickham, *Foucault and Law: Toward a Sociology of Law as Governance* (London: Pluto Press, 1994). It was only after I had begun work on this book that I came across Hunt's reference to Foucault's depiction of the disciplinary state as a "negative utopia." For a more general overview of Foucault's approach to law, see Jerry Leonard, *Foucault: Genealogy, Law, Praxis*, 14 LEGAL STUDIES FORUM 3 (1990); Jerry Palmer and Frank Pearce, *Legal Discourse and State Power: Foucault and the Juridical Relation*, 11 INT'L J. OF SOCIOLOGY OF LAW 361 (1983); and Gerald Turkel, *Michel Foucault: Law, Power, and Knowledge*, 17 J. OF LAW AND SOCIETY 170 (1990).

5. See Gillian Rose, *Dialectic of Nihilism: Post-Structuralism and Law* (Oxford: Basil Blackwell, 1984), 171–207; and Daniel Williams, *Law, Deconstruction, and Resistance: The Critical Stances of Derrida and Foucault*, 6 CARDOZO ARTS AND ENTERTAINMENT L. REV. 359 (1988).

6. On privacy see, e.g., Jed Rubenfeld, *The Right of Privacy*, 102 HARVARD L. REV. 737, 770 (1989); and Kendall Thomas, *Beyond the Privacy Principle*, 92 COLUMBIA L. REV. 1431, 1478 (1992). On intellectual property, see David Lange, *At Play in the Fields of the Word: Copyright and the Construction of Authorship in the Post-Literate Millennium*, 55(2) LAW AND CONTEMPORARY PROBLEMS 139 (1992). Regarding punishment, see Adrian Howe, *Punish and Critique* (New York: Routledge, 1994), especially chapter 3: "The Foucault Effect: From Penology to Penalty."

7. Duncan Kennedy has pointed out that Foucault sometimes refers to the view which he is challenging as the "Law-and-Sovereign" model. *The Stakes of Law, or Hale and Foucault*, 15 LEGAL STUDIES FORUM 327 (1991). While this formulation is used occasionally by Foucault, I will stay with Foucault's more common terminology for the liberal approach to political and legal theory.

8. Michel Foucault, "Two Lectures," in *Power/Knowledge: Selected Interviews and Other Writings, 1972–77*, trans. Colin Gordon et al. and ed. Colin Gordon (New York: Pantheon, 1980), 97–98.

9. Ibid., 88.

10. Thomas Hobbes, *Leviathan* (New York: Penguin, 1968) 276, 264.

11. Ibid., 261.

12. Foucault's most explicit discussion of Nietzsche is set forth in the essay "Nietzsche, Genealogy, History," trans. Donald Bouchard and Sherry Simon, in *The Foucault Reader*, ed. Paul Rabinow (New York: Pantheon, 1984). For a brief discussion of Foucault's debt to Nietzsche, see Barry Smart, *Michel Foucault* (New York: Tavistock, 1985), 14–15.

13. Friedrich Nietzsche, *On the Genealogy of Morals,* trans. Walter Kaufman (New York: Vintage, 1989), especially the second essay: " 'Guilt,' 'Bad Conscience,' and the Like."

14. Nietzsche, " 'Guilt,' 'Bad Conscience,' and the Like," #13, p. 45.

15. Friedrich Nietzsche, *Daybreak,* trans. R. J. Hollingdale (Cambridge: Cambridge University Press, 1982), #112. One should add that Nietzsche flatly rejected social contract theory: "Human society is a trial: thus I teach it. . . . A trial, O my brothers, and *not* a 'contract.' Break, break, this word of the softhearted and half-and-half." *Thus Spoke Zarathustra,* trans. Walter Kaufman (New York: Penguin, 1966), part 3, chap. 12, #25, p. 212.

16. See the final passages from Foucault's *Order of Things: An Archaeology of the Human Sciences* (New York: Vintage, 1994).

17. Michel Foucault, "The Subject and Power," in *Michel Foucault: Beyond Structuralism and Hermeneutics,* Hubert Dreyfus and Paul Rabinow (Chicago: University of Chicago Press, 1982), 208 (emphasis added).

18. Michel Foucault, *Discipline and Punish,* trans. Alan Sheridan (New York: Vintage, 1979), 194.

19. Foucault uses the term "disciplines" to designate procedures whereby the body is regulated, coerced, and subjected to constant surveillance: "These methods, which made possible the meticulous control of the operations of the body, which assured the constant subjection of its forces and imposed upon them a relation of docility–utility, might be called disciplines." *Discipline and Punish,* 137. Note, however, that the disciplines were not entirely repressive since they also *constituted* the subject. In other words, the disciplines gave us a framework for understanding the subject, and thus *created* the subject. For example, the discipline of psychiatry once held that gays were aberrant and disturbed. This label, in part, constituted the identity of gays at that time. The method of classifying, isolating, and medicalizing gay behavior was not only a repressive but also a productive act, a way of turning gays into subjects, albeit subjects of a denigrated variety. Of course, it is this very "subjectivization" of homosexuals that can serve as the rallying point for a "queer politics" which resists their marginalization at the hands of the dominant culture. See David Halperin, "The Queer Politics of Michel Foucault," *Saint Foucault* (New York: Oxford University Press, 1995), 15–125.

20. Foucault, "Nietzsche, Genealogy, History," 76–100.

21. Nietzsche argued, in effect, that there have been two paradigms of morality and law since the beginning of recorded history. The first epoch of law was based on the discharge of power relations among the strong, the so-called master morality. The second epoch coincided with the Christian-based ethic of *ressentiment,* in which the weak banded together to rebel against the strong, the so-called slave morality. See Nietzsche, *Beyond Good and Evil* (New York: Vintage, 1989), #260.

22. Foucault, "Nietzsche, Genealogy, History," 85 (emphasis added).

23. Foucault, "Two Lectures," 95.

24. In addition to distancing himself from the liberal understanding of power as state power, Foucault also wishes to distance himself from the Marxist understanding of

power as class power. He feels the Marxist position is too reductionist because it sees power solely in terms of economic relations and therefore views social relations as a reflection of the relations of production. Foucault argues that while some law and discipline can be explained as the mechanism by which one class tries to control another, the disciplines cannot be wholly explained as mechanisms which provide for the smooth functioning of capitalism. Furthermore, Foucault rejects the Marxist notion of the self ("species being") and hence disagrees with the Marxist concept of emancipation through the abolition of private property. See Foucault, *Discipline and Punish*, 220–21. See also Best and Kellner, *Postmodern Theory*, 56–59.

25. Foucault's overall conception of social contract theory is best substantiated by Rousseau's *Social Contract*, which first devotes several chapters to establishing the legitimacy of the state and then turns to mechanisms for controlling the population, including the establishment of a civil religion and the right of the state to censor. See Foucault, "Governmentality," trans. Rosi Braidotti and Colin Gordon, in *The Foucault Effect: Studies in Governmentality*, ed. Graham Burchell, Colin Gordon, and Peter Miller (Chicago: University of Chicago Press, 1991), 101.

26. Michel Foucault, *The History of Sexuality. Volume 1: An Introduction*, trans. Robert Hurley (New York: Vintage, 1990), 87.

27. Foucault, "Two Lectures," 103.

28. Foucault certainly recognizes that while the juridical system as a whole has been adopted to benefit the monarchies, this system also gave rise to certain rights (privacy, autonomy, property) which have been used to justify rebellion against the monarchies: "Moreover, law, particularly in the 18th Century, was a weapon of the struggle against the same monarchical power which had initially made use of it to impose itself." "Power and Strategies," trans. Colin Gordon et al., in *P/K*, 140–41.

29. Foucault, "Two Lectures," 96 (emphasis added).

30. Foucault, "Governmentality," in *The Foucault Effect*, 87–104.

31. Foucault, "Two Lectures" 102.

32. Ibid., 104.

33. Foucault, *Discipline and Punish*, 194.

34. Foucault, "Two Lectures" 97 (emphasis added).

35. Foucault, *The History of Sexuality*, 89.

36. Foucault, "Truth and Power," 121 (emphasis added).

37. Foucault, "Two Lectures," 105–8.

38. Ibid., 105.

39. Ibid., 106–7.

40. Foucault, *Discipline and Punish*, 194.

41. Foucault, "Power and Strategies," 141.

42. This position is what separates Foucault from the Marxists, who trace the rise of disciplines to the need for docile laborers in a capitalist economy. While Foucault acknowledges that certain disciplines had this function (viz. creating a class of docile workers), he thinks that the disciplines arose for reasons other than capitalism, although "each makes the other possible and necessary." *Discipline and Punish*, 221.

43. Ibid, 222.

44. Ibid. (emphasis added).

45. Ibid.

46. Ibid., 223.

47. Foucault, *The History of Sexuality*, 144 (emphasis added).

48. Michel Foucault, "The Dangerous Individual," *Foucault: Philosophy, Politics, and Culture*, trans. Alain Baudot and Jane Couchman, ed. Lawrence Kritzman (New York: Routledge, 1988), 125.

49. Ibid., 126. Of course, one can turn this analysis back on Foucault by arguing that the question of the perpetrator's intent is without doubt a relevant question, and that any system of penology which failed to take this into account is flawed. For example, the perpetrator may have been under a delusion during the attacks, or he may have committed the attacks under the influence of drugs, which would affect the sentence to be passed. One could argue, *contra* Foucault, that there is nothing sinister about questioning the mental state of a criminal. After all, even Socrates was asked to say something in his defense at his own trial!

50. Foucault, *Discipline and Punish*, 223.

51. Nietzsche, *The Will to Power*, trans. R. J. Hollingdale and Walter Kaufmann, ed. Walter Kaufmann (New York: Vintage, 1968) #2, p. 9.

52. According to Foucault, *Discipline and Punish*, "The 'Enlightenment,' which discovered the liberties, also invented the disciplines" (222).

53. Foucault, "On the Genealogy of Ethics: An Overview of a Work in Progress," in *Michel Foucault: Beyond Structuralism and Hermeneutics*, 231.

54. Michel Foucault, "Space, Knowledge, and Power," trans. Christian Hubert, in *The Foucault Reader*, 249.

55. Foucault, "Human Nature: Justice Versus Power" (debate with Noam Chomsky), *The Foucault Reader*, 6.

56. Ibid., 6.

57. This point is stressed in Richard Posner's complaint against postmodern theory: "When the ethnocentric, embedded, socially constructed character of the self is emphasized, social criticism becomes an oxymoron; it presupposes an external standpoint that postmodernism denies." *Overcoming Law* (Cambridge, Mass.: Harvard University Press, 1995), 316.

58. Foucault, "Two Lectures," 108.

59. Ibid.

60. Foucault, "On the Genealogy of Ethics: An Overview of Work in Progress," in *The Foucault Reader*, 351. For a discussion of the shift in Foucault's later work, see Best and Kellner's *Postmodern Theory*, 60–61; see also Jon Simons, "From Resistance to Polaesthics: Politics After Foucault," *Philosophy and Social Criticism* 17 (1991): 41.

61. Foucault, "The Subject and Power," 216.

62. Colin Gordon, afterword to *P/K*, 246.

63. Foucault, *Discipline and Punish*, 301.

64. Michel Foucault, "Sexual Choice, Sexual Act: Foucault and Homosexuality," trans. James O'Higgins in *Foucault: Philosophy, Politics, and Culture*, 286, 294.

65. In his final works, Foucault said that power relations are inevitable ("I don't believe there can be a society without relations of power"), yet he seemed to advocate a system in which there would be a "minimum of domination." See Foucault's essay "The Ethics of Care for the Self as a Practice of Freedom," trans. J. D. Gauthier, in *The Final Foucault*, ed. J. Bernauer and D. Rasmussen (Cambridge, Mass.: MIT Press, 1988), 18.

66. A series of critical articles which appeared in the early and mid eighties pointed out that Foucault lacked a normative basis for decrying the rise of the disciplinary state. See, e.g., Michael Walzer, "The Politics of Michel Foucault," *Dissent* 30 (1983): 481; Charles Taylor, "Foucault on Freedom and Truth," *Political Theory* 12 (1984): 152; and Nancy Fraser, "Michel Foucault: A 'Young Conservative?,'" *Ethics* 96 (1985): 165. Some commentators have responded by arguing that Foucault's "aesthetics of the self" (set forth in his later writings) could ground a political program of localized resistance to domination. See, e.g., Simons, "From Resistance to Polaesthics," 48–53.

67. In his interesting book on punishment, Mark Tunick confirms that Foucault takes an external perspective on the legal system. See his *Punishment: Theory and Practice* (Berkeley: University of California Press, 1992), 18.

5: DERRIDA

1. See, e.g., J. M. Balkin, *Deconstructive Practice and Legal Theory*, 96 YALE L. J. 743 (1987); Clare Dalton, *An Essay in the Deconstruction of Contract Doctrine*, 94 YALE L. J. 997 (1985).

2. Jacques Derrida, "Declarations of Independence," trans. Tom Keenam and Tom Pepper, *New Political Science* 15 (1986): 7–17.

3. Jacques Derrida, "'The Laws of Reflection': Nelson Mandela, in Admiration," in *For Nelson Mandela*, trans. Mary Ann Caws and Isabelle Lorenz, ed. Jacques Derrida and Mustapha Tlili (New York: Holt, 1987); idem, "Before the Law," in Jacques Derrida, *Acts of Literature*, ed. Derek Attridge (New York: Routledge, 1992).

4. The proceedings of the symposium, including the text of Derrida's lecture and the responses thereto, were published as *Deconstruction and the Possibility of Justice*, 11 CARDOZO L. REV. 919 (1989). Many of these papers, along with Derrida's text, were later revised and collected in the volume *Deconstruction and the Possibility of Justice*, ed. Drucilla Cornell, Michel Rosenfield, and David G. Carlson (New York: Routledge, 1992). Subsequent references to Derrida's lecture will be to the 1992 version published by Routledge.

5. Due to time constraints, Derrida presented only the first half of his text during the colloquium. The remaining half was delivered at UCLA in 1990, at a conference on "Nazism and the 'Final Solution': Probing the Limits of Representation." See *Deconstruction and the Possibility of Justice*, 3. The first half of the lecture (upon which I will be focusing) deals directly with issues of law and justice, while the second half involves a close reading of Walter Benjamin's essay "Critique of Violence." Derrida's reading of Benjamin was the subject of a second symposium at Cardozo Law School, the papers of which were published in 13 CARDOZO L. REV. 1081 (1991).

6. On the notion that deconstruction cannot generate a coherent ethical program, see Thomas McCarthy, "The Politics of the Ineffable: Derrida's Deconstructivism," *Ideals and Illusions: On Reconstruction and Deconstruction in Contemporary Critical Theory* (Cambridge, Mass.: MIT Press, 1991). On the notion that deconstruction ultimately lapses into a sort of conservative inaction, see Jürgen Habermas, *The Philosophical Discourse of Modernity* (Cambridge, Mass.: MIT Press, 1987), 161–84. For a possible line of defense against Habermas' critique, see David C. Hoy, "Splitting the Difference: Habermas' Critique of Derrida," in *Working Through Derrida*, ed. Gary Madison (Evanston, Ill.: Northwestern University Press, 1993), 230–51.

7. This text will be supplemented by some of Derrida's other writings that deal more or less directly with the issues of justice and law (of which there are surprisingly quite a few). In "Force of Law" Derrida points out that many of his earlier works address the problematic of law and justice. See especially "Declarations of Independence"; "'The Laws of Reflection': Nelson Mandela, in Admiration"; "Before the Law"; and "Violence and Metaphysics," in *Writing and Difference*, trans. Alan Bass (Chicago: University of Chicago Press, 1978), 79–153.

Some of Derrida's more recent work also touches upon issues of justice and law. See *Specters of Marx*, trans. Peggy Kamuf (New York: Routledge, 1994), xix, 59, 183–84; *Aporias*, trans. Thomas Dutoit (Stanford, Calif.: Stanford University Press, 1993), 16–20; and *The Other Heading: Reflections on Today's Europe*, Pascale-Anne Brault and Michael Nass (Bloomington: Indiana University Press, 1992), 76–83.

8. See Derrida, "Différance," in *Margins of Philosophy*, trans. Alan Bass (Chicago: University of Chicago Press, 1982), 1. Note that the word "différance" is a variant of the accepted spelling so as to emphasize Derrida's point about how meaning is created through differences.

9. Derrida, "Différance," 1. Derrida writes: "The sign, in this sense, is deferred presence. . . . The first consequence to be drawn from this is that the signified concept is never present in and of itself, in a sufficient presence that would refer only to itself" (9, 11).

10. See Derrida's discussion of logocentrism in his *Of Grammatology*, trans. Gayatri Spivak (Baltimore, Md.: Johns Hopkins University Press, 1976), 10–15.

11. Jacques Derrida, *Positions*, trans. Alan Bass (Chicago: University of Chicago Press, 1981), 72.

12. For an interesting postmodern discussion with deconstructive overtones, see Stanley Fish's examination of how mainstream legal theory uses the Parole Evidence Rule to draw an artificial boundary between what is inside a contract and what is outside. "The Law Wishes to Have a Formal Existence," in *There's No Such Thing as Free Speech and It's a Good Thing, Too* (New York: Oxford University Press, 1994), 144–56. Fish points out that mainstream legal theory wishes the law to have a "formal existence" divorced from politics, but the boundary which separates law from politics is artificial and untenable.

13. In this vein, see J. M. Balkin's innovative deconstructive reading of a Supreme Court case in *Tradition, Betrayal, and the Politics of Deconstruction*, 11 CARDOZO L. REV. 1613 (1990).

14. Derrida, "Force of Law," 3–5.

15. Ibid., 19.

16. Ibid.

17. Ibid., 10.

18. Ibid., 16.

19. Ibid., 17.

20. Ibid., 16.

21. Ibid., 22. Derrida stops short of wholesale adoption of Levinas' notion of justice toward the other, since Levinas' analysis carries additional commitments (presumably of a religious character) that Derrida wants to avoid in his lecture on law. Derrida's appropriation of Levinas in this lecture serves to extend and solidify his earlier discussion of Levinas in "Violence and Metaphysics": "Ethics, in Levinas' sense, is an Ethics without law and without concept, which maintains its non-violent purity only before being determined as concepts and laws. . . . Levinas does not seek to propose laws or moral rules, does not seek to determine a morality, but rather the essence of the ethical relation in general." *Writing and Difference*, 111. Interestingly, in this relatively early essay Derrida was critical of the transcendental elements of Levinas' work, although (as I will argue) Derrida's own later works contain a strong transcendental component.

22. Jacques Derrida, *Given Time 1. Counterfeit Money*, trans. Peggy Kamuf (Chicago: University of Chicago Press, 1992).

23. "Force of Law," 25.

24. The notion of a duty beyond law is further explored in *Aporias:* "Duty must be such an over-duty, which demands acting without duty, without rule or norm (therefore without law). . . . [A] responsible decision must obey an 'it is necessary' that owes nothing, it must obey a duty that owes nothing, that must owe nothing in order to be a duty, a duty that has no debt to pay back, a duty without debt and therefore without duty" (16). That is, a genuine duty is categorically binding, regardless of the empirical situation in which one finds oneself, and regardless of whether one will be rewarded for doing one's duty.

25. Wittgenstein provides an excellent example of this process of tracing justifications back to their source in mere customs: "If I have exhausted the justifications I have reached bedrock, and my spade is turned. Then I am inclined to say: 'This is simply what I do.' *Philosophical Investigations*, trans. G. E. M. Anscombe (New York: Macmillan, 1958), sec. 217, p. 85e.

26. Quoted by Derrida in "Force of Law," 12.

27. Ibid.

28. Ibid., 13.

29. There are problems with Derrida's claim that the founding of every state involves an act of interpretive violence. This formulation renders every foundation violent, thereby obscuring the fact that some foundations are truly violent (apartheid South Africa, the former military dictatorship in Haiti) while others are largely based on the consent of the governed (as in the United States). By saying that all law involves force, Derrida fails to distinguish between *legitimate* force, which follows a rule of law,

and *illegitimate* force, which occurs at the whim of the powers that be. I discuss this point in "Derrida and Lyotard's Misreading of Founding Documents" (in author's manuscript possession). A similar point is made by Nancy Fraser, *The Force of Law: Metaphysical or Political?* 13 CARDOZO L. REV. 1325 (1991).

30. "Force of Law," 14.

31. Derrida, "Before the Law," 191–94, and "The 'Laws of Reflection,'" 18.

32. Derrida's more recent work affirms that the call to responsibility requires an experience of the impossibility of justice. By experiencing this *aporia,* one avoids "good conscience," a term which denotes the mistaken belief that one has successfully encapsulated the infinite demand of justice into a technical rule. See *Aporias,* 19; and *The Other Heading,* 81. The notion of "good conscience" has a Sartrean ring to it, and in essence Derrida's "good conscience" resembles Sartre's "bad faith" in that both represent a flight from infinite responsibility.

33. "Force of Law," 14.

34. Ibid., 14. Drucilla Cornell has focused on Derrida's notion that deconstruction exposes the structural conditions which make a legal system possible in the first instance but which are themselves outside the system. See her book *The Philosophy of the Limit* (New York: Routledge, 1992).

35. At times Derrida seems to contradict this claim that justice cannot be (fully) present. For example, he argues that it is just to address the other in the language of the other, and that it is unjust for one group of people (say, imperialists) to impose its language upon a minority. I think that in such cases Derrida is committed to saying that a particular action is "just" or "unjust," which seems to entail that justice or injustice is present in such cases. Of course, since Derrida eschews the metaphysics of presence, he has difficulty explaining (without using metaphysical language) how justice can be present as such in these cases.

36. "Force of Law," 15.

37. Ibid.," 16.

38. Ibid., 22.

39. Ibid., 23.

40. There is some uncertainty as to whether this is a genuine "paradox" or *aporia.* For example, H. L. A. Hart points out that legal rules must be open-textured to allow for flexible application to new situations, so uncertainty is built into the judicial process for good reason. *The Concept of Law* (Oxford: Oxford University Press, 1961), 127–28. No doubt Derrida is correct that a judge should not be a mere "calculating machine," nor can a judge ignore precedent altogether; this makes the judge "regulated yet unregulated" in a certain sense. However, *contra* Derrida, it seems quite possible for a judge to successfully juggle these two demands. That is, a judge could avoid the *aporia* by following the law in most cases, unless he or she felt the law was unconstitutional or unjust, in which case the judge would overrule the law in deference to a higher authority. Hence there is no true *aporia* here but only contradictory demands between following precedent and being free to ignore precedent when equity demands it. Indeed, one could use similar reasoning to dissolve all three of Derrida's *aporias* of justice,

since the mere existence of competing demands on a judge does not necessarily give rise to impassable *aporias*.

41. "Force of Law," 24.

42. Ibid., 26.

43. Ibid.

44. Ibid., 27–28.

45. Derrida, *Specters of Marx*, 184.

46. "Force of Law," 28.

47. Ibid.

48. Derrida, *Specters of Marx*, 59, xix. In *Aporias,* Derrida also speaks of a call to the other which involves the duty of action without repayment (16).

49. It might be argued that Derrida's project is not to erect a notion of "deconstructive justice," in the sense of providing a positive program for jurisprudence, but rather to provide a method for questioning the very possibility of a successful and complete legal theory. This reading of Derrida would be similar to that of David C. Hoy in "Splitting the Difference," 251. Yet I think that "Force of Law" is an attempt to explain the essence of justice and law. On my reading, Derrida appears to sketch the outlines of justice and law as such, attempting to provide the grounds for a positive legal theory over and above his critique of classical jurisprudence. That is, he is not concerned merely with deconstructing but also with explaining legal principles that can be used in actual cases.

50. For the notion that Derrida's theory of law employs a type of Platonic transcendentalism (including at least some of the accompanying metaphysical baggage), see J. M. Balkin, *Transcendental Deconstruction, Transcendental Justice,* 92 MICHIGAN L. REV. 1131 (1994).

51. See, e.g., *Phaedo* at 100d: "The one thing that makes the object beautiful is the presence in it or association with it, in whatever way the relation comes about, of absolute beauty. . . . [I]t is by beauty that beautiful things are beautiful." *Collected Dialogues of Plato,* ed. Edith Hamilton and Huntington Cairns (Princeton, N.J.: Princeton University Press, 1961), 81–82. Similarly, it is by means of justice that various actions are deemed just.

52. See the *Republic* at 479e, in *Collected Dialogues,* 719–20.

53. "Force of Law," 25.

54. Ibid., 16.

55. As some of Derrida's critics have pointed out, Derrida has a tendency to speak of certain concepts as if they were quasi-transcendental and hence similar to Platonic forms. This is especially true of Derrida's notion of "différance" and "arche-writing," which sometimes appear as transcendental forces with causal powers. See Dieter Freudlieb, "Deconstructionist Metaphysics and the Interpretation of Saussure," *Journal of Speculative Philosophy* 4 (1986): 113.

56. Derrida discusses certain Kantian elements of his work in the afterword ("Toward an Ethic of Discussion") to *Limited Inc,* trans. Samuel Weber (Evanston, Ill.: Northwestern University Press, 1988). There Derrida speaks of an unconditional

responsibility that is not quite outside all contexts but manages to penetrate all contexts (152–53).

57. Immanuel Kant, *Critique of Pure Reason*, trans. Norman Kemp Smith (New York: St. Martin's, 1965), secs. A644, B672, p. 533; idem, *Groundwork of the Metaphysic of Morals*, trans. H. J. Paton (New York: Harper & Row, 1964), 126–31.

58. Kant, *Groundwork*, 127.

59. In an interesting parallel, Kant foreshadowed Derrida's point that law should not be confused with justice: "[The jurist] can indeed state what is laid down as right, that is, what the laws in a certain place and at a certain time say or have said. But whether what these laws prescribed is also right, and what the universal criterion is by which one could recognize right as well as wrong—this would remain hidden from him. . . . Like the wooden head in Phaedrus' fable, a merely empirical doctrine of Right is a head that may be beautiful but unfortunately it has no brain." *The Metaphysics of Morals, Part I: Metaphysical First Principles of the Doctrine of Right*, trans. Mary Gregor (Cambridge: Cambridge University Press, 1991), secs. 229–30, p. 55.

60. "Force of Law," 24–25.

61. The key question is whether Derrida would embrace a version of Kantian theory that has been sufficiently denuded of metaphysics. One example of an ethical theory that fits this description would be Habermas' discourse ethics, which incorporates certain Kantian notions of universality and reciprocity yet purportedly eschews Kantian metaphysics. It appears that Derrida finds Habermas' program weighed down by too many metaphysical assumptions, especially concerning the primacy of communicative speech over other forms of expression, the stability of communicative contexts, and the shared horizons of understanding between persons in an ideal speech scenario. For a discussion of a possible rapprochement between Derrida and Habermas (perhaps suggested by Christopher Norris), see Terry Hoy, "Derrida: Postmodernism and Political Theory," *Philosophy and Social Criticism* 19 (1993): 243–57.

62. Merold Westphal, "Derrida as a Natural Law Theorist," *International Philosophical Quarterly* 34 (1994): 250.

63. Derrida's comments against "logocentrism" (the idea that metaphysical entities can be made fully present and completely understandable) are set forth most fully in *Of Grammatology*, 6–12.

64. Westphal, "Derrida as a Natural Law Theorist," 252.

65. Derrida, *Limited Inc*, 152 (emphasis added).

66. Ibid., 153 (emphasis added).

67. Derrida, "Structure, Sign and Play," in *Writing and Difference*, 278–93.

68. See, e.g., "Force of Law," 22.

69. Derrida is quoting from Emmanuel Levinas' *Totality and Infinity* (Pittsburgh, Pa.: Duquesne University Press, 1969); see especially the section on "Truth and Justice."

70. "Force of Law," 15.

71. See "Différance" and "The Ends of Man," in *Margins of Philosophy*, 109–53. My point is that there is a potential contradiction at work in Derrida's simultaneous denial of the unified subject and his notion that justice involves a duty from one subject to

another subject. William Richardson explains the problem as follows: "How can one talk about emancipation without a conception of a subject that is free and inviolable? . . . But there is nothing in Deconstruction that can account for a subject that is stable enough to be capable of response, responsibility or freedom." *Law and Right,* 13 CARDOZO L. REV. 1339, 1340 (1991). Richardson's point captures the key argument in this chapter: for Derrida to generate a notion of justice, he must make metaphysical assumptions (regarding the self, others, communication, stability of contexts) which he has elsewhere rejected.

72. Like Derrida, Dworkin feels that positive law must be interpreted in light of principles of justice. However, Dworkin feels that these principles are historically contingent, whereas Derrida seeks a more transcendental source of justice.

73. It would be interesting to explore the ways in which Derrida's brand of Kantianism is similar to Rawls'. Both agree with Kant that laws should be assessed on the basis of whether they respect fundamental justice owed to others. But Rawls argues that particular arrangements of positive law can be deemed "just" if they satisfy certain enumerated principles of justice, whereas Derrida thinks that one can never say that the law is just. Derrida's view is more utopian (and vaguer) in the sense that he holds out justice as a transcendental idea that cannot be instantiated in the imminent legal order. For a brief comparison, see Cornell, *The Philosophy of the Limit,* 182.

74. Ibid., 1.

75. "The 'Laws of Reflection,'" 20.

76. "Force of Law," 8 (emphasis added).

77. It might be argued that Derrida conceives of justice solely as the procedure of questioning the foundations of legal systems, and that he does not put forth a *substantive* theory of justice. That is, Derrida sees justice as procedural since he does not provide substantive principles of justice but only a procedure for interrogating the law. From my perspective, this view fails to capture the fact that Derrida spends a great deal of time discussing justice per se, as if it were something apart from the mere process of interrogating the legal system. I take Derrida's account to be *both* procedural and substantive.

78. "Différance," 10.

79. "Force of Law," 15.

80. Ibid., 27.

81. Ibid., 27–28 (emphasis added).

82. In "Before the Law" Derrida makes a similar claim that the duty to the other is beyond history: "To be invested with its categorical authority, the [moral] law must be without history, genesis, or any possible derivation. That would be the law of the law. Pure morality has no history: as Kant seems at first to remind us, no intrinsic history" (191).

83. "Signature, Event, Context," in *Margins of Philosophy,* 320.

84. Cornell, *Philosophy of the Limit,* 8.

85. Ibid., 182–83.

86. Some of the problems at issue between Derrida and Gadamer (and, though less

directly, Habermas) are discussed by Ernst Behler in "Deconstruction Versus Hermeneutics," *Confrontations: Nietzsche/Heidegger/Derrida* (Stanford, Calif.: Stanford University Press, 1991), 137–57. Interestingly, Habermas argues that his discourse ethics is sufficiently removed from traditional philosophic claims about truth, presence, and totality: "So little is this totalitarian, that there is no call for a totalizing critique of reason against it." *The Philosophical Discourse of Modernity*, 408–9. Habermas claims that since discourse ethics is fallibilist and nonmetaphysical, there is no reason for deconstructionists to suppose that he is caught in a totalizing metaphysics of presence. As for Derrida's engagement with J. L. Austin's speech-act theory (and with John Searle), see *Limited Inc.*

87. It may even be the case, as J. M. Balkin has argued, that deconstruction requires some sort of positive commitments, such as a notion of the self who is doing the deconstructing and an antipathy toward the values which are being deconstructed: "Deconstruction, therefore, does not alleviate the need for the existence of a set of political committments that preexist the deconstructive act." *Tradition, Betrayal, and the Politics of Deconstruction*, 11 CARDOZO L. REV. 1613, 1629 (1990). Balkin's view seems correct. One always deconstructs for a particular reason and toward a particular end. Honesty requires that one clearly state the ends that one hopes to advance through the deconstructive project.

6: LYOTARD

1. The shift in Lyotard's work is chronicled by Geoffrey Bennington in *Lyotard: Writing the Event* (New York: Columbia University Press, 1988), 1–5.

2. Jean-François Lyotard, *The Postmodern Condition: A Report on Knowledge*, trans. Geoff Bennington and Brian Massumi (Minneapolis: University of Minnesota Press, 1984); *Just Gaming*, trans. Wlad Godzich with Jean-Loup Thébaud (Minneapolis: University of Minnesota Press, 1985); *The Differend: Phrases in Dispute*, trans. Georges Van Den Abbeele (Minneapolis: University of Minnesota Press, 1988).

3. Of particular interest is Lyotard's recent essay on Kafka's story "In the Penal Colony," in *Toward the Postmodern* (Atlantic Highlands, N.J.: Humanities Press International, 1993), as well as some of the political essays in *Lyotard: Political Writings*, trans. Bill Readings and Kevin Paul (Minneapolis: University of Minnesota Press, 1993), and *The Lyotard Reader*, trans. Andrew Benjamin (Oxford: Basil Blackwell, 1989). Lyotard's views on political legitimation and totalitarianism are reiterated in *The Postmodern Explained: Correspondence, 1982–1985*, trans. Julian Pefanis and Morgan Thomas (Minneapolis: University of Minnesota Press, 1993).

4. Immanuel Kant, "An Answer to the Question: 'What Is Enlightenment,'" in *Perpetual Peace and Other Essays*, trans. Ted Humphrey (Indianapolis, Ind.: Hackett, 1983).

5. *The Postmodern Condition*, 31–37.

6. Ibid., 37.

7. Ibid., 37.

8. Ibid.

9. *The Differend,* 179–80.

10. *The Postmodern Condition,* xxiii–iv.

11. Ibid., 26.

12. Ibid., xxiv. Lyotard amplified this point in an interview published in *Diacritics: A Review of Contemporary Criticism* 14 (Fall 1984): 17.

13. *The Postmodern Condition,* xxv.

14. *Just Gaming,* 100.

15. *The Postmodern Condition,* xxv.

16. *Just Gaming,* 3, 81.

17. *The Postmodern Condition,* 40.

18. Ibid., 36.

19. Ibid., 63–64.

20. Ibid., 82.

21. *The Differend,* 158.

22. *Just Gaming,* 95.

23. Ibid., 3.

24. Ibid., 31.

25. Ibid., 30.

26. Ibid., 34 (emphasis added).

27. Ibid., 31.

28. Ibid., 28.

29. Ibid., 82.

30. Ibid., 14.

31. Ibid., 7, 59.

32. Ibid., 65.

33. Ibid., 24.

34. Ibid., 64.

35. Ibid., 45.

36. Ibid., 45.

37. Ibid., 77.

38. Ibid., 68–69.

39. Ibid., 69–70.

40. Immanuel Kant, *Groundwork of the Metaphysic of Morals,* trans. H. J. Paton (New York: Harper & Row, 1964), 88.

41. *Just Gaming,* 100.

42. Ibid., 100 (emphasis added).

43. I take it that this principle would prevent, say, neo-Nazis from physically harming immigrants because in so doing they would be imposing their own game on others, which would violate the universal prescription that the games must be kept autonomous and distinct. But notice how this approach not only rules out undesirable behavior but also such desirable coercive behavior as taxation, which involves the

imposition of one form of life (redistribution of wealth) on many people who do not share in this language-game, such as tax resisters. It seems that in law and politics there is an inescapable amount of coercion, such that one language-game must overtake others for society to function at all. If this is correct, then Lyotard will have difficulty explaining how a just political arrangement will keep language-games heteronomous and distinct.

44. *Just Gaming,* 28.

45. Ibid., 100.

46. Ibid., 71–72.

47. Ibid., 100.

48. Lyotard also finds heterogeneity at the level of names (words), which exist one level below the level of phrases (which consist of names) (*The Differend,* 47). For Lyotard names are loci of conflicting meanings, such that a given name (e.g., "Stalin") has a fluid meaning depending on context. This means that Lyotard finds our language permeated with heterogeneity and dissensus from the most elementary level (names) all the way up to phrase systems and discursive genres.

49. *The Differend,* 9, xi.

50. Ibid., xi.

51. See Allen Dunn, "A Tyranny of Justice: The Ethics of Lyotard's Differend," *Boundary* 2, no. 20 (1993): 192–220. Dunn is skeptical of Lyotard's attempt to derive ethical implications from his discussion of the differend: "Not surprisingly, Lyotard encounters formidable difficulties in his efforts to present the ethical implications of the differend" (197).

52. See Ward Churchill, "Perversions of Justice: Examining the Doctrine of U.S. Rights to Occupancy in North America," in *Radical Philosophy of Law,* ed. David Caudill and Steven J. Gold (Atlantic Highlands, N.J.: Humanities Press International, 1995).

53. See *The Differend,* 128. For Lyotard each "universe" involves four basic components: a referent, a meaning, an addressor, and an addressee. (*The Differend,* 14). These components undergo strategic shifts, depending on the type of statement being offered.

54. Ibid., xii.

55. *Just Gaming,* 59.

56. Ibid., 82, 65.

57. Ibid., 96.

58. Immanuel Kant, *Critique of Judgment,* trans. James Meredith (Oxford: Clarendon Press, 1980). My discussion of Kant's views borrows from James Clarke, "A Kantian Theory of Political Judgment," *Philosophy Today* 38 (1994): 135–48, and David Ingram, "The Postmodern Kantianism of Arendt and Lyotard," *Review of Metaphysics* 42 (1988): 51–77.

59. Jean-François Lyotard, *Instructions Païennes* (Paris: Galilee, 1977), 36. For more on Lyotard's reading of Kant, see Bill Readings, *Introducing Lyotard: Art and Politics* (New York: Routledge, 1991).

60. For some cautions about whether aesthetics can ground political action, see Terry Eagleton, "The Kantian Imaginary," *The Ideology of the Aesthetic* (Cambridge: Basil

Blackwell, 1990), 76. For a similar concern, see Christopher Norris, "From the Sublime to the Absurd (Lyotard)," *Uncritical Theory* (London: Lawrence & Wishart, 1992), 70–86.

61. *The Differend*, 13.

62. Readings, *Introducing Lyotard*, 125.

63. *The Postmodern Condition*, 82.

64. Honi F. Haber, *Beyond Postmodern Politics* (New York: Routledge, 1994), 32.

65. This suggestion is made by David Ingram in "Legitimacy and the Postmodern Condition: The Political Thought of Jean-François Lyotard," *Praxis International* 7, nos. 3–4 (1987–88): 286–87.

66. Aristotle, *Politics*, sec. 1287a28, in *The Basic Works of Aristotle*, ed. Richard McKeon (New York: Random House, 1941), 1202.

67. Aristotle, *Nichomachean Ethics*, 1103b, in *The Basic Works of Aristotle* (emphasis added).

68. Ibid., 1094b.

69. Ibid., 1134b.

70. Aristotle, *Politics*, 1287b3 (emphasis added).

71. *Just Gaming*, 14.

72. For more on Lyotard's (mis)reading of Kant, see Michael Drolet, "The Wild and the Sublime: Lyotard's Postmodern Politics," *Political Studies* 42 (1994): 267.

73. Immanuel Kant, *The Metaphysics of Morals*, trans. Mary Gregor (Cambridge: Cambridge University Press, 1991), 80 (property rights), 96 (marriage rights), and 177 (the right to rebel).

74. Immanuel Kant, "On the Proverb 'That May Be True in Theory But Is of No Practical Use,'" in *Perpetual Peace and Other Essays*, trans. Ted Humphries (Indianapolis, Ind.: Hackett, 1983), 77 (emphasis added).

75. Ibid., 79 (emphasis added).

76. Kant, *The Metaphysics of Morals*, 176.

77. Immanuel Kant, "To Perpetual Peace: A Philosophic Sketch," in *Perpetual Peace and Other Essays*, 112.

78. Kant, "On the Proverb," 72.

79. Ludwig Wittgenstein, *The Blue and Brown Books* (New York: Harper & Row, 1958), 17.

80. Ludwig Wittgenstein, *Philosophical Investigations* (New York: Macmillan, 1958), sec. 7, p. 5 (emphasis added).

81. Ibid., sec. 19, p. 8.

82. Ibid., 200 (emphasis added).

83. David Hume, *A Treatise of Human Nature* (Oxford: Clarendon Press, 1978), 469–70.

84. John Searle, "How to Derive 'Ought' from 'Is,'" *Philosophical Review* 73 (1964): 43.

85. This claim is set forth by Lyotard in *The Differend*, 128.

86. John Searle, "What Is a Speech Act?" in *Language and Social Context*, ed. Pier Giglioli (Harmondsworth, Eng.: Penguin, 1972), 136–54, 139.

87. *The Differend*, 147.

88. This is also the title of a chapter in Lyotard's *Just Gaming*.

89. See Donald Davidson, "On the Very Idea of a Conceptual Scheme," *Proceedings and Addresses of the American Philosophical Association* 47 (1973–74): 5–20.

90. *The Postmodern Condition*, 82.

7: RORTY'S POSTMODERN ANTIFOUNDATIONALISM

1. Michel Foucault, "The Order of Discourse," trans. Rupert Swyer in *Untying the Text*, ed. Robert Young (Boston: Routledge, 1981), 65.

2. Louis Althusser, "Freud and Lacan," *Lenin and Philosophy*, trans. Ben Brewster (New York: Monthly Review Press, 1971), 218–19. Foucault also speaks of the "decentering" of the subject in *The Archaeology of Knowledge*, trans. A. M. Sheridan Smith (New York: Pantheon, 1972), 13.

3. Jacques Lacan, *Écrits*, trans. Alan Sheridan (New York: Norton, 1977), 1.

4. Alasdair MacIntyre, *After Virtue* (Notre Dame: University of Notre Dame Press, 1984), 265–66.

5. Michael Walzer, *Spheres of Justice* (New York: Basic Books, 1983), 312–13.

6. Richard Rorty, "Wild Orchids and Trotsky," in *Wild Orchids and Trotsky*, ed. Mark Edmundson (New York: Penguin, 1993), 33.

7. Richard Rorty, *Contingency, Irony, and Solidarity* (Cambridge: Cambridge University Press, 1989), 198.

8. Richard Rorty, *Unger, Castoriadis, and the Romance of a National Future*, 82 NORTHWESTERN L. REV. 335 (1988); idem, *The Banality of Pragmatism and the Poetry of Justice*, 63 SO. CAL. L. REV. 1811 (1990); idem, *What Can You Expect from Anti-Foundationalist Philosophers? A Reply to Lynn Baker*, 78 VIRGINIA L. REV. 719 (1992).

9. See Richard Posner, *The Problems of Jurisprudence* (Cambridge, Mass.: Harvard University Press, 1990); Ronald Dworkin, "Pragmatism, Right Answers, and True Banality," in *Pragmatism in Law and Society*, ed. Michael Brint and William Weaver (Boulder, Colo.: Westview Press, 1993), 359–88.

10. Richard Rorty, "Postmodern Bourgeois Liberalism," *Journal of Philosophy* 80 (1983): 583–89; rpt. in Richard Rorty, *Objectivity, Relativism, and Truth: Philosophical Papers, Vol 1* (Cambridge: Cambridge University Press, 1991). All references to this article will be to the version in *Philosophical Papers*.

11. *Philosophical Papers*, 198.

12. In a recent interview, when asked why democracy was important if it could not be justified, Rorty stated: "There are lots of things you can't justify that are important. Your mother, for example. There are things that are so basic to one's identity that one wouldn't know who one was if one stopped cherishing them. John Dewey felt that way about democratic institutions and I suppose I do, too." Martin Oliver, "Towards a Liberal Utopia: An Interview with Richard Rorty," *Times Literary Supplement*, June 24, 1994, 14.

13. *Philosophical Papers*, 198.

14. Rorty has said that he meant the term "postmodern bourgeois liberalism" as a joke. See his comments in "Towards a Liberal Utopia," 14.

15. *Philosophical Papers*, 199.

16. Ibid., 200.

17. Ibid., 201.

18. This essay was originally published in *The Virginia Statute of Religious Freedom*, ed. Merrill Peterson and Robert Vaughan (Cambridge: Cambridge University Press, 1988), 257–88; rpt. in *Philosophical Papers*, 175–97.

19. Rawls' remark is quoted in *Philosophical Papers*, 185.

20. See Richard Rorty, "On Ethnocentrism: A Reply to Clifford Geertz," *Michigan Quarterly Review* 25 (1986): 525–34; rpt. in *Philosophical Papers*, 203–10.

21. *Philosophical Papers*, 15.

22. Richard Rorty, "Cosmopolitanism Without Emancipation: A Response to Jean-François Lyotard," in *Philosophical Papers*, 211–22. Rorty put the same point differently in a more recent interview: "I don't think that anybody is ever able to escape more than about one percent of his or her past or the institutions in which they have grown up." "Towards a Liberal Utopia," 14.

23. *Philosophical Papers*, 29.

24. Richard Rorty, "Thugs and Theorists: A Reply to Bernstein," *Political Theory* 15, no. 4 (1987): 564–80.

25. Ibid., 565.

26. Francis Fukuyama, *The End of History and the Last Man* (New York: Free Press, 1992).

27. Quoted in Rorty, *Contingency, Irony, Solidarity*, 46.

28. Ibid.

29. Ibid., 189.

30. Ibid., 53. Of course, this raises the problem of the forces (economics, race, gender) which prevent certain people from articulating a voice for the future. Thus, we may have to make a special effort to find "strong poets" who are not simply a collection of white males intended to speak for all others. See Allan Huchinson, *The Three Rs: Reading Rorty Radically*, 103 HARVARD L. REV. 555, 565 (1989).

31. See *Contingency, Irony, Solidarity*, 196. Rorty sees an important role for separatist groups (radicals, feminists) who work outside the mainstream to create new narratives and linguistic practices as a way of articulating their marginalized status. These groups try to formulate "new ways of speaking" which enable them to "gather the moral strength to go out and change the world." "Feminism and Pragmatism" (The Tanner Lecture on Human Values at the University of Michigan, December 1990), *Michigan Quarterly Review* 30 (1991): 247. Rorty also stresses that dominant social groups (such as white males) should sensitize themselves to the sufferings of marginalized groups by reading novels and manifestos produced by such groups. "Two Cheers for the Cultural Left," *South Atlantic Quarterly* 89 (1990): 227–29.

32. Rorty's emphasis on redescription explains his reluctance to "answer Hitler" by

refuting him (i.e., by proving that Hitler was morally wrong in some objective or trans-cultural sense). Rorty thinks that if we were in a conversation with a philosophically sophisticated Nazi, we couldn't prove Hitler wrong; the best that we could do would be to redescribe Hitler in language that might convince the Nazi that Hitler is not a great man, or that the Nazi state is not a utopia. But there is no way to demonstrate conclu-sively that Hitler is wrong in any sense deeper than the fact that he stands opposed to the things we value. "Truth and Freedom: A Reply to Thomas McCarthy," *Critical Inquiry* 16 (Spring 1990): 636–37.

33. Rorty, *Contingency, Irony, Solidarity*, 191.

34. Ibid.

35. Ibid., 192.

36. Ibid., xvi.

37. Ibid., 63.

38. Ibid., 65.

39. Rorty, "Feminism and Pragmatism," 242.

40. Oliver Wendell Holmes, *The Common Law* (Boston: Little, Brown, 1881), 1.

41. See Thomas C. Grey, *Langdell's Orthodoxy*, 45 PITT. L. REV. 1, 2 (1983). According to Langdell, "legal judgments are made by applying pre-existing law to facts" (n. 6).

42. Dworkin has vehemently rejected the pragmatist label. See his "Pragmatism, Right Answers, and True Banality."

43. Rorty, "The Banality of Pragmatism," 1815.

44. Rorty makes a similar point in his essay, "Thugs and Theorists": "I cannot find much use for philosophy in formulating means to the ends that we social democrats share, nor in describing either our enemies or the present danger. Its main use lies, I think, in thinking through our utopian visions" (569).

45. 381 U.S. 479 (1965).

46. Rorty, "The Banality of Pragmatism," 1818.

47. Rorty cites Dewey's famous position: "It is no longer enough for a principle to be elevated, noble, universal, and hallowed by time. It must present its birth certifi-cate, it must show under just what condition of human experience it was generated, and it must justify itself by its works, present and potential." John Dewey, *Reconstruc-tion in Philosophy*, quoted in "What Can You Expect from Anti-Foundationalist Philosophers?" 722.

48. Rorty, "Thugs and Theorists," 566.

49. Rorty, "What Can You Expect . . . ?" 719.

50. Ibid., 724.

51. Rorty, *Contingency, Irony, Solidarity*, xv.

52. Recall Holmes' list of the forces outside of logic which undoubtedly affect a judge's decision: "The felt necessities of the time, the prevalent moral and political theories, intuitions of public policy avowed or unconscious, even the prejudices which judges share with their fellow men, have had a good deal more to do than the syllogism in deter-mining how men should be governed." Oliver Wendell Holmes, *The Common Law*, quoted in Thomas Grey, *Holmes and Legal Pragmatism*, 41 STAN. L. REV. 787, 806 (1990).

53. Rorty, "The Banality of Pragmatism," 1818.

54. Rorty's position here is quite similar to that set forth by Stanley Fish, who argues that one's choice of a legal theory or method does not determine outcomes in particular legal cases. Hence, a legal theory is not a sine qua non for advocating a particular solution to a case. See Fish's "Play of Surfaces: Theory and the Law," *There's No Such Thing as Free Speech* (New York: Oxford University Press, 1994), 180. Fish runs counter to well-known liberal thinkers (such as Ronald Dworkin and Michael Perry) who argue that cases should be decided with reference to theoretical positions about law, politics, and democracy. For Dworkin and Perry, a theoretical conception of democracy is essential to properly resolve constitutional cases; indeed, it is the theory that determines the outcome of the case. Fish seems to hold that the law consists of rhetorical devices all the way down, so one can twist legal doctrine and precedent to get any result that one desires; for example, one can favor or reject abortion rights regardless of one's theoretical commitment to formalism/nonformalism, originalism/nonoriginalism. Since legal theorists don't really need a theory to support particular outcomes, they should drop the pretentious theoretical appeals and simply engage in the actual practice of law.

Fish's position seems incorrect. One's theoretical commitments do seem to affect one's decisions, at least in a general way. It is well known that originalists tend to be conservatives and that nonoriginalists tend to be liberals; this is not a mere accident but a result which issues from the fact that liberals adopt a theoretical posture which looks beyond specific texts to general considerations of the legal system as a whole. It is precisely the liberal's theoretical attitude which allows him or her to make the move beyond the text of the Constitution (which is silent on key issues like abortion and affirmative action) to higher-level principles of autonomy and integrity. Furthermore, *contra* Fish, there is no simple way to practice law without engaging in theoretical debates; even a simple First Amendment case about whether it is acceptable to pass out flyers in a shopping mall raises theoretical concerns about the interplay of free speech and private property. One's theory on such questions will affect how one decides the case.

55. Rorty, "The Banality of Pragmatism," 1815.

56. Ibid. Rorty also says that "we do not need 'a unified principle that would provide the basis for judicial decisions.'" Ibid., 1818, quoting Farber, *Legal Pragmatism and the Constitution*, 72 MINN. L. REV. 1331 (1988).

57. See Richard Posner, *What Has Pragmatism to Offer Law?* 63 S. CAL. L. REV. 1653 (1990).

58. Hilary Putnam, *A Reconsideration of Deweyan Democracy*, 63 S. CAL. L. REV. 1671 (1990).

59. Oliver Wendell Holmes, *The Common Law* (Boston: Little, Brown, 1949), 1.

60. Benjamin Cardozo, *The Nature of the Judicial Process* (New Haven, Conn.: Yale University Press, 1921), 112–13.

61. Benjamin Cardozo, *The Growth of the Law* (Westport, Conn.: Greenwood Press, 1975), 59.

62. Fitz-James Stephen, *Liberty, Equality, Fraternity,* quoted in William James, "The Will to Believe," *Essays in Pragmatism* (New York: Hafner Press, 1948), 109.

63. Jean-Paul Sartre, *Existentialism and Human Emotions,* trans. Bernard Frechtman (New York: Citadel Press, 1990), 43.

64. This argument has been made by Vince Samar in *The Right of Privacy* (Philadelphia: Temple University Press, 1991).

65. Rorty, "Unger, Castoriadis, and the Romance of a National Future," 349–50.

66. Elizabeth Mensch, "The History of Mainstream Legal Thought," in *The Politics of Law,* ed. David Kairys (New York: Pantheon, 1990), 13.

67. Ronald Dworkin, "Pragmatism, Right Answers, and True Banality," 370.

68. See Georgia Warnke, *Justice and Interpretation* (Cambridge, Mass.: MIT Press, 1993), vii.

69. Quoted in Dworkin, "Pragmatism, Right Answers, and True Banality," 369 (emphasis added).

70. See Posner, *The Problems of Jurisprudence,* 197–219, 286–89; Ronald Dworkin, "Is Wealth a Value?" *A Matter of Principle* (Cambridge, Mass.: Harvard University Press, 1985), 237–66.

71. Rorty, "The Banality of Pragmatism," 1815.

8: CONCLUSION

1. See Mark Tushnet, "The Politics of Constitutional Law," in *The Politics of Law,* ed. David Kairys (New York: Pantheon, 1990), 232.

2. Michel Foucault, *Madness and Civilization,* trans. Richard Howard (New York: Vintage, 1973).

3. David Kairys, introduction to *The Politics of Law,* 6.

4. Jean-François Lyotard, *The Differend: Phrases in Dispute,* trans. Georges Van Den Abbeele (Minneapolis: University of Minnesota Press, 1988).

5. Jacques Derrida, "Tympan," *Margins of Philosophy,* trans. Alan Bass (Chicago: University of Chicago Press, 1982), xxiii.

6. Michel Foucault, "The Subject and Power," in *Michel Foucault: Beyond Structuralism and Hermeneutics* (Chicago: University of Chicago Press, 1983).

7. For more on this issue, see Ward Churchill, "Perversions of Justice: Examining the Doctrine of U.S. Rights to Occupancy in North America," in *Radical Philosophy of Law,* ed. David Caudill and Steven J. Gold (Atlantic Highlands, N.J.: Humanities Press International, 1995).

8. F.R.C.P. 12(b)(6).

9. Catharine MacKinnon, "Sexual Harassment: Its First Decade in Court," *Feminism Unmodified* (Cambridge, Mass.: Harvard University Press, 1987), 103.

10. See Nadine Taub and Elizabeth Schneider, "Women's Subordination and the Role of Law," in *The Politics of Law,* 151–76.

11. "Polish Group's Suit Accuses NBC of Slur Campaign," *Chicago Sun-Times,* January 3, 1996, p. 7.

12. Lyotard, *The Differend*, 13.

13. For a useful discussion of this point, see Madan Sarup, *An Introductory Guide to Post-Structuralism and Postmodernism* (Athens.: University of Georgia Press, 1993), 50–51.

14. Clare Dalton, "An Essay in the Deconstruction of Contract Law," in *Critical Legal Studies*, ed. Allan Hutchinson (Totowa, N.J.: Rowman & Littlefield, 1989), 195–208.

15. See Duncan Kennedy, *Form and Substance in Private Law Adjudication*, 89 HARVARD L. REV. 1685 (1976); rpt. in *Critical Legal Studies*, 36–55.

16. See my article *Dworkin and Critical Legal Studies on Right Answers and Conceptual Holism*, 18 LEGAL STUDIES FORUM 135 (1994).

17. Michel Foucault, *The Archaeology of Knowledge*, trans. A. M. Sheridan Smith (New York: Pantheon, 1972).

18. For example, Patricia Williams writes about her experience as a law school professor in *The Alchemy of Race and Rights* (Cambridge, Mass.: Harvard University Press, 1991).

19. Duncan Kennedy, "Legal Education as Training for Hierarchy," in *The Politics of Law*, 38.

20. Ronald Dworkin, *Law's Empire* (Cambridge: Harvard University Press, 1986), 12–15.

21. 347 U.S. 483, 74 S. Ct. 686 (1954).

22. Richard Delgado, *Discussion*, 45 STAN. L. REV. 1671 (1993).

23. Ludwig Wittgenstein, *Philosophical Investigations*, trans. G. E. M. Anscombe (New York: Macmillan, 1958), sec. 124.

24. David Kairys, introduction to *The Politics of Law*, 4.

25. Ibid., 3–4.

26. Duncan Kennedy, "Legal Education as Training for Hierarchy," 47 (emphasis added).

27. Catharine MacKinnon, "Feminism, Marxism, Method, and the State: Toward Feminist Jurisprudence," in *Critical Legal Studies*, 61.

28. Richard Posner, *The Problems of Jurisprudence* (Cambridge, Mass.: Harvard University Press, 1990), 468.

29. For an example of this argument, see D. W. Haslett, "Is Inheritance Justified?" *Philosophy and Public Affairs* 15, no. 2 (1986), 122–25.

30. Ronald Dworkin, *A Matter of Principle* (Cambridge, Mass.: Harvard University Press, 1985), 2.

31. See J. M. Balkin, *Understanding Legal Understanding: The Legal Subject and the Problem of Legal Coherence*, 103 YALE L. J. 105 (1993), who writes: "A critical perspective does not reject the importance of the internal perspective. . . . Instead of taking for granted the primacy of the internal viewpoint of the participants in the legal system, a critical perspective asks how this internal perspective comes about" (110). This project allows the external perspective to "check" the internal pespective and vice versa.

32. Hilary Putnam, *Reason, Truth, and History* (Cambridge: Cambridge University Press, 1981), 216.

33. Dworkin, *Law's Empire*, 80 (emphasis added).

34. See his comments in "Thugs and Theorists: A Reply to Bernstein," *Political Theory* 15, no. 4 (1987): 571.

35. The restrictions on women's rights were laid out by the Supreme Court in *Frontiero v. Richardson*, 411 U.S. 677 (1973).

36. *Bradwell v. Illinois*, 83 U.S. (16 Wall.) 130, 141 (1873).

37. On the status of woman as other and man as subject, Simone de Beauvoir, *The Second Sex*, trans. H. M. Parshley (New York: Vintage, 1989), has written: "He is the Subject, he is the Absolute—she is the Other" (xxii).

38. Lani Guinier, *The Tyranny of the Majority* (New York: Free Press, 1994).

39. Thomas Kuhn, *The Structure of Scientific Revolutions* (Chicago: University of Chicago Press, 1970).

40. According to Bruce Ackerman, *We The People I: Foundations* (Cambridge, Mass.: Harvard University Press, 1991), "Modern lawyers are perfectly prepared to admit that the Constitutional Convention was acting illegally in proposing its new document in the name of We the People" (41).

41. 5 U.S. (1 Cranch) 137 (1803).

42. 381 U.S. 479, 85 S. Ct. 1678 (1965).

43. Robert Bork, *The Tempting of America: The Political Seduction of the Law* (New York: Free Press, 1990), 95–100.

44. See Benjamin Cardozo, *The Nature of the Judicial Process* (New Haven, Conn.: Yale University Press, 1921). There is something of a charade which takes place when judges announce what is undeniably a new rule, only to claim that the rule is a well-established principle of law. This charade is somewhat necessary, given the basic notion that citizens of a democratic society should be given reasonable advance notice of the laws which will govern their conduct. Basic considerations of due process and notice mandate that judges refrain from subjecting litigants to ad hoc principles of law. On the other hand, judges must have the flexibility to announce new rules to fit the cases brought before them. This need to satisfy the demands of precedent while also fashioning new remedies gives rise to the curious practice where a judge announces a new rule while denying that the rule is new.

45. Herbert Marcuse, *One-Dimensional Man* (Boston: Beacon Press, 1964), 199.

Index